Mechanical Systems
for Architects

Mechanical Systems for Architects

Aly S. Dadras, N.C.A.R.B.

Architect - Planner

Professor of Architecture

New York Institute of Technology

McGraw-Hill, Inc.

New York San Francisco Washington, D.C. Auckland Bogotá
Caracas Lisbon London Madrid Mexico City Milan
Montreal New Delhi San Juan Singapore
Sydney Tokyo Toronto

Library of Congress Cataloging-in-Publication Data

Dadras, Aly S.
    Mechanical systems for architects / Aly S. Dadras.
        p.   cm.
    Includes bibliographical references.
    ISBN 0-07-015080-X
    1. Buildings—Mechanical equipment.   I. Title.
TH6010.D28 1995
696—dc20   94-37995
                                     CIP

1 2 3 4 5 6 7 8 9 0 KGP/KGP 9 0 9 8 7 6 5 4

ISBN 0-07-015080-X

The sponsoring editor for this book was Joel Stein, the editing supervisor was Christine Furry, and the production supervisor was Donald Schmidt.

It was set in Helvetica by North Market Street Graphics.

Printed and bound by Arcata Graphics/Kingsport Press.

McGraw-Hill Books are available at special quantity discounts to use as premiums and sales promotions, or for use in corporate training programs. For more information, please write to the Director of Special Sales, McGraw-Hill, Inc., 11 West 19th Street, New York, NY 10011. Or contact your local bookstore.

This book is printed on acid-free paper

Dedicated

to the

New York Institute of Technology

where I have been honored and privileged to be a part of its

distinguished faculty for thirty years,

to the

University of Miami

where I received my undergraduate education and was

honored to receive the first

"Alumnus of Distinction Award" in 1970,

and to

Every one of my thousands of students

who have helped me to learn and

encouraged me to write.

About the Author

Aly S. Dadras is a registered architect and professor of architecture at the New York Institute of Technology, where he was one of the founders of the School of Architecture in 1964. He received a B.S. in Architectural Engineering (cum laude) from the University of Miami in 1954, and an M.S. in Planning from the School of Architecture at Columbia University in 1956. He has obtained many honors and awards, and is a member of Tau Beta Pi (National Engineering Honor Society), Pi Mu Epsilon (National Mathematics Honor Society), and other professional societies both in the United States and abroad. His biography has been published in Marquis' *Who's Who in Finance and Industry, Who's Who in the East, Who's Who in the World,* and *Dictionary of International Biography,* and he has been the winner of several architectural and master planning competitions.

Professor Dadras has worked as a designer with several outstanding architects from 1950 to 1964 on such distinguished projects as House of Seagram, Daily News Building, Time and Life Building, Metropolitan Opera at Lincoln Center, and the Chrysler Pavilion at the 1963–64 New York World's Fair. He has been practicing in his own firm, Dadras International (Architects, Engineers, Planners), for the past 30 years. His work includes a number of commercial, educational, cultural, recreational, industrial, religious, and residential buildings, as well as master planning projects here and abroad. He and his wife, Ursula, live in Douglas Manor, New York, where they are visited often by their four children and two grandchildren.

OTHER RELATED McGRAW-HILL BOOKS BY ALY S. DADRAS

Forthcoming books will be:

Electrical Systems for Architects

HVAC Systems for Architects

CONTENTS

Part 1

GENERAL INFORMATION

G

General Information

CONTENTS

Part 2

WATER AND ITS USE IN BUILDINGS

Basic Information

Design of Water Systems

Water Distribution

Hot Water Systems

Design of Hot Water System

Hot Water Distribution

CONTENTS

Part 3

SEWAGE DISPOSAL SYSTEMS

S

Basic Information

Sewage Treatment

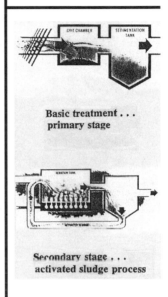

Basic treatment . . .
primary stage

Secondary stage . . .
activated sludge process

CONTENTS

Part 4

D

STORM DRAINAGE SYSTEMS

Drainage Systems

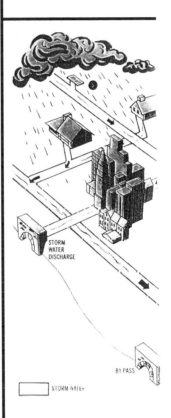

CONTENTS

PLUMBING SYSTEMS

Design of Plumbing Facilities

Plumbing Systems for Water Supply and DWV in Buildings

Pipes and Tubing Used for Water Distribution Systems

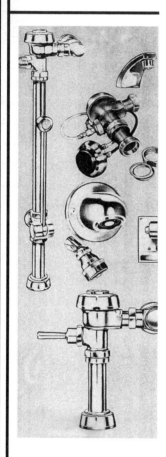

Design of Water Supply Main

Sanitary Drainage System
Drainage, Waste, and Vent (DWV)

Design of Drainage, Waste, and Vent (DWV)

CONTENTS

Part 6

LIGHTNING PROTECTION

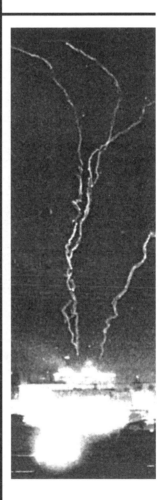

CONTENTS

Part 7

FIRE PROTECTION

F

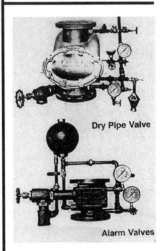

Dry Pipe Valve

Alarm Valves

Standard Spray

Bulb Sprinkler

CONTENTS

Part 8

BUILDING SERVICES

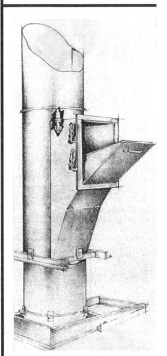

Sanitation and Disease

Odor Within the Building

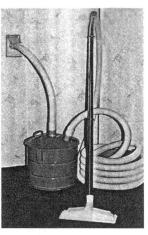

Control and Removal of Waste

Central Vacuum Cleaning Systems

Snow-Melting Systems

Preface

This book is written with an understanding of the feelings of architects, architectural designers, and architectural students, who are so much involved in design and drawings and whose artistic enthusiasm does not allow them to get involved in technical and research problems which are complicated and difficult to follow.

This book is written in such a way that it is easy to follow and understand. All answers to questions are readily available. All problems are solved step by step, using the American system of measurements in order to eliminate confusion. When the problem is solved, the result may be converted to the metric system (by using a conversion-factor table) for the projects designed for the countries or regions using the metric system.

I have followed the procedure successfully for many years in my practice and lectures.

WHY ARCHITECTS AND ARCHITECTURAL STUDENTS MUST BE KNOWLEDGEABLE IN THIS FIELD

Based on my 30 years of experience in education and practice, architects, designers, and architectural students must be knowledgeable regarding how mechanical and electrical systems are designed, calculated, and placed in structures, because approximately 42 percent of the total budget of a project is allocated for mechanical and electrical equipment, and the architect is directly responsible to the owner for the work performed by his or her consultant(s). Therefore, architects *must* be able to check the design and calculations done by their consultant(s) in order to protect themselves as well as their clients.

It is a matter of survival in the professional practice

In a small project, the architect should be able to design and calculate and produce the construction documents for the mechanical and electrical equipment, thus earning the fee otherwise given to a consultant(s).

Profit is made by knowing the field.

Furthermore, architects and architectural students cannot begin to design a successful building(s) without knowing the space requirements for toilet facilities, kitchen equipment, vertical transportation, mechanical rooms, and the effect of mechanical systems on their structure(s).

Successful design cannot be accomplished without knowledge of the field.

All information and calculations, etc., given in this book are based on the American system. Tables of conversion are provided for converting the American system to the metric system. It is suggested that all calculations be performed using the American system in the United States, and the following procedures if the work is to be done in the countries where the metric system is in practice:

1. Convert all dimensions and other requirements from the metric system to the American system by using Fig. G-24.
2. Use these figures to solve the problems.
3. When you solve the problem using the American system, convert the solution to the metric system by using Fig. G-25.

Aly S. Dadras

Acknowledgments

I would like to give my sincere thanks and appreciation to:

Dr. Matthew Schure, Ph.D.

President

New York Institute of Technology

Dr. King V. Cheek, J.D., L.C.D., L.H.D.

Vice President of Academic Affairs

New York Institute of Technology

Mr. Joel E. Stein

Senior Editor, Architecture

McGraw-Hill, Inc.

Professional Book Group

Mrs. Ursula M.S. Dadras, B.F.A., M.P.S.

Editor of this book

for the devoted guidance, moral support, and encouragement which they have given me in writing
and preparing this book.

Mrs. Hannelore R. Leavy

for the technical assistance in preparing this book.

Aly S. Dadras

References

The author is grateful for the use of reference materials from the following sources:

American National Standards Institute Inc.

American Society of Heating, Refrigerating and Air Conditioning Engineers, Inc.

Briggs Plumbingware, Inc.

Broadway Industries, Inc.

Crain Plumbing Corporation

Dadras International (Architects-Engineers-Planners)

Elkay Corporation

The Illustrated Columbia Encyclopedia

The International Association of Plumbing and Mechanical Officials

Manual of Individual Water Supply Systems

Nassau County Department of Health

Nassau County Comprehensive Water Management Plan

National Fire Protection Association

National Standard Plumbing Code

Robbins Lightning Inc.

Southern Building Code Congress International

Sloan Corporation

Uniform Plumbing Code

U.S. Environmental Protection Agency

U.S. HUD-FHA

U.S. Weather Bureau

W.H. Sadlier, Inc.

Whirlpool Corporation

Mechanical Systems
for Architects

CONTENTS

Part 1

GENERAL INFORMATION

G

General Information

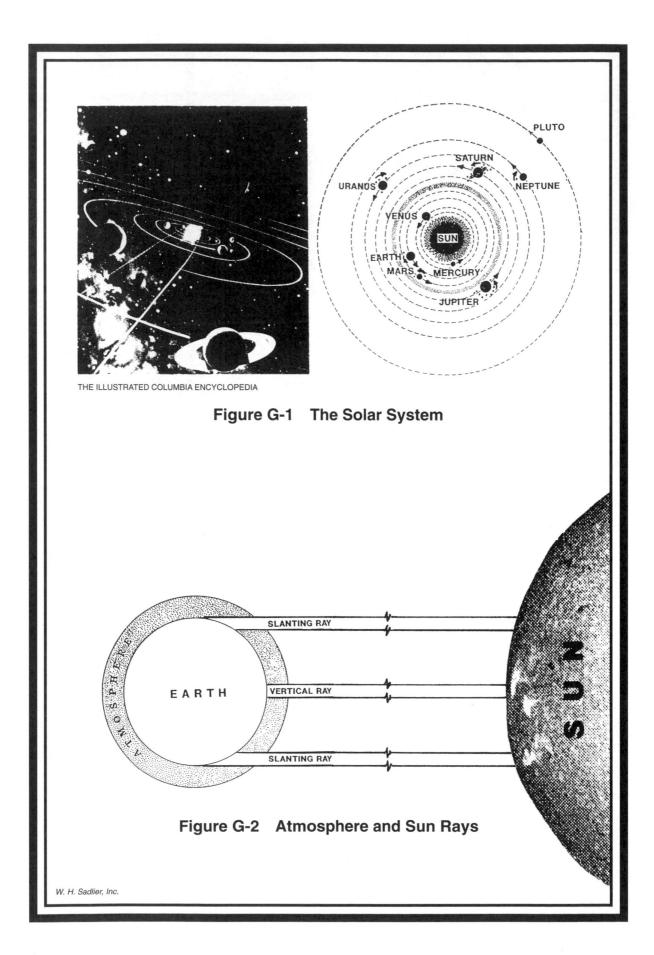

THE ILLUSTRATED COLUMBIA ENCYCLOPEDIA

Figure G-1   The Solar System

Figure G-2   Atmosphere and Sun Rays

GENERAL INFORMATION

G-1   INFORMATION

The following general information will directly or indirectly affect the mechanical equipment systems in a structure. The knowledge obtained shall enable us to understand the contents of this book.

G-2   EARTH

Earth is the fifth largest planet in the solar system (Fig. G-1).

The age of the earth has been estimated at from 2 to 4 billion years.

a. The equatorial diameter of the earth is 7926 mi. The circumference at the equator is 24,830 mi. The surface of the earth is divided into 57,469,923 sq. mi. of land and 139,480,841 sq. mi. of oceans.

b. The earth is surrounded by an envelope of gases called **atmosphere,** the greater part of which is made up of nitrogen and oxygen (Fig. G-2).

c. The distance from the earth to the sun is 92,960,800 mi. The path of the earth's orbit is an ellipse; consequently, the earth is nearer to the sun at some seasons than at others (Fig. G-7). The difference between its maximum and its minimum distance from the sun is 3 million mi. This difference is not great enough to affect the climate on the earth.

d. Conjectured internal composition of the earth is driven by the behavior of earthquake waves and is illustrated in Fig. G-3.

e. The earth rotates from west to east once every 24 hours on its axis. This makes the sun appear to move 15° in a westerly direction every hour.

f. The earth revolves around the sun once in 365¼ days (1° per day). We have 365 days in all years except in leap years, which have 366 days and occur every fourth year. The earth is nearest to the sun in January, and is farthest from the sun in July (Fig. G-4).

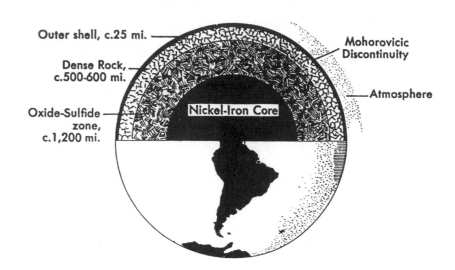

Outer shell, c.25 mi.

Dense Rock, c.500-600 mi.

Oxide-Sulfide zone, c.1,200 mi.

Mohorovicic Discontinuity

Atmosphere

Nickel-Iron Core

Figure G-3 The Earth Internal Composition

Summer Solstice — June 21

94,500,000 Miles.

SUN

91,500,000 Miles.

December 21

Winter Solstice

W. H. Sadlier, Inc.

Figure G-4

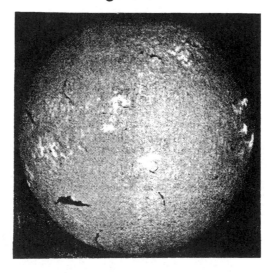

Figure G-5 The Sun

G-3   SUN

a.   The sun is intensely hot. Its temperature is approx. 10,832°F (6000°C). It is a self-luminous body of gases which is the center of our solar system. The sun is actually a star of about medium size. Its diameter is 865,400 mi., and its volume is about 1.3 million times that of the earth. Its mass is almost 700 times the total mass of all the bodies in the solar system, and 332,000 times that of the earth.

b.   Its gravitational force on the surface is almost 28 times that of the earth. The sun rotates on its axis from east to west. Because of its gaseous nature, its rate of rotation varies somewhat with latitude, the speed being greatest (a period of 28 days) in the equatorial region and least at the poles (a period of almost 35 days).

c.   The axis of the sun is inclined at an angle of about 7° to the plane of the ecliptic.

d.   Without the heat and light of the sun, life could not exist on the earth (Fig. G-5).

G-4   SEASONS (Fig. G-7)

The change in seasons is the result of the fact that the earth's axis is inclined to the plane of its orbit making an angle of 23.5° (Fig. G-6).

a.   **March 21:** The rays of the sun shine from pole to pole; the days and nights are of equal length everywhere. This is the beginning of spring in the northern hemlsphere— the ***spring equinox.***

b.   **June 21:** The rays of the sun go beyond the north pole, and the south pole is dark. The days are longer than the nights in the northern hemisphere. This is the beginning of the summer in the northern hemisphere, or ***summer solstice.***

c.   **September 23:** The rays of the sun shine from pole to pole. The days and nights are of equal length everywhere. This is the beginning of autumn in the northern hemisphere, or ***autumnal equinox.***

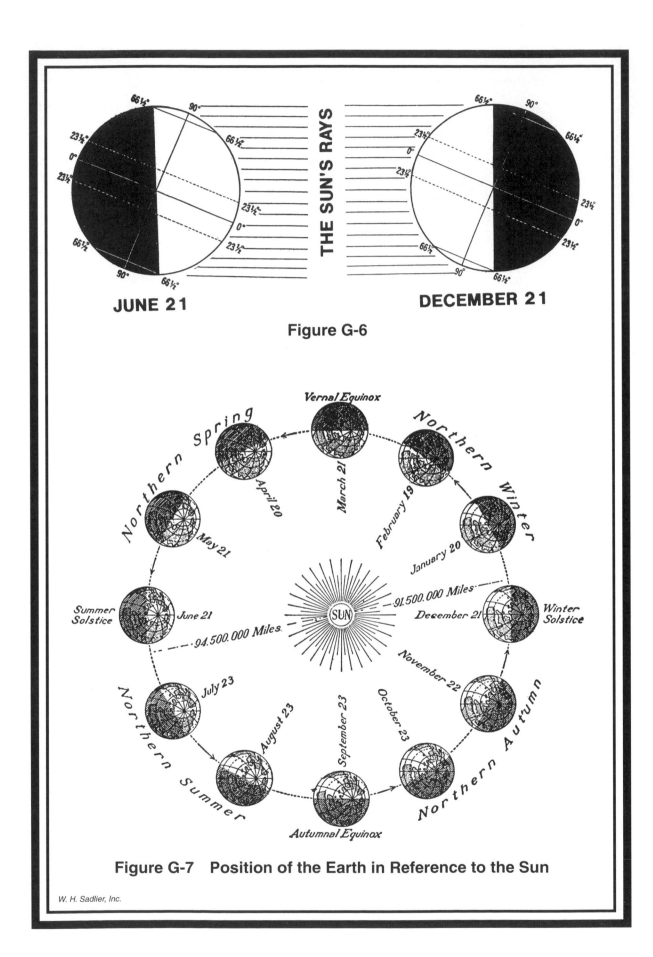

THE SUN'S RAYS

JUNE 21

DECEMBER 21

Figure G-6

Figure G-7   Position of the Earth in Reference to the Sun

d. **December 21:** The north pole region is dark, and the south pole region is lighted. The days in the northern hemisphere are shorter than the nights. This is the beginning of winter in the northern hemisphere, or **winter solstice.**

Note: When the northern hemisphere receives the most direct rays, it has its warmest season—summer. At that time, the southern hemisphere has winter, because it is receiving indirect rays (Fig. G-6).

G-5 LATITUDE (PARALLELS)

The distance north or south of the equator is called *latitude.* This distance is measured in degrees along a meridian (Figs. G-8 and G-10).

a. North of the equator is north latitude, and south of the equator is south latitude. The equator is always 0° latitude. The north pole is 90° north latitude, and the South Pole is 90° south latitude.

b. In general, the areas in low latitudes are hot, and the areas in high latitudes are cold.

c. The circumference of the latitude around the equator is 24,830 mi. Therefore, the length of 1° latitude is 24,830 mi. ÷ 360° = 68.97 mi.

G-6 LONGITUDE

The prime meridian passes through the Royal Observatory of Greenwich, England (Figs. G-8 and G-10).

a. The conventional dividing line between the eastern and western hemispheres starts from Greenwich, England. The geographical longitude is computed from 0 to 180° east and 180° west of Greenwich.

b. Since the circumference of the meridian is (the same as latitude) 24,830 mi., the length of 1° longitude is also 68.97 mi.

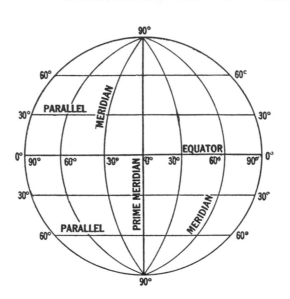

Figure G-8   Parallels and Meridians

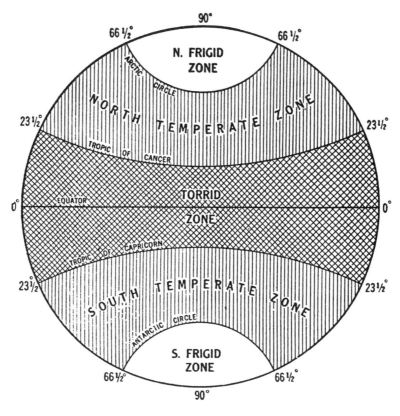

Figure G-9   Heat Zones of the Earth

G-7 STANDARD TIME ZONE

Every 15 degrees of longitude represents a difference of one hour in time (Fig. G-11). *Light year* is the unit of length, in astronomy, equal to the distance light travels in one year. The speed of light is 186,000 miles per second.

$$60 \text{ s/m} \times 60 \text{ m/h} \times 24 \text{ h/d} \times 365 \text{ d/y} = 31,530,000 \text{ s/y}$$

Therefore, light year = 31,530,000 s/y $\times$ 186,000 mi/s = 58,657 $\times$ 10^8 mi/year

where s = second, m = minute, h = hour, d = day, and y = year.

G-8 TEMPERATURE OF THE EARTH

a. The earth is divided into five (5) temperature zones (Figs. G-9 and G-10).

1. North frigid zone: 66½ to 90° north latitude; it is called *north cold belt.*

2. North temperate zone: 23½ to 66½° north latitude; it is called *north temperate belt.*

3. Torrid zone: 23½° south latitude to 23½° north latitude; it is referred to as *hot belt.*

4. South temperate zone: 23½ to 66½° south latitude; it is called **south temperate belt.**

5. South frigid zone: 66½ to 90° south latitude; it is referred to as **south cold belt.**

b. The temperature decreases as the heighth of the land increases. The temperature falls 3° Fahrenheit for every 1000 feet that land rises vertically. Approximately every 1000 miles toward the north pole or south pole from the equator, the temperature decreases by 16° Fahrenheit.

G-9 CLIMATE

Activities of people are greatly influenced by climate. The climate of a region largely determines the kinds of plants and animals which live there.

a. The people in a region where the climate is hot and moist are likely to be slow-moving, and they don't feel very ambitious. People become depressed in a cloudy and damp climate.

9

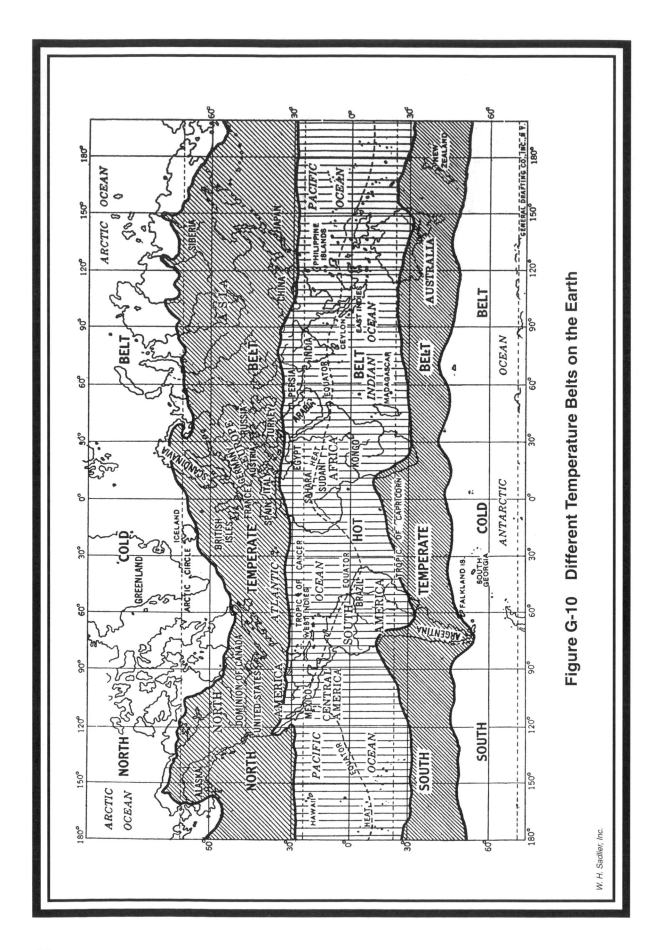

Figure G-10 Different Temperature Belts on the Earth

W. H. Sadlier, Inc.

b. The climate of a region is determined by weather conditions over a long period of time and is driven by temperature, precipitation, humidity, wind, barometric pressure, etc.

c. The major influences governing the climate are the latitude of the area, water, altitude, topography, and prevailing winds.

d. The average weather conditions over a number of years in a region are called *climate* of the place.

G-10 WEATHER

The weather is the condition of the atmosphere at a certain time, and is based on temperature, barometric pressure, wind, humidity, cloudiness, and precipitation. Weather is distinguished from climate in that it is concerned with conditions over short periods of time.

G-11 ATMOSPHERE (AIR)

Atmosphere, or air, which surrounds the earth is the mixture of gases (Fig. G-2).

a. Approximately 90 percent of the mass of the atmosphere is within 10 mi. of the earth's surface. This is called **troposphere.**

b. The composition of the troposphere is 78.09 percent nitrogen, 20.95 percent oxygen, 0.93 percent argon, 0.03 percent carbon dioxide, and other gases.

c. The air is very elastic and can be greatly compressed. Therefore, the weight of the upper air pressing down makes the air which closely surrounds the earth's crust very dense. At sea level, under average conditions, the air pressure is 14.7 psi, or 30 inches of mercury.

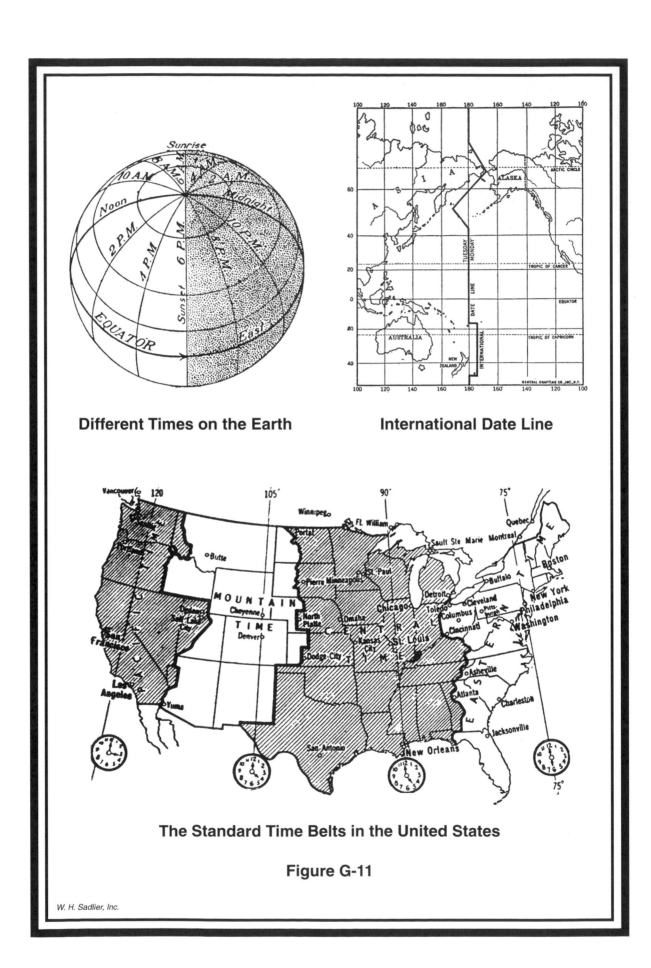

Different Times on the Earth

International Date Line

The Standard Time Belts in the United States

Figure G-11

d. The pressure of air is measured by a *barometer* (Fig. G-12) consisting of a hollow glass tube about 36 inches long. One end of the tube is closed. The tube is filled with mercury, and the open end is placed in a dish of mercury. When the tube stands upright, the pressure of air moves the mercury up and down as the pressure changes. At sea level, when the pressure of air is 14.7 psi, the mercury level is at 30 inches.

e. The pressure or weight of the air is not always the same at sea level, or anywhere else. When the air is warmed, it expands and becomes lighter. Therefore, the pressure will be lower. When the air is cold, it contracts and becomes heavier. Hence, the pressure will be higher.

f. When the pressure of air is 14.7 psi, water will boil at 212°F (psi = pounds per square inch, F = Fahrenheit). If the pressure is lower, the boiling point will decrease, and with higher pressure the boiling point will increase.

G-12 HUMIDITY

The amount of water vapor in the air is a primary element of *climate*. Humidity measurements include the following.

a. Absolute Humidity

The mass of water vapor per unit volume of natural air. Absolute humidity has a great application in air-conditioning and ventilating systems.

b. Relative Humidity

The ratio of the actual water vapor content of the air to its total capacity at a given temperature.

c. Specific Humidity

The mass of water vapor per unit mass of natural air, and mixing ratio. The mass of water vapor per unit mass of dry air.

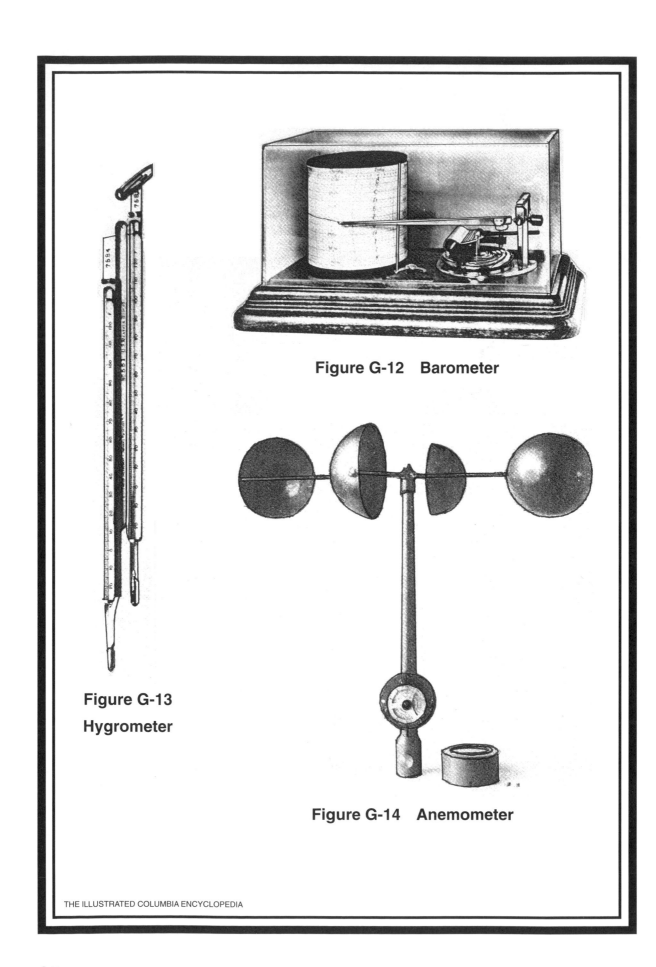

Figure G-12   Barometer

Figure G-13

Hygrometer

Figure G-14   Anemometer

d. **Humidity is measured by a *hygrometer*** (Fig. G-13). The most widely used device is the ***dry-wet-bulb psychrometer.*** It consists of two identical mercury thermometers, one of which has a wet liner wick around its bulb. Water evaporating from the wick absorbs heat from the thermometer bulb, causing the thermometer reading to drop. The person conducting the measurement after recording the dry-bulb temperature and the drop in wet-bulb temperature by looking at the appropriate table can determine the temperature-humidity index.

e. ***Temperature-Humidity Index***

This is defined as follows

$$Ith = 0.4\ Fd + Fw + 15$$

where   Ith = temperature-humidity index

Fd = dry-bulb temperature

Fw = wet-bulb temperature

Ith of 70 is most comfortable

Ith of 75 is satisfactory

Ith of 80 is uncomfortable

f. ***Humidity decreases with altitude.*** Cold air with high relative humidity feels colder than dry air of the same temperature, because high humidity in cold weather increases the conduction of heat from the body. Conversely, hot air attended by high relative humidity feels warmer than it actually is, because of an increased conduction of heat from the body combined with a lessening of the cooling effect afforded by evaporation. A low relative humidity modifies the effect of temperature extremes on the human body.

G-13   **WIND**

Wind is the movement of air from high-pressure areas to low-pressure areas.

a. The greater the difference in pressure, the stronger the wind. The direction of the wind is not always the same near the surface of the earth as it is some miles above the earth. Winds generally blow more steadily and with more force over the oceans than over land. Winds help to bring sudden changes in our weather.

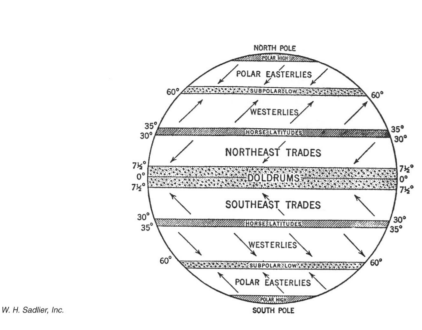

W. H. Sadlier, Inc.

Figure G-15   The Great Wind Belts

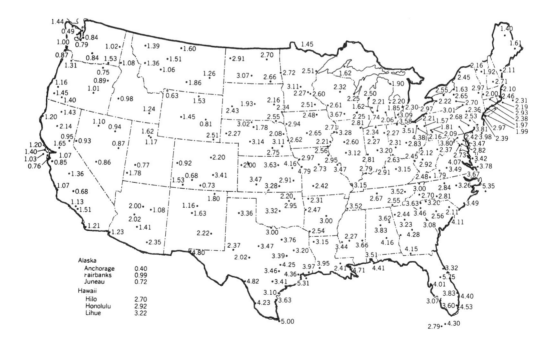

Figure G-17   Max. Hourly Rainfall U.S. Weather Bureau (1961)

b. Around the equator where the heated air is expanding and rising, low pressure is created and is known as **doldrums** (Fig. G-15).

About 30° north latitude and 30° south latitude, there are belts of high pressure known as the **horse latitudes.**

Near 60° north latitude and 60° south latitude, there are belts of low pressure.

Finally, there are the north polar and south polar caps of high pressure. The prevailing wind systems of the earth blow from the several belts of high pressure toward adjacent low-pressure belts. Because of the earth's rotation, winds are deflected to the right in the northern hemisphere, and to the left in the southern hemisphere (Fig. G-16).

c. The U.S. Weather Bureau uses numbers from 0 to 12 to represent the following:

0—calm wind (less than 1 mi/hour)

1—light air	7—near gale
2—light breeze	8—gale
3—gentle breeze	9—strong gale
4—moderate breeze	10—storm
5—fresh breeze	11—violent storm
6—strong breeze	12—hurricane (over 70 mi/hour)

Tornado winds have reached 500 ml/hour.

e. In winter, areas of high pressure tend to build up over cold continental land masses, while vigorous low-pressure development takes place over the adjacent, relatively warm oceans. Exactly the opposite conditions occur to a lesser degree during the summer. These contrasting pressures over land and water areas are the cause of **monsoon winds,** which reverse their direction with the seasons.

f. Wind velocity is commonly measured by means of a **cup-anemometer.** The direction of the wind is determined by a *wind vane,* also called a *weather vane* (Fig. G-14).

g. The water in the oceans is moving from warmer to cooler regions or from cooler to warmer regions. The prevailing winds cause currents on the oceans (Fig. G-16).

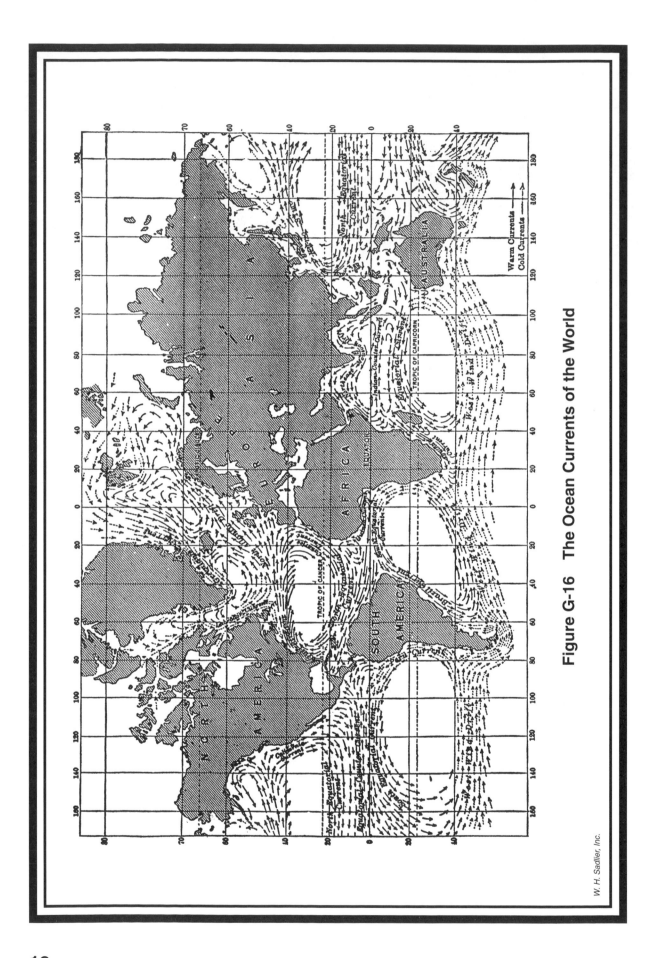

Figure G-16   The Ocean Currents of the World

W. H. Sadlier, Inc.

18

G-14 RAIN

When the particles of moisture in clouds are heavy enough, they fall as drops of rain.

a. Precipitation is formed by further condensation of the moisture in a cloud. The rain-drops formed are enlarged by coalescing with others on impact and by condensing on their colder surfaces the moisture in the air through which they pass.

From the time they leave the bottom of the cloud, evaporation takes place, and, if the air is warm and dry and the cloud is high, the raindrops are small and they fall slowly, or they may evaporate completely before they reach the earth.

b. Rainfall is one of the primary elements in climate.

c. Rainfall in the United States ranges from less than 2 in. in Death Valley to more than 100 in. on the coast of Washington state. In the rest of the country, the average rainfall is between 15 and 45 in. annually (Fig. G-17).

d. Areas near the sea and ocean receive more rain than inland regions, because the winds constantly lose moisture and may be quite dry by the time they reach the interior of a continent.

e. Rainfall is measured in terms of inches of depth, by means of a simple receptacle-and-gauge apparatus or electrical or weighing devices placed where eddies of air will not interfere with the normal fall of the raindrops. Rainfall is measured in daily, monthly, and annual totals. Amounts are also recorded during a specific period of hours or min-utes.

G-15 CLOUDS

In the regions with moist air, there are more clouds than in areas with dry air. Clouds are of different shapes, colors, and thicknesses. There are four kinds of clouds (Fig. G-18):

Cumulus Clouds

Stratus Clouds

Cirrus Clouds

Figure G-18

1. *Cumulus clouds*

   On a hot summer afternoon, thick clouds frequently appear in the sky. They look like cotton balls pulled apart or large piles of smoke. The bottom of this cloud is about 2000 to 4000 feet above the ground, and the top may be 3 or 4 mi. above the ground. They may turn into clouds which bring rain.

2. *Nimbus clouds*

   These are thick, dark clouds from which rain or snow falls. They are generally not more than 3000 ft. from the ground.

3. *Cirrus clouds*

   Sometimes, feathery-shaped clouds are seen high in the sky. They are light and commonly white, and generally do not bring rain.

4. *Stratus clouds*

   These clouds are seen near the earth. They are a little too high to form fog. Sometimes they denote stormy weather.

Figure G-19   Lightning Striking

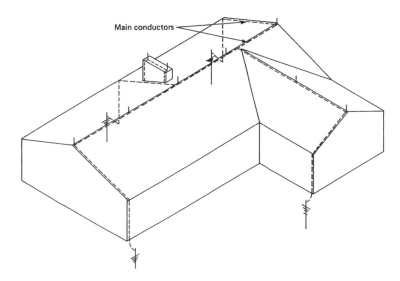

Main conductors

Figure G-20   Lightning Rods and Conductors

G-16 LIGHTNING

Lightning is an electrical discharge accompanied by thunder, which is commonly occurring during a thunderstorm. The discharge may take place between one part of a cloud and another part of a cloud, or between one cloud and another cloud, or between a cloud and the earth.

a.   In general, there are four types of lightning:

1.   ***Forked lightning.***   Lightning appears as a jagged streak (Fig. G-19).

2.   ***Sheet Lightning.***   Appears as a vast flash in the sky.

3.   ***Ball Lightning.***   Illuminates as a brilliant ball.

4.   ***Heat Lightning.***   Illumination from lightning flashes occurring near the horizon, often with clear sky overhead, and with the accompanying thunder too distant to be audible.

b.   **Lightning rod**

When correctly installed on a building, a lightning rod offers a certain degree of protection to the structure during electrical storms (Fig. G-20).

See Part 6 for more information.

AMERICAN AND BRITISH SYSTEM

Linear Measure

12 inches = 1 foot
3 feet = 1 yard
5½ yards = 1 rod
220 yards = 1 furlong
5,280 feet = 1 mile
6 feet = 1 fathom
6,076.1 feet = 1 nautical mile

Square Measure

144 square inches = 1 square foot
9 square feet = 1 square yard
30¼ square yards = 1 square rod
160 square rods = 1 acre
4,840 square yards = 1 acre
640 acres = 1 square mile

Cubic Measure

1,728 cubic inches = 1 cubic foot
27 cubic feet = 1 cubic yard

Liquid Measure

16 ounces = 1 (U.S.) pint
20 ounces = 1 imperial (British) pint
2 cups = 1 pint
2 pints = 1 quart
4 quarts = 1 gallon
1.2 U.S. gallons = 1 imperial (British) gallon

Weights: Avoirdupois

16 drams = 1 ounce
16 ounces = 1 pound
112 pounds = 1 long hundredweight
2000 pounds = 1 short ton
2240 pounds = 1 long ton

Weights: Troy and Apothecary

480 grains = 1 ounce
12 ounces = 1 pound

Figure G-21

G-17 WEIGHTS AND MEASURES

The crude versions of the weights and measures probably date back to prehistoric times. Early units were commonly based on body measurements and on plant seeds.

As civilization progressed, technological and commercial requirements led to increased standardization of weights and measures.

Today the chief systems are:

> *a. American and British system* (Fig. G-21)
>
> *b. Metric system* (Fig. G-22)

a. American and British System

This system evolved in England and was carried to America by English colonists. In 1856 it became the official weights and measures system in the United States. In the American and British system, two sets of weights are employed:

1. *Avoirdupois.* Used in general commerce, it was legalized in England in 1303, and is based on 16 ounces per pound.

2. *Troy.* Used for weighing precious metals, it was legalized in England in 1527, and is based on 12 ounces per pound.

b. Metric System

This is a system of measurements and weights planned and adopted in France in accordance with a law passed in 1799 (Fig. G-22). It was subsequently adopted by many nations. The use of the metric system was permitted in England, and the U.S. government permitted the use of the metric system in 1866.

METRIC SYSTEM

Linear Measure

10 millimeters = 1 centimeter
10 centimeters = 1 decimeter
10 decimeters = 1 meter
10 meters = 1 dekameter
1,000 meters = 1 kilometer

Square Measure

100 square millimeters = 1 square centimeter
100 square centimeters = 1 square decimeter
10,000 square centimeters = 1 square meter
100 square meters = 1 are
100 ares = 1 hectare
10,000 ares = 1 square kilometer

Cubic Measure

1,000 cubic millimeters = 1 cubic centimeter
1,000 cubic centimeters = 1 cubic decimeter
1,000 cubic decimeters = 1 cubic meter

Liquid Measure

10 milliliters = 1 centiliter
100 centiliters = 1 liter
1,000 liters = 1 kiloliter

Weights

10 milligrams = 1 centigram
10 centigrams = 1 decigram
10 decigrams = 1 gram
100 centigrams = 1 gram
10 grams = 1 dekagram
10 dekagrams = 1 hectogram
10 hectogram = 1 kilogram
1,000 grams = 1 kilogram
1,000 kilograms = 1 ton

Figure G-22

G-18 CONVERSION FACTORS

All information and calculations, etc., given in this book are based on the American system. Tables of conversion are provided for converting the American system to the metric system. It is suggested that all calculations be performed in the American system which is commonly used in the United States, and if the work is to be done in the countries where the metric system is in practice, use the following procedures:

1. **Convert all dimensions and other requirements from the metric system to the American system by using Fig. G-23.**

2. **Use these figures to solve the problems.**

3. **When you solve the problem using the American system, convert the solution to the metric system by using Fig. G-24.**

CONVERSION FACTORS
METRIC SYSTEM TO AMERICAN SYSTEM

Length	millimeter	mm	× 0.0393	= inch	in
	meter	m	× 3.2808	= foot	ft
	meter	m	× 1.0936	= yard	yd
	kilometer	km	× 0.6213	= mile U.S.	mi
Area	sq. millimeter	mm²	× 0.00155	= sq. inch	in²
	sq. meter	m²	× 10.7639	= sq. foot	ft²
	sq. meter	m²	× 1.1959	= sq. yard	yd²
	sq. kilometer	km²	× 0.3861	= sq. mile	mi²
	sq. meter	m²	× 0.000247	= acre	A
	hectare	h	× 2.471	= acre	A
Volume	cubic millimeter	mm³	× 0.000061	= cubic inch	cu. in.
	cubic meter	m³	× 35.3146	= cubic foot	cu. ft.
	cubic meter	M³	× 1.3079	= cubic yard	cu. yd.
	liter	l	× 0.2641	= gallon U.S.	gal
	liter	l	× 1.0566	= quart U.S.	qt
Mass	gram	g	× 0.03527	= ounce (avo)	oz
	kilogram	kg	× 2.2046	= pound (avo)	lb
	kilogram	kg	× 0.001102	= short ton	t
Pressure	kilopascal	KPa	× 0.145	= pound-force/m² psi	
	kilopascal	KPa	× 0.3345	= foot of water 1 psi	
	kilopascal	KPa	× 0.2953	= in. of mercury-32°F	
Power	watt	W	× 0.7375	= ft-lbf/s	
	watt	W	× 3.4121	= Btuh	
	kilowatt	kW	× 1.341	= HP (550 ft-lbf/s)	
Angle	radian	rad	× 57.2957	= degree	deg
Temperature Celsius		C	(1.8×°C + 32)	= degree Fahrenheit	

Figure G-23

CONVERSION FACTORS
AMERICAN SYSTEM TO METRIC SYSTEM

Length	inch	in	× 25.4	= millimeter	mm
	foot	ft	× 0.3048	= meter	m
	yard	yd	× 0.9144	= meter	m
	mile U.S.	mi	× 1.6093	= kilometer	km
Area	sq. inch	in^2	× 645.16	= sq. millimeter	mm^2
	sq. foot	ft^2	× 0.0929	= sq. meter	m^2
	sq. yard	yd^2	× 0.8361	= sq. meter	m^2
	sq. mile U.S.	mi^2	× 2.5899	= sq. kilometer	km^2
	acre	A	× 4046.873	= sq. meter	m^2
	acre	A	× 0.4046	= hectare	h
Volume	cubic inch	in^3	× 16387.06	= cubic millimeter	cu. mm
	cubic foot	ft^3	× 0.0283	= cubic meter	cu. m
	cubic yard	yd^3	× 0.7645	= cubic meter	cu. m
	gallon U.S.	gal	× 3.7854	= liter	l
	quart U.S.	qt	× 0.9463	= liter	l
Mass	ounce (avo)	oz	× 28.3495	= gram	g
	pound (avo)	lb	× 0.4535	= kilogram	kg
	short ton	t	× 907.185	= kilogram	kg
Pressure	pound-force/m^2	psi	× 6.8947	= kilopascal	KPa
	foot of water	1 psi	× 2.9889	= kilopascal	KPa
	Inch of mercury	(32°F)	× 3.3863	= kilopascal	KPa
Power	ft-lb-f/s		× 1.3558	= watt	W
	btuh		× 0.293	= watt	W
	HP (550 ft. lb/s)		× 0.7457	= kilowatt	kW
Angle	degree	deg	× 0.01745	= radian	+ad
Temperature Fahrenheit		F	(°F − 32 ÷ 1.8)	= degree Celsius	C

Figure G-24

G-19 ABBREVIATIONS

A	area
AD	area drain
AFD	area floor drain
AGA	American Gas Association
AHAM	Association of Home Appliance Manufacturers
AIA	American Institute of Architects
AISI	American Iron and Steel Institute
ASA	American Standard Association
ASCE	American Society of Civil Engineering
ASHRAE	American Society of Heating, Refrigeration and Air Conditioning Engineers
ASME	American Society of Mechanical Engineers
ASSE	American Society of Sanitary Engineering
ASTM	American Society of Testing Materials
A.V.	air vent
B	bidet
B.S.	bar sink
B.T.	bathtub
Btu	British thermal unit
Btuh	British thermal units per hour
Bwv	back water valve
c	capita (person)
°C	temperature, Celsius
C°	temperature, difference
C.B.	catch basin
C to C	center to center
CI	cast iron
CISPI	Cast Iron Soil Pipe Institute
C.L.	condensate line

CO	cleanout
CODP	cleanout deck plate
C.W.	cold water
CWR	cold water return
cu. ft.	cubic feet
cu. in.	cubic inches
C.W.M.	clothes washing machine
C.V.	check valve
D (DIA)	diameter
D.B.	distribution box
DD	degree days
DEG	degree, temperature difference
DHW	domestic hot water
DL	developed length
DWV	drainage waste and vent
D.P.	distribution leaching pool
D.F.	drinking fountain
D.S.	down spout
D.W.	dish washer
DR	drain
D.W.	dry well
D.T.	drain tile
E to C	end to center
Elev.	elevation
EWC	electric water cooler
°F	degrees Fahrenheit
F°	Fahrenheit
F.B.	foot bath
F.D.	floor drain
F.F.	finish floor

F.C.O.	floor cleanout
F.D.C.	fire department connection
F.D.R.	feeder
F.E.C.	fire extinguisher cabinet
F.E.	fire extinguisher unit
F.G.	fire grade (final)
F.H.	fire hose
F.H.C.	fire hose cabinet
F.L.	fire line
FL	flow line
F.P.	fire plug
F.S.P.	fire standpipe
F.T.	flush tank
F.U.	fixture unit
F.V.	flush valve
fpm	feet per minute
ft	foot, feet
gpd	gallons per day
gpm	gallons per minute
GR	grade
G.T.	grease trap
H	height
H.B.	hose bibs
Hd or H.D.	head
H.W.	hot water
H.W.C.	hot water circulating line
H.W.R.	hot water return
H.W.S.	hot water supply
HWT	hot water tank
HWP	hot water pump

I.B.R.	Institute of Boiler and Radiator Manufacturers
ID	inside diameter
IW	indirect waste
IPS	iron pipe size

k	heat conductivity
K.S.	kitchen sink
kW	kilowatt(s)
kWh	kilowatt-hour

L	length
L. or LAV	lavatory
LDR	leader
L.T.	laundry tray
lb	pound
L.P.	leaching pool

m	meter
m^2	square meter
max.	maximum
Mbh	thousands of British thermal units per hour
mfr.	manufacturer
M.H.	manhole
min.	minimum
MRT	mean radiant temperature

NAPHCC	National Association of Plumbing, Heating and Cooling Contractors
NBFU	National Board of Fire Underwriters
NBS	National Bureau of Standards
NFPA	National Fire Protection Association
NPS	nominal pipe size

O	oxygen
O.D.	outside diameter
oz	ounce
P	person (capita)
P.D.	planter drain
P.P.	pool piping
psi	pounds per square inch
%	percent
pf	power factor
R	symbol for resistance
R19,R7,etc.	thermal resistances
(R)	roughing only
rad.	radius
R.C.P.	reinforced concrete pipe
R.D.	roof drain
red	reducer
R.L.	roof leader
R.S.	residential
S.	sink
san.	sanitary
SC	sink cock
S.B.	sitz bath
SH	shower
S.O.V.	shutoff valve
S.P.	swimming pool
spec.	specification
sq.	square
sq. ft.	square foot, feet
sq. in.	square inch, inches
SS	service sink

std.	standard
SV	service
SW	service weight
S&W	soil and waste
T	temperature
TEL	total equivalent length
TOIL	toilet
U	transmission factor
U or Urn	urinal
V	volume
V.	vent
V.C.P.	vitrified clay pipe
V.C.T.	vitrified clay tile
V.S.	vent stack
Vtr	vent through roof
W	waste
W.C.	water closet
W.C.O.	wall cleanout
W.H.	water heater
W.H.	wall hydrant
W.S.	waste stack
XH	extra heavy
Y.D.	yard drain

G-20 DEFINITIONS

acidity   An acid condition of water.

approved   Approved by office in charge.

area drain   A receptacle used to collect surface or rain water from an open area.

air gap   The unobstructed vertical distance between the lowest opening from any pipe or faucet supplying water to a tank in a water supply system.

air changes   The number of times the air is changed per hour in a room, in a ventilation system.

air density   The weight of air in pounds per cubic foot.

airflow pattern   Method by which air is introduced into a space and removed.

airfoil vanes   Blades in a register that can be turned to positions that direct the airstream.

airstream   Airflow through filters, coils, registers, and ducts.

air vent valve   Used for escape of air at high points in a hot water heating system.

anaerobic   Bacteria found in septic tanks are beneficial in digesting organic matter living without oxygen.

auxiliary resistance heating   Electric resistance heaters that supplement the heat from the heat pump.

average water temperature   Average between temperature of water leaving and returning to the boiler.

backfill	Filling the trench excavated up to the original line after the sewer or other piping has been laid.
backflow	The flow of water or other substances into the pipes of a potable water supply line.
backflow preventer	A device to prevent backflow into the potable water system.
back siphonage	The flow of water or other substances into the pipes of a potable water supply source, due to negative pressure in the pipe.
base	The lowest point of any vertical pipe.
battery of fixtures	Group of two or more similar adjacent plumbing fixtures which discharge into a common horizontal soil branch.
blower-coil unit	Blower moving the airstream across heating coils, cooling coils, and filter.
boiler	A unit that produces hot water or steam for a heating system.
boiler blow-off	Outlet on a boiler used for discharging of water or sediment in the boiler.
branch	Any part of a piping system other than a main or riser.
branch interval	A length of soil or waste stack connected into the horizontal branches.
branch vent	The vent that connects one or more individual vents with a vent stack.
breathing wall	Incremental system that has an exterior wall opening for heat and moisture, fresh air supply, and discharge.

37

British thermal unit	Quantity of heat (Btu).
building drain	The main horizontal sanitary system inside the wall of the building.
building sewer	That part of the horizontal drainage system which connects to the end of the building drain and to a public sewer or individual sewage disposal system.
building storm drain	A drain used to receive rain water, surface water, ground water, and discharge into a building storm sewer or a combined building sewer.
building storm sewer	Connects to the end of the building storm drain and conveys the contents to a public storm sewer or combined sewer.
building subdrain	Drainage system which cannot drain by gravity into the building sewer.
caulking	Any approved method of rendering joint water and gas pipes tight. For cast-iron pipes with hub joints, caulking the joint with lead and oakum.
centralized	A system with one heating or cooling source for HVAC distribution network.
chassis	The parts of an incremental conditioner, shaped to fit into a sleeve.
check valve	A valve that allows fluid to flow in one direction.
chilled water	The refrigerated water used to cook the air in HVAC system.
circulator	Centrifugal pump or "booster."
cleanout	A removable plug in a drainage system (CO) where a vertical pipe is connected to horizontal building drain.

38

closet carrier An iron or steel frame to support a water closet hangs from a wall.

code Regulations and their subsequent amendments adopted to control the plumbing work by the local authority.

combined sewer Pipe carrying storm and sanitary drainage.

combined building sewer A building sewer which receives storm water and sewage.

common vent The vertical vent portion serving to vent two or more fixtures at the same level in a vertical stack.

compression Produces high pressure in Freon gas.

condensing Liquifies high-pressure Freon gas.

continuous waste A drain connecting a single fixture with more than one compartment or other permitted fixtures to a common trap.

continuous circulation Blower runs continuously; evaporator or burner runs intermittently.

contract documents Includes the contract, the working drawings, and the specifications.

convector Heating element that warms the air passing over it by convection.

covering Thermal insulation on ducts.

cross connection Any connection between two separate piping systems, one with potable water and the other water of questionable source.

curb box Access to an underground valve at the street curb. It controls water service to a building.

curved blade A register blade that directs the airstream.

edge loss factor	Heat loss, slab to earth.
effective opening	The minimum area of a circle at the point of water supply discharge.
effluent	The liquid flowing from the septic tank into the drainfield or cesspool(s).
electronic air cleaners	A filter used for the removal of small, suspended particles from air.
energy	Expressed in kilowatt-hours (kWh), the product of power and time.
energy layout	A drawing that is the basis for shop drawings.
evaporation	Freon liquid absorbs heat as Freon becomes a gas.
expansion fitting	A device to allow for the expansion of pipes and tubings.
face velocity	The speed in feet per minute by which air leaves a register.
fall per foot	The slope of a drainage pipe.
feed line	A pipe that supplies water to a boiler or a domestic hot water tank.
feet of head	Pressure loss in psi divided by the factor 0.433.
fill and vent	Pipes to fill and vent an oil storage tank.
finned-tube	Used for heat transfer between water and air.
fixture clearance	Distance between fixtures or from a fixture to an obstruction.
fixture unit	An index of the relative rate of flow of water to a fixture or sewage leaving a fixture.

fixture branch	The drain from the fixture to the junction of that drain with a vent.
fixture drain	The drain from the fixture branch to any other drain pipe.
fire lines	The system includes the water service, standpipe, roof manifold, Siamese connections and pumps.
flood-level rim	The top edge of a plumbing fixture from which water will overflow.
floor drain	An opening located at floor level connected to a trap to receive the discharge from indirect waste and floor drainage.
floor sink	An opening made of enameled cast iron located at floor level which is connected to a trap, to receive indirect waste and floor drainage; used for restaurants and hospitals.
flow pressure	The pressure adequate to supply a fixture(s).
flow rate	Cubic feet per minute (cfm) of air circulated in an air system.
flue gas	Carbon monoxide, carbon dioxide, and others.
flush tank	A tank that refills automatically and flushes a water closet.
flush valve	A valve that, when operated, delivers water to flush a water closet.
flushometer valve	A device actuated by water pressure which discharges water to fixtures for flushing purposes.
foot of head	The pressure at the bottom of a column of water 1 ft high.
fossil fuels	Oil, gas, and coal.
Freon	Refrigerant gas.

fresh air inlet	A vent that admits air to the house drain.
furnace	A unit that warms the air in warm air heating systems.
grade	The slope or pitch, the "fall," expressed in drainage piping as a fraction of an inch per foot.
gpm	Gallons per minute.
grills	Perforated frame used for air return.
gutter	Rainwater-collecting trough at the edge of a roof.
gutterspace	The empty spaces around the sides, top, and bottom of a panelbox.
hardness	Calcium compounds in water.
heat pump	An all-electric heating/cooling device that takes energy from outdoor air or groundwater.
horsepower (hp)	A unit of power which equals 746 watts.
hose bibb	Connection for supplying water to a garden hose.
house trap	A trap between the house drain and the house sewer.
hydronic	Heating or cooling by water.
humidifier	A device to vaporize water and to use it to increase the realative humidity of air.
I.B.R.	Institute of Boiler and Radiator Manufacturers.

indirect wastes	A waste pipe charged to convey gray water wastes by discharging them into an open plumbing fixture such as floor drain or floor sink.
industrial waste	Liquid waste, free of body waste, resulting from the processes used in industrial establishments.
infiltration	Cold air that leaks inside of building.
insanitary	Contrary to sanitary principles, injurious to health.
interceptor	A device installed to separate and retain deleterious or hazardous matter from normal wastes and discharge by gravity into the sewer.
latent heat	Inherent heat in the form of water vapor.
lavatory	A wash basin.
layout	First drawing of a system showing the relationship of the system components.
leader	A pipe that carries storm water down from a gutter or a roof drain fixture.
liquid waste	The discharge from any fixture or appliance connected to a plumbing system, not including black water.
load factor	The percentage of the total connected fixture unit flow rate.
loop or circuit waste and vent	Plumbing fixtures on the same floor level connected to a common horizontal branch waste pipe.
M	Means thousands.

main	The principal continuous piping to which branches are connected.
main vent	The principal venting system to which vent branches are connected.
Mbh	Thousands of British thermal units per hour.
mean radiant temperature	Average temperature, interior surfaces.
milinches per foot	The head lost in 1 ft of tubing as caused by friction of water flow.
net output	Applied to a boiler, the value of the Mbh delivered by the boiler to heat the building.
one-way throw	A register that delivers air in only one direction.
opposed blade dampers	Controls for the regulation of the flow of air in ducts.
outdoor design temperature	Temperature to which heat is lost.
output	The heat delivered to a room by heating units.
package unit	A boiler plus a number of its controls and accessories.
performance data	Ratings for heating, cooling cfm.
pitch	Referred to as the *slope* of pipe, also called *grade.*
planting screen	Bushes that hide a refrigerant compressor.
plumbing	Includes materials such as pipe, fittings, valves, fixtures, and appliances which are part of a system for the purpose of maintaining sanitary conditions in buildings.

plumbing fixtures	Receptables, devices, or appliances which are supplied with water.
plumbing official inspector	Administrative officer charged with the enforcement of the plumbing code.
plumbing system	The drainage system, water supply, water supply distribution pipes, plumbing fixtures, traps, soil pipes, waste pipes, vent pipes, building drains, building sewers, building storm drain, building storm sewer, liquid waste piping, water treating, water-using equipment, sewage treatment, sewage treatment equipment, fire standpipes, fire sprinklers, and related appliances and appurtenances within the private property.
potable	Water that is safe to drink.
primary air	Heated or cooled air directly from the HVAC.
"process" hot water	Hot water needed for manufacturing processes over and above the "domestic hot water" that is for the personal use of industrial workers.
psi	Pounds per square inch pressure.
public use	Fixture use in a public building.
private sewer	A sewer privately owned, such as a septic system or private sewage treatment plant.
public sewer	A common sewer directly controlled by public authority.
range hood	Hood over a stove to collect odor-laden air that is to be exhausted.
recessed unit	A heating element flush with the floor.

recharge

Putting water back into the ground.

register

Slotted frame for control of the direction of air delivered to the space and its flow rate.

reverse return

A return main that does not get directly back to the boiler but is reversed to serve all the further convectors.

roof drain

A metal water collector flashed into a flat roof.

roof slope

Pitch of a flat roof to direct rainwater to a roof drain.

roughing dimensions

Locations of water supply and drainage pipes to ensure proper fit of a plumbing fixture.

roughing-in

Parts of a plumbing system that are completed prior to the installation of plumbing fixtures.

runout

A branch pipe from a hot water main to a convector.

R-value

Resistance rating of thermal insulation of building materials.

sanitary drainage

Removal of sewage from a building.

sanitary sewer

A pipe which carries sewage only.

Sealtite

Trade name for waterproof flexible steel conduit.

secondary air

Air from the space that is drawn along with the primary air, resulting in a milder mixture.

seepage pit

Receives the effluent of a septic tank and allows it to seep into the earth.

sensible heat	Heat that raises the air temperature.
septic tank	A rectangular concrete tank which receives the discharge of a drainage system designed and constructed to separate solids from liquid and digest organic matter through a period of detention.
service sink	Also called a *slop sink;* a sink used for mopping operations.
sewage	Any liquid waste containing human, mineral, or vegetable matter in suspension or solution.
shop drawings	Also called *contractors'* or *manufacturers' drawings* giving details of equipment for architect's approval.
shutoff valve	A valve near a plumbing fixture for turning off the water.
soil	Major pollutants in plumbing.
soil pipe or waste pipe	Any pipe which receives discharge from the water closets and fixtures, etc., and discharges into the building drain.
stack	The vertical pipe such as soil, waste, or vent piping.
stack vent	The extension of a soil or waste stack above the highest horizontal drain connected to the stack.
standpipe system	A system of piping installed for fire protection purposes.
storm sewer	A sewer used for conveying rainwater and/or surface water.
storm drainage	Removal of rainwater from a roof or other area.
static head	Frictional resistance to airflow in a system.

surface drain	A drain which receives subsurface water and discharges it to a place of disposal.
sump	A pit which receives liquid waste located below the grade of the gravity system and discharges into the house drain by sump pump.
support	Or *anchors* or *hangers.* Devices used for supporting and securing pipe and fixtures to walls, ceilings, floors, and structural members of the building.
supply well	Water from a well used for public, semipublic, or private use.
sweat fitting	A soldered connection of a tube to a fitting.
tankless heater	A coil in a boiler for heating domestic hot water.
temperature difference	The difference between indoor and outdoor temperature.
temperature drop	The difference in temperature of water leaving and returning to the boiler or the difference in temperature of the return air and the heated air delivered.
temperature rise	The difference in temperature of the return air and the delivered cooled air.
thermal transfer	Moving heat into or out of occupied space.
trap	A fitting which provides a liquid seal which will prevent the back-passage of gases.
trap seal	The vertical depth of liquid that a trap will retain.
U coefficient	Overall coefficient of heat transmission.
upfeed system	Boiler located below convectors.

upflow, downflow, horizontal	Furnace types classified by direction of airflows.
vacuum breaker	A device to stop suction in a water pipe.
valve	A control used for flow of water or gas.
ventilation	Control for use of outdoor air.
venturi tee	Directs water through the convector.
vent stack	A vertical vent pipe used for providing circulation of air to and from any part of the drainage system.
vent system	A pipe or pipes used to provide a flow of air to or from a drainage system.
vertical pipe	A pipe which is installed in a vertical position.
water cooler	An electric, refrigerated drinking fountain.
water hammer	Banging of pipes caused by the shock of closing faucets.
waste	Pollutants in a plumbing system.
waste pipe	Any pipe which receives the discharge of any fixture or appliances.
water-distributing pipe	A pipe which conveys water from the water service pipe to the plumbing fixtures.
water main	Water supply pipe.
water outlet	Used in connection with the water-distributing system.
water service pipe	The pipe from the source of water supply.

G-21 PLUMBING SYMBOLS

DESCRIPTION	ABBREVIATION	SYMBOL
Wet standpipe	W.S.P.	—— WSP ——
Dry standpipe	D.S.P.	—— DSP ——
Main supplies sprinkler	S.	—— S ——
Branch and head sprinkler	B.H.S.	——O——O——O——
Gas—low pressure	G.	—— G ——
Gas—medium pressure	M.G.	—— MG ——
Gas—high pressure	H.G.	—— HG ——
Compressed air	A.	—— A ——
Vacuum	V.	—— V ——
Vacuum cleaning	V.C.	—— VC ——
Oxygen	O.	—— O ——
Liquid oxygen	L.OX.	—— LOX ——
Nitrogen	N.	—— N ——
Liquid nitrogen	L.N.	—— LN ——
Hydrogen	H.	—— H ——
Helium	H.E.	—— HF ——
Argon	A.R.	—— AR ——
Liquid petroleum gas	L.P.G.	—— LPG ——
Sewer—cast iron	C.S.I.	—— CSI ——
Sewer—clay tile bell and spigot	S.C.T.	—— SCT ——
High-pressure steam	H.P.S.	—#—#—#—
Medium-pressure steam	M.P.S.	—/—/—/—

DESCRIPTION	ABBREVIATION	SYMBOL
Low-pressure steam	L.P.S.	————————————
Cold water	C.W.	——— - ——— - - ———
Hot water	H.W.	——— - - ——— —— -
Hot water return	H.W.R.	——— - - - ——— - - -
Waste line	W.L.	——— **WL** ———
Vent line	V.L.	— — — — — —
Sanitary sewer	S.S.	——— **SS** ———
Condensate line	C.	——— **C** ———
Storm drain	S.D.	——— **SD** ———
Rain water leader	R.W.L.	——— **RWL** ———
Indirect waste	I.W.	——→ ——→ ——→
Fire line	F.	——— **F** ———
Soil, waste, or leader (above grade)	S.W.L.A.	————————————
Soil, waste, or leader (below grade)	S.W.L.B.	——— ——— ———
Combination waste and vent	C.W.V.	——— **CWV** ———
Acid waste	A.W.	——— **AW** ———
Acid vent	A.V.	— — — **AV** — — —
Indirect drain	D.	——— **D** ———
Chilled drinking water supply	D.W.S.	——— **DWS** ———

DESCRIPTION	ABBREVIATION	SYMBOL
Chilled drinking water return	D.W.R.	——— DWR ———
Sanitizing hot water supply (180°F.)	S.H.W.	— — — — — —
Tempered water supply	T.S.	——— TS ———
Fuel oil supply	F.O.S.	——— FOS ———
Fuel oil return	F.O.R.	——— FOR ———
Fuel oil tank vent	F.O.V.	– · – · — FOV – · – ·
Hot water heating supply	H.W.	——— HW ———
Recessed tub	R.T.	
Angle tub	A.T.	
Roll rim tub	R.R.T.	
Corner tub	C.T.	
Shower	SH.	
Shower stall	SH.T.	
Water closet (tank)	W.C.	

DESCRIPTION	ABBREVIATION	SYMBOL
Water closet (flush)	F.T.	
Urinals	U.	
Bidet	B.	
Lavatory	L.	
Drinking fountain	D.F.	DF DF DF
Kitchen sink	K.S.	
Gas range	G.R.	GR
Electric range	E.R.	ER
Oven	O.	O
Dishwasher	D.W.	DW
Washing machine	W.M.	WM
Dryer	D.	D

DESCRIPTION	ABBREVIATION	SYMBOL
Laundry trays	L.T.	
Manhole	M.H.	
Dry well	D.W.	
Leader	L.	
Meter	M.	
Gate valve	Ga.V.	
Globe valve	Gl.V.	
Check valve	C.V.	
Floor cleanout	F.C.O.	
Floor drain	F.D.	
Planter drain	P.D.	
Roof drain	R.D.	

CONTENTS

Part 2

WATER AND ITS USE IN BUILDINGS

Basic Information

Design of Water Systems

Water Distribution

Hot Water Systems

Design of Hot Water System

Hot Water Distribution

WATER AND ITS USE IN BUILDINGS
AND IN DEVELOPMENTS

BASIC INFORMATION

W-1 WATER

Since the late 19th century water has been used inside structures for drinking, cooking, washing, bathing, and fire fighting.

Water is a liquid which is odorless, tasteless, and colorless in small amounts, but exhibits a bluish tinge in large quantities.

Water is necessary for life; it constitutes a great part of the fundamental substances (protoplasm) of which human, animal, and plant bodies are composed. The blood of humans and animals and the sap of plants contain large quantities of water.

W-2 PROPERTY OF WATER

a.   Chemically, water is a compound of **hydrogen (H) and oxygen (O).**

Its molecule consists of **two atoms of hydrogen and one atom of oxygen = H_2O.**

Water composition by weight is one part of hydrogen to eight of oxygen, i.e., 11.1 percent hydrogen and 88.9 percent oxygen.

b.   Unlike other liquids, water expands when it freezes. When cooled, it freezes at 32°F and changes into a colorless, crystalline solid (ice) which is less dense than liquid.

c.   When heated to its boiling point of 212°F (under standard pressure of 14.7 psi), it vaporizes into steam.

d.   Water stores heat readily, removes large quantities of heat when it evaporates, and has a remarkable cooling potential. For this reason, we use it as a heat-transfer medium in heating, ventilating, and air-conditioning systems (HVAC).

e.   Completely pure water is a poor conductor of electricity.

W-3 QUANTITY OF WATER AND SOURCE

a. Water covers approximately 70 percent of the earth's surface in oceans, lakes, rivers, and glaciers. Over 97 percent of this water is inaccessible because it is salty or frozen in the polar ice caps.

b. The primary source of a water supply is rainfall. Water constantly circulates, powered by the earth's solar energy (hydrolic cycle).

c. Removal of salts from brackish water is accomplished commercially by distillation (or evaporation), electrodialysis, freezing, and ion exchange. It has a limited application for water supply, because of the fuel cost involved in converting salt water to steam.

N-4 IMPURITY OF WATER AND TREATMENT

a. Surface water and groundwater contain some degree of impurities. Rain or runoff water, when it percolates down through the soil, may dissolve minerals, entrap gases, and pick up pollution.

b. All potable water to be used for human drinking, cooking, and washing must be tested before being put to use and also be tested periodically during use.

The test can be performed by the local Department of Health or by an approved private testing laboratory. The testing agency checks the water for the following.

c. *Hardness.* Caused by magnesium and calcium salts, hardness will affect food preparation and laundering, and causes clogging of the pipes. It can be corrected by an ion-exchanger.

d. *Acidity.* Entrapped gases, such as carbon dioxide and oxygen, can corrode nonferrous pipes, cause rust, and clog steel pipes. This can be corrected by adding sodium silicate, which neutralizes the acid.

e. ***Pollution.*** Caused by sewage and organic matters. This will cause ill health and disease. It can be corrected by chlorination.

f. ***Color.*** Caused by manganese and iron; can be corrected by ozonation and filtration.

g. ***Taste and odor.*** Caused by organic matter; normally found in shallow wells, problems can be corrected by the use of activated carbon filtration.

W-5 POTABLE WATER

Water which is tested and corrected to be suitable for human drinking, cooking, and bathing.

W-6 NONPOTABLE WATER

Surface water, groundwater, or collected rainwater which contains some degree of impurity. This water can be used for any purpose except human drinking, cooking, and bathing.

W-7 GRAY WATER

Water discharged from dishwashers, washing machines, bathtubs, sinks, and other fixtures, except wastewater from toilets or urinals.

W-8 BLACK WATER

Water containing toilets' and urinals' wastes.

W-9 DISTILLATION OF WATER

The process generally employed in making nearly pure water by using distillation. It is commonly used in laboratories, and is not economical for the use in a water supply because of the expenses involved in boiling the water.

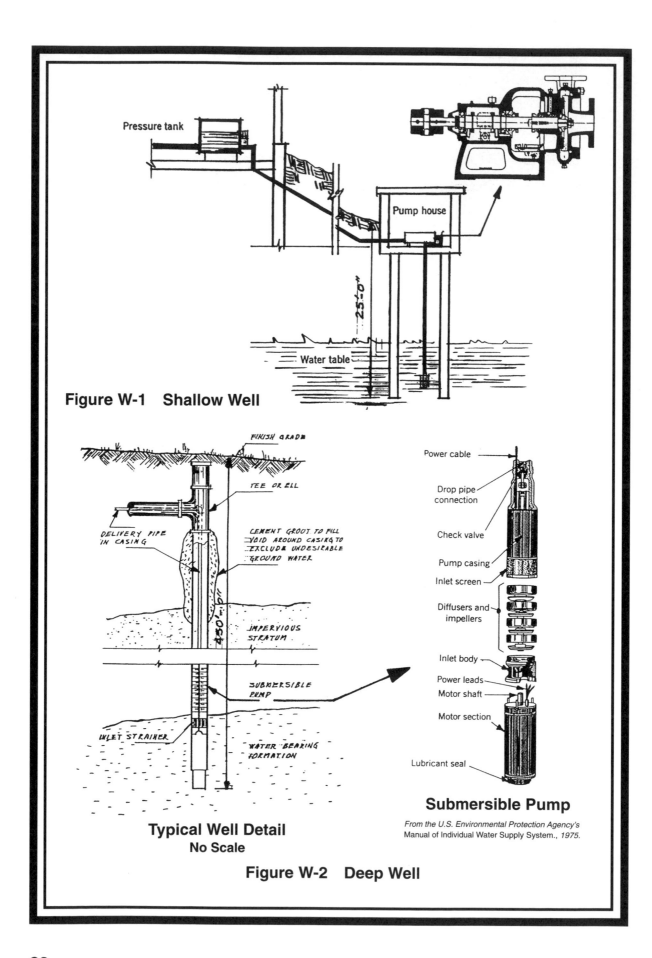

Figure W-1   Shallow Well

Pressure tank

Pump house

25'-0"

Water table

Typical Well Detail
No Scale

FINISH GRADE

TEE OR ELL

DELIVERY PIPE IN CASING

CEMENT GROUT TO FILL VOID AROUND CASING TO EXCLUDE UNDESIRABLE GROUND WATER

450'-0"

IMPERVIOUS STRATUM

SUBMERSIBLE PUMP

INLET STRAINER

WATER BEARING FORMATION

Power cable

Drop pipe connection

Check valve

Pump casing

Inlet screen

Diffusers and impellers

Inlet body

Power leads

Motor shaft

Motor section

Lubricant seal

Submersible Pump

From the U.S. Environmental Protection Agency's Manual of Individual Water Supply System., 1975.

Figure W-2   Deep Well

W-10 WATER DESALINIZATION

Several processes used for removing soluble salts from water to render it suitable for drinking or other purposes. The principal methods used include distillation (evaporation), electrodialysis, freezing, and ion exchange. The cost of energy to operate these systems is very high; consequently, it is not widely used for a water supply.

W-11 SURFACE WATER

The rainwater, melted snow, and ice that runs off the surface of the ground into streams, rivers, and other bodies of water.

W-12 GROUNDWATER

Water that seeps and percolates through the soil, building a supply of water below the surface of the earth.

W-13 WATER TABLE AND DEPTH OF WATER TABLE

Water present in the earth. Its upper level is called *water table,* which is caused either by the downward seepage of rainwater (vadose water) or the forcing upward of the magmatic water (juvenile water) originating in the molten rock of the earth's interior.

Depth of the water table is the distance from the ground surface to the water level (water table).

W-14 SHALLOW WELL

When the depth of the water well is less than 25 feet, it is called *shallow well.* Shallow wells are dug, driven, or drilled. They are normally protected by circular masonry or a concrete wall (Fig. W-1).

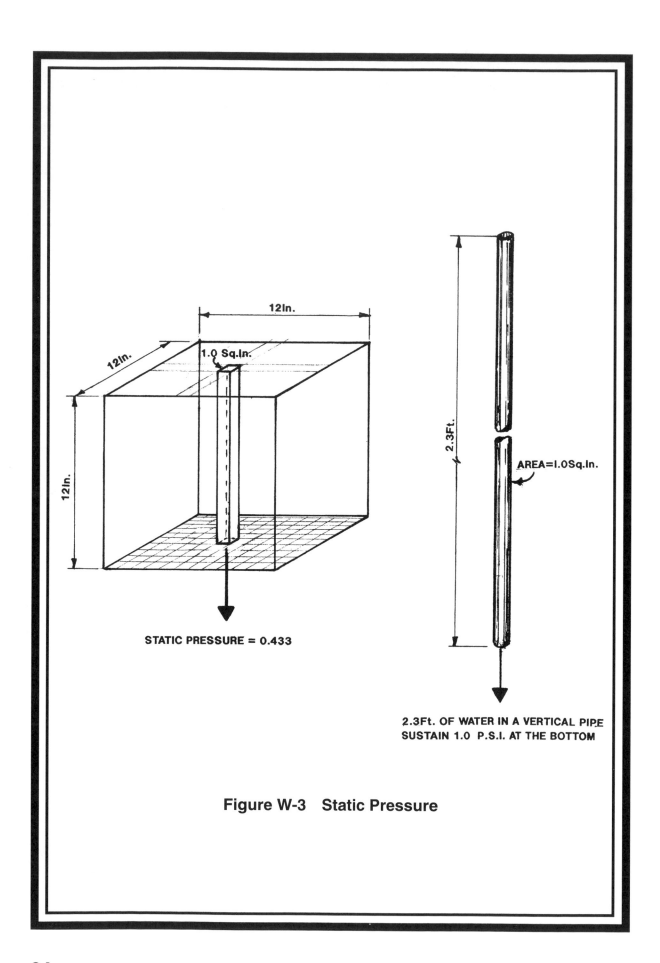

12In.

12In.

1.0 Sq.In.

12In.

STATIC PRESSURE = 0.433

2.3Ft.

AREA=1.0Sq.In.

2.3Ft. OF WATER IN A VERTICAL PIPE SUSTAIN 1.0 P.S.I. AT THE BOTTOM

Figure W-3   Static Pressure

W-15 DEEP WELL

When the depth of the water well is over 25 feet, it is called *deep well.* These are drilled or bored. Deep wells of 500 feet or more are not uncommon. They are drilled through earth and rock; the casing (steel tube) is sent down in sections until it reaches the water (Fig. W-2).

W-16 ARTESIAN WELL

The impervious stratum has water bearing soil below it. A breakthrough causes water to flow out of its own accord because of the pressure of trapped water.

W-17 WATER MEASUREMENT

One gallon of water weighs 8.33 pounds. By volume, 1 gallon of water is 231 cu. in., or 0.134 cu. ft.

240 gallons of water weigh 1 ton.

One acre of water (43,560 sq. ft.) 1 foot deep is equal to 325,851 gallons.

W-18 WATER PRESSURE

The pressure of water in the system is measured in **pounds per square inch (psi).** Eight psi of pressure is considered sufficient for all fixtures in a system, except when a flush valve is used, requiring approximately 15 psi. The maximum permissible pressure for fixtures in a system is 50 psi. Pressure tanks (pneumatic) for a residence operate at approximately 35 psi. Pressure of a municipality water supply. For a residence it is about 35 psi, and approximately 50 psi for other structures. The architect should contact the Department of Water Supply to obtain the amount of pressure available to supply the structure. Water pressure above 80 psi will damage the fixtures.

W-19   STATIC PRESSURE

The pressure of the water at the bottom of a pipe is directly related to the weight of water and its height.

One cubic foot of water weighs 62.352 pounds at 60°F at the bottom of 1 cubic foot. We have (see Fig. W-3):

$$12 \text{ in} \times 12 \text{ in} = 144 \text{ in}$$
$$62.352 \text{ lb} \div 144 \text{ in/ft}^2 = 0.433 \text{ psi/ft of height}$$

Therefore, **Static pressure = 0.433 psi/ft of height**

How many feet of water will sustain a static pressure of 1 psi?

$$1 \text{ psi} \div 0.433 \text{ psi/ft} = 2.3 \text{ ft}$$
1 psi = 2.3 ft of height

which means that 2.3 ft of water in a vertical pipe sustain 1 psi at the bottom.

W-20   FEET OF HEAD

This is the distance from the point of water to be used up or down to the level of a water supply.

W-21   DESIGN OF RESERVOIR

Example

We have toilet facilities on the 12th floor of a building, and a water supply is to be supplied from a reservoir above the roof. The pressure required in fixtures on the 12th floor is 16 psi.

What is the height of the reservoir above the 12th floor and roof? The floor height is 12 ft.

Solution

$$16 \text{ psi} \times 2.3 \text{ psi/ft} = 36.8 \text{ ft above the roof}$$
$$36.8 \text{ ft} + 12 \text{ ft} \doteq 48.8 \text{ ft above the 12th floor}$$

W-22   DESIGN OF UPFEED DISTRIBUTION

Example

The city supply of water entering the building is 50 psi. How many stories can this pressure serve? Floor to floor is 12 ft, and the pressure required on the top floor is 16 psi.

Solution

$$50 \text{ psi} - 16 \text{ psi} = 34 \text{ psi}$$
$$34 \text{ psi} \div 0.433 \text{ psi/ft} = 78.522 \text{ ft} \approx 78.5 \text{ ft}$$
$$78.5 \text{ ft} \div 12 \text{ ft/F} = 6.54 \text{ no. of floors}$$

The building can be six stories in height.

W-23   SPECIFIC HEAT OF WATER

To raise the temperature of 1 pound of water 1°F, the heat required is one Btu (British thermal unit).

1 Btu raises temp. of 1 lb of water 1°F

Daily Usage Per Capita (As Listed)	Gallons
Airports (per passenger)	3–5
Apartments, multiple family (per resident)	60
Cottages with seasonal occupancy (per resident)	50
Courts, tourist, with individual bath units (per person)	50
Clubs	
Country (per resident member)	100
Country (per nonresident member present)	25
Dwellings	
Boardinghouses (per boarder)	50
Additional kitchen requirements for nonresident boarders	10
Luxury (per person)	100–150
Multiple-family apartments (per resident)	40
Rooming houses (per resident)	60
Single family (per resident)	50–75
Estates (per resident)	100–150
Factories (per person per shift)	15–35
Highway rest area (per person)	5
Hotels with private baths (two persons per room)	60
Hotels without private baths (per person)	50
Institutions other than hospitals (per person)	75–125
Hospitals (per bed)	250–400
Laundries, self-service (per washing)	50
Motels with bath, toilet, and kitchen facilities (per bed space)	50
With bed and toilet (per bed space)	40
Restaurants with toilet facilities (per patron)	7–10
Without toilet facilities (per patron)	2½–3
With bar/cocktail lounge (additional quantity per patron)	2
Schools	
Boarding (per pupil)	75–100
Day, with cafeteria, gymnasium, and showers (per pupil)	25
Day with cafeteria but no gymnasiums or showers (per pupil)	20
Day without cafeteria, gymnasiums, or showers (per pupil)	15
Service stations (per vehicle)	10
Stores (per toilet room)	400
Swimming pools (per swimmer)	10
Theaters	
Drive-in (per car space)	5
Movie (per auditorium seat)	5

These values may be reduced as follows: with flow controls, up to 25% reduction; with water recycling, up to 50% reduction.

Figure W-4   Planning Guide for Water Supply

Manual of Individual Water Supply Systems (1975).

DESIGN OF WATER SYSTEMS

W-24   WATER SYSTEMS

The first step in planning and designing any project is to determine the availability of water that will serve the project. There are two types of water systems:

1. Community or municipality water system
2. Private water system

W-25   COMMUNITY OR MUNICIPALITY WATER SYSTEM

Water system which is owned by a private entity or by local government (public).

Usually hydrants in the street(s) adjacent to the site of the project indicate that the community is being served by a central water system. However, your project may or may not be served by this central water system. In order to clarify this question follow these steps:

1. Determine the approximate quantity of water your project needs in gallons/day by using Fig. W-4.
2. Contact the owner of the water supply (Department of Water Supply or private water company).
3. If they are able to furnish a water supply for your project, obtain *in writing* a confirmation from them stating:

   a. The quantity of water in gallons/day your project will receive

   b. The approximate amount of water pressure (psi) entering your project

   c. Location of the water main and its elevations

   d. The requirements for connecting to the water main (tapping)

   If your project will not be served by a central water system, then you can design a private water system as outlined in the following pages.

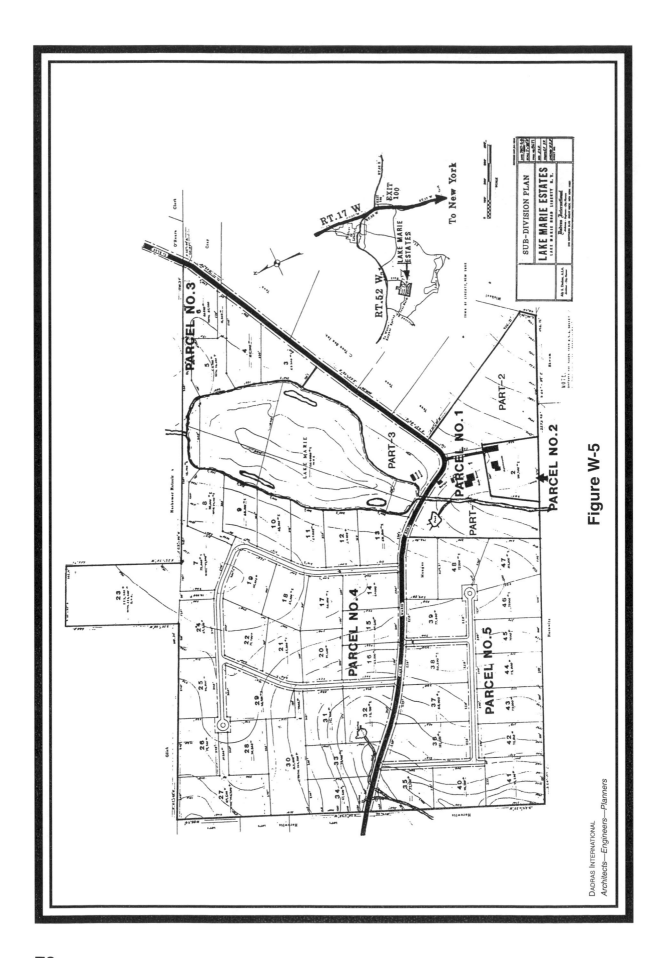

Figure W-5

W-26 DESIGN OF PRIVATE WATER SUPPLY

Before planning and designing a private water system, you *must* contact the local Department of Health and obtain the rules, regulations, and criteria with regard to the following:

1. Design of the water system
2. Location of the wells
3. Testing the water for quantity, quality, and correction

The principal of designing a private water system is the same for a nonresidential project and a residential project.

In the following, the design procedures are given for residential projects. There are commonly three conditions governing the design of a water system for a housing project or a subdivision. These conditions are given in W-27, W-28, and W-29.

W-27 HOUSING PROJECT OR SUBDIVISION LOTS WITH INDIVIDUAL WELL AND SEPTIC SYSTEM

In general, when a community contains less than 50 lots, and each lot is more than 1 acre, regulations may allow each lot to be served with a well for the water supply and a septic system for disposal of sewage.

For example, a proposed housing project, Lake Marie Estate, located in Liberty, New York, planned by Dadras International (architects, engineers, planners), is illustrated in Fig. W-5. The land contains over 125 acres and has been divided into 48 lots of 1½ acres and more. Each lot will have an individual well and a septic system. (Design of septic system is shown in S-22.)

DESIGN OF WELL FOR EACH LOT DESIGN PROCEDURE

1. The well has to be located on the lot with a radius of 75 ft from any waste line or house sewer (50 feet is minimum but not recommended).
2. The well must be in a watertight casing.
3. Calculate the gallons of water required for each house by using Fig. W-4.
4. Use a pneumatic tank (pressurized tank, Fig. W-11) to create adequate pressure for the house.

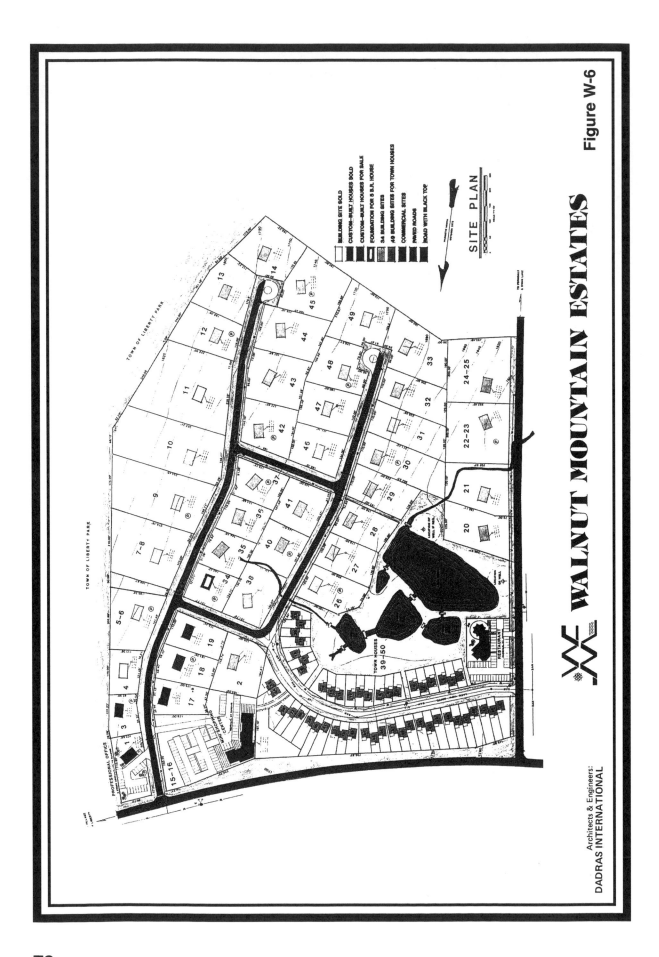

WALNUT MOUNTAIN ESTATES

Architects & Engineers:
DADRAS INTERNATIONAL

Figure W-6

SITE PLAN

Legend:
- BUILDING SITE SOLD
- CUSTOM-BUILT HOUSES SOLD
- CUSTOM-BUILT HOUSES FOR SALE
- FOUNDATION FOR B.R. HOUSE
- 34 BUILDING SITES
- 49 BUILDING SITES FOR TOWN HOUSES
- COMMERCIAL SITES
- PAVED ROADS
- ROAD WITH BLACK TOP

TOWN OF LIBERTY PARK

PROFESSIONAL OFFICE

MINI SHOPPING CENTER

TOWN HOUSES 39-50

RESTAURANT

72

Example

Design a water supply for a residence with five bedrooms.

Solution

Note: P = person, B.R. = Bedroom, H = hour, M = minute, G = gallon, d = day.

Step 1. Find number of persons.

$$5 \text{ B.R.} \times 2 \text{ P/B.R.} = 10 \text{ P}$$

Step 2. From Fig. W-4, 50 to 75 G/P/d is required. Using 75 G/P/d:

$$10 \text{ P} \times 75 \text{ G/P/d} = 750 \text{ G/d}$$

Step 3. Assume a pumping period of 20 H (4 H resting period for pump):

$$750 \text{ G/d} \div 20 \text{ H} = 37.5 \text{ G/H}$$

$$37.5 \text{ G/H} \div 60 \text{ M/H} = 0.63 \text{ G/M}$$

We need a well to produce 2 to 3 G/M

(Normally, well should produce 3 to 5 G/M)

Step 4. It is a good practice to design a pneumatic tank to supply water for 6 hours.

$$6 \text{ H} \times 37.5 \text{ G/H} = 225 \text{ G} \approx 250 \text{ G}$$

A 250 G pneumatic tank is required.

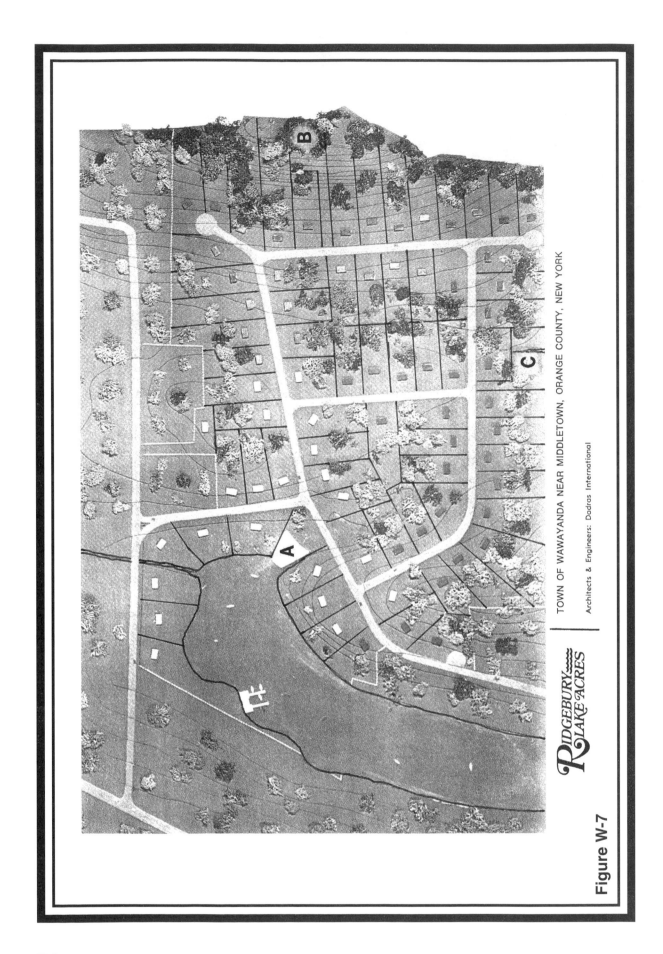

RIDGEBURY LAKE ACRES

TOWN OF WAWAYANDA NEAR MIDDLETOWN, ORANGE COUNTY, NEW YORK

Architects & Engineers: Dodras International

Figure W-7

W-28 HOUSING PROJECT OR SUBDIVISION LOTS WITH EITHER INDIVIDUAL WELL OR SEPTIC SYSTEM

When a housing project contains less than 50 lots, and each lot is less than 1 acre, the requirements usually call for either a central water system with an individual septic system, or a central sewage treatment plant and an individual well for the water system.

(*Note:* Individual septic system is more practical and economical.)

To illustrate this condition, reference is made to the housing project (Walnut Mountain Estates, located in Liberty, New York) shown in Fig. W-6.

The land is approximately 60 acres, and it was originally divided into 49 lots for individual houses, plus lot No. 50. Lot No. 50 later was used for 49 town houses because a town sewage system became available.

The water supply for this project is obtained from the Loomis Water District; therefore, lot sizes are less than 1 acre, and each house is served with an individual septic system, except for the 49 town houses and restaurant, which will discharge to the town sewer main. (The design of the septic system is illustrated in S-22.)

W-29 HOUSING PROJECT OR SUBDIVISION, LOTS WITH CENTRAL WATER AND CENTRAL SEWAGE SYSTEM

If a housing project is planned for more than 50 lots, regardless of the size of lots, a central water system and a central sewage treatment plant are required. Reference is made to Ridgebury Lake Acres, Middletown, New York (Fig. W-7).

This housing project was planned for more than 50 lots; therefore, the central water system and central sewage treatment plant were designed to serve this community. We discuss the design of the central water system in the following. (The design of the sewage treatment plant is given in S-24.)

The land was 87 acres, divided into 78 lots, 75 lots for houses, one lot allocated for park and the location of wells (A), one lot designated for a park and the location of a reservoir (B), and one lot for the sewage treatment plant (C).

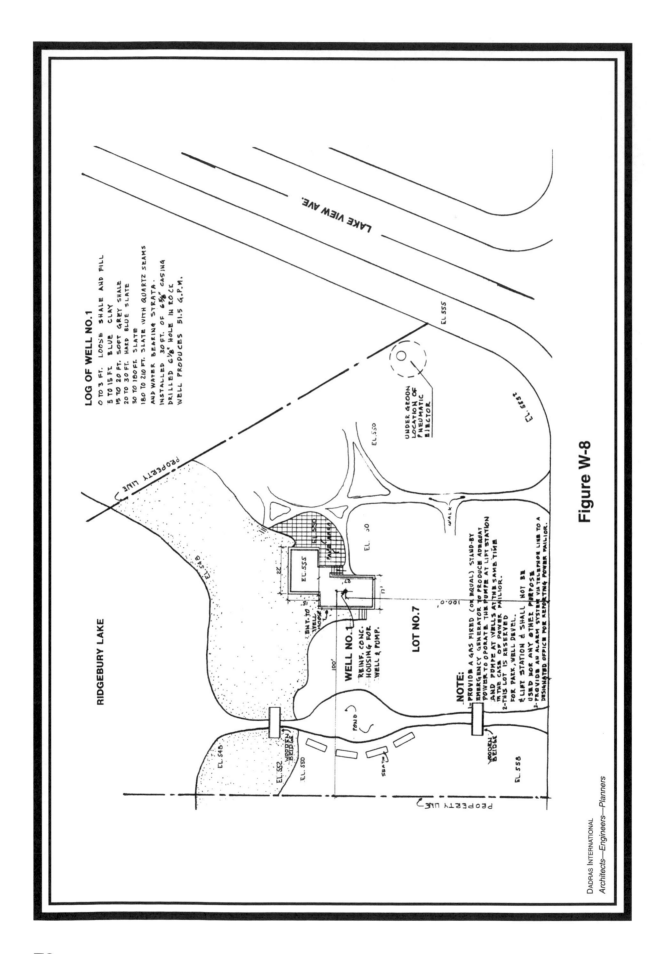

Figure W-8

DESIGN OF WELLS

Since the project is located in New York state, the requirements of the N.Y. State Department of Health were used, and their approval has been obtained.

Note: B.R. = Bedroom, H = House, P = Person, d = day, m = minute, h = hour, g = gallons.

Step 1.
$$75 \text{ H} \times 3 \text{ B.R./H} = 225 \text{ B.R.}$$
$$225 \text{ B.R.} \times 2 \text{ P/B.R.} = 450 \text{ P}$$

Step 2. From Fig. W-4, 50 to 75 G/d/P is required. Use 75 G/P/d:
$$450 \text{ P} \times 75 \text{ G/P/d} = 33{,}750 \text{ G/d}$$

Step 3. Assume pumping period of 20 h (4 h resting period for pump):
$$33{,}750 \text{ G/d} \div 20 \text{ h/d} = 1687.5 \text{ G/h}$$

Step 4. *Note:* Water obtained from well(s) and the rating of the pump used are based on gallons per minute.

Therefore, $1687.5 \text{ G/h} \div 60 \text{ m/h} = 28.125 \text{ G/M}$

Step 5. A well with a yield of 28 G/m is needed for this project.

Note

1. If the amount of water needed for the project cannot be obtained by one well, then other well(s) have to be developed to produce the amount of water required.
2. The wells must be 100 ft apart in order not to receive water from the same source.
3. When the required water is obtained from the well(s), then one additional well is required as a standby well (emergency well) to operate in the case the pump of the supply well becomes unoperational. This well can be located within 20 to 30 ft of the supply well.
4. No structures or sewer lines of any kind or type shall be located within a 100-ft radius of the well(s). It is a good practice to allocate the ground around the well(s) as park, play area, or picnic area.

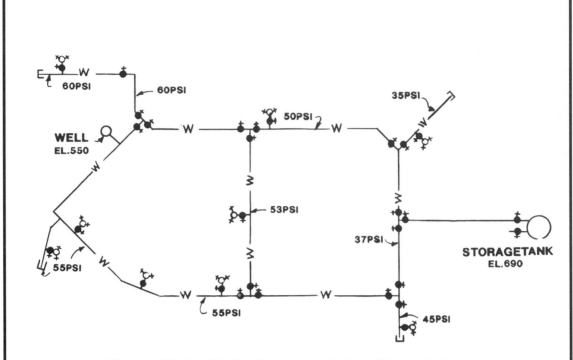

Figure W-9   Static Pressure in the Water Mains

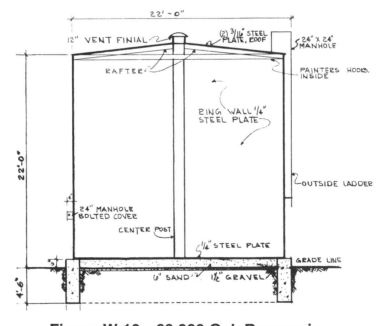

Figure W-10   60,000 Gal. Reservoir

Step 6. The well for this project was located on lot 7, which is a park with an elevation of 562 ft, shown on Fig. W-7 as "A."

The well produced 56 G/M, which was well above the water required. A standby well was drilled 35 ft from the supply well, and housing for the wells and pump were constructed (Fig. W-8).

W-30 DESIGN PROCEDURE OF WELL(S) FOR ANY PROJECT

1. Determine the number of persons using the project.
2. Use the planning guide for the water supply (Fig. W-4) to determine the approximate amount of water needed.
3. Follow the steps given supra.

W-31 DESIGN OF WATER RESERVOIR

Example

Design a reservoir for Ridgebury Lake Acres (Fig. W-7).

Total water required is

$$33,750 \text{ G/d}—1687.5 \text{ G/h.}$$

Solution

Step 1. Assume the hours of use to be 7 A.M. to 9 P.M. (14 hours required):

$$1687.5 \text{ G/h} \times 14 \text{ h} = 23,625 \text{ G}$$

Step 2. The total amount of water needed in 14 hours (hours in use) is 33,750 G. The pump is delivering 23,625 G in 14 hours. Therefore,

$$33,750 \text{ G} - 23,625 \text{ G} = 10,125 \text{ G}$$

10,125 G need to be stored in the reservoir to be used in 14 hours.

Step 3. Add 20 percent safety requirement

$$10,125 \text{ G} \times 0.2 = 2025 \text{ G}$$

$$10,125 \text{ G} + 2025 \text{ G} = 12,150 \text{ G}$$

The capacity of the reservoir for domestic water use is 12,150 gallons.

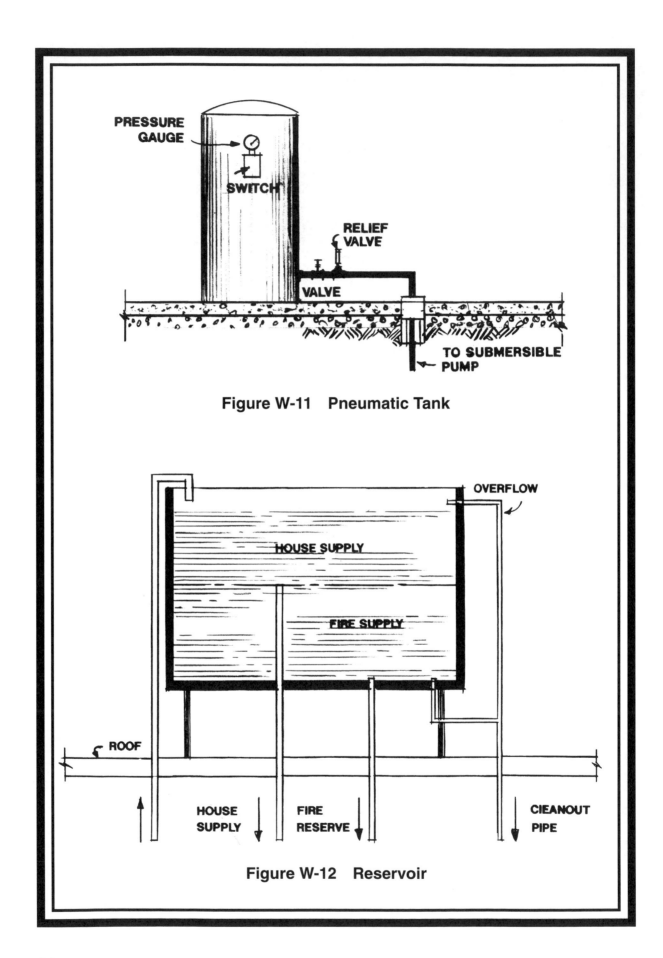

Figure W-11   Pneumatic Tank

Figure W-12   Reservoir

Step 4. Contact the local fire marshal and obtain his or her requirements *in writing* for the amount of water needed to be stored in the reservoir for fire fighting.

For this project, the fire marshal required 40,000 gallons of water. Therefore,

$$12,150 \text{ G} + 40,000 = 52,150 \text{ G}$$

The closest storage tank available was a 60,000-G tank, which was used (Fig. W-10).

Step 5. *Location of reservoir.* In this project, the reservoir was located on lot 53 at an elevation of 690 ft. The elevation of the well housing was 552 ft.

$$690 \text{ ft} - 552 \text{ ft} = 138 \text{ ft of head}$$
$$\text{(from W-19) 1 psi} = 2.3 \text{ ft or } 2.3 \text{ ft/psi}$$

$$138 \text{ ft} \div 2.3 \text{ ft/psi} = 60 \text{ psi water pressure at well housing}$$

Fig. W-9 shows the water pressure in the water main for this project. Fig. W-10 shows the installation of the reservoir for this community.

W-32 RESERVOIR AND PNEUMATIC TANK

Water obtained from the well(s) (or from a water main with inadequate pressure) must be pressurized in order to be usable in structures or for any other purpose (see W-18). Commonly, there are two systems used to pressurize the water:

a. Pneumatic tank (pressure tank) Fig. W-11.

b. Reservoir (gravity tank) Fig. W-12.

W-33 PNEUMATIC TANK (PRESSURIZED TANK)

A pneumatic tank is normally located below the fixtures to be supplied. When water is used, the air pressure on the top portion of the tank forces the water into the system. When a portion of water is used, the air pressure in the tank will drop, actuating the starting switch and causing the pump to start delivering water to the tank and increasing the air pressure. This system is generally favored for small structures.

W-34   RESERVOIR (GRAVITY TANK)

A reservoir is supported on the top of a structure in a multistory building and, when used to supply water to a community, is located on the top of a tower (water tower) or, if the community is on the hilly side, it may be economical to locate it on the top of the hill (Fig. W-7).

W-35   HEIGHT OF RESERVOIR

The height of a reservoir above the roof is directly related to the pressure requirements of the fixtures on the top floor of the structure.

Example

Determine the height of a reservoir to create a pressure of 210 psi in the street main.

| *Solution* | 2.3 ft = 1 psi or 2.3 ft/psi |
| From W-19, | 210 psi × 2.3 ft/psi = 483 ft height of reservoir |

W-36   DESIGN OF RESERVOIR

Example

A reservoir is to be located on the roof of a five-story building. The height of floor to floor is 12 ft. Pressure required on the fifth floor to operate fixtures is 16 psi.

1.   What is the height of the reservoir above the fifth floor?
2.   What is the water pressure on each floor?

Solution   1 psi = 2.3 ft or 2.3 ft/psi

From W-19,

1.   16 psi × 2.3 ft/psi = 36.8 ft minimum height of reservoir above fifth floor.

2.   *a.* Water pressure on the fifth floor is 16 psi.

    b.   Water pressure on the fourth floor:

$$36.8 \text{ ft} + 12 \text{ ft} = 48.8 \text{ ft}$$

$$48.8 \text{ ft} \div 2.3 \text{ ft/psi} = 21.218 \text{ psi}$$

c. Water pressure on the third floor:

48.8 ft + 12 ft = 60.8 ft

60.8 ft ÷ 2.3 ft/psi = 26.435 psi

d. Water pressure on the second floor:

60.8 ft + 12 ft = 72.8 ft

72.8 ft ÷ 2.3 ft/psi = 31.653 psi

e. Water pressure on the first floor:

72.8 ft + 12 ft = 84.8 ft

84.8 ft ÷ 2.3 ft/psi = 36.87 psi

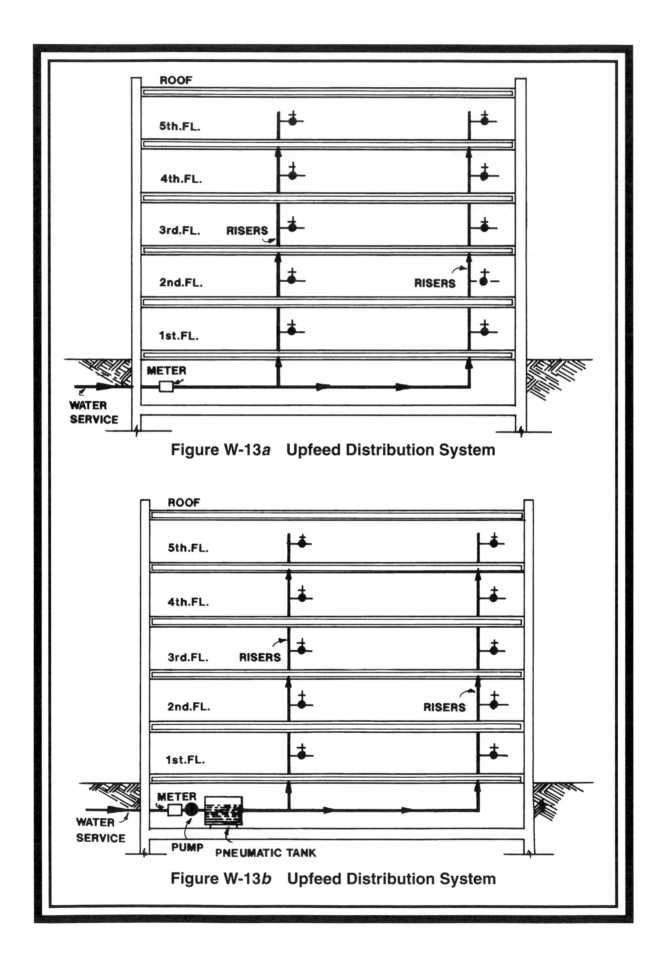

Figure W-13a Upfeed Distribution System

Figure W-13b Upfeed Distribution System

WATER DISTRIBUTION

W-37   COLD WATER DISTRIBUTION

There are two basic types of water distribution systems for buildings:

1.   Upfeed distribution system

2.   Downfeed distribution system

W-38   UPFEED DISTRIBUTION SYSTEM

There are two methods commonly used for upfeed distribution systems.

1.   The supply of water for the building is received from a public street main

(usually 35 psi for residential structures, and about 50 psi for other buildings)

(Fig. W-13a).

2.   Private water supply enters into a pneumatic tank (pressurized tank) and is pres-

surized from approximately 35 to 60 psi (Fig. W-13b).

In both systems the height of the building is directly proportional to the pressure of water.

W-39   DESIGN OF UPFEED DISTRIBUTION SYSTEM

Example

The cold water has a pressure of 60 psi. How many stories can a building have in order to

receive an upfeed distribution system? Assume the following cases:

1.   Using a flush valve for water closet

2.   Using a flush tank for water closet

Solution

1.   ***Using a flush valve.***   Pressure required is 10 to 20 psi (Fig. P-31); use 15 psi.

From W-19, 1 psi = 2.3 ft or 2.3 ft/psi

Therefore,   60 psi − 15 psi = 45 psi

45 psi × 2.3 ft/psi = 103.5 ft

103.5 ft ÷ 10 ft/stories = 10.35 ≈ 10 stories

103.5 ft ÷ 12 ft/stories = 8.625 ≈ 8 stories

85

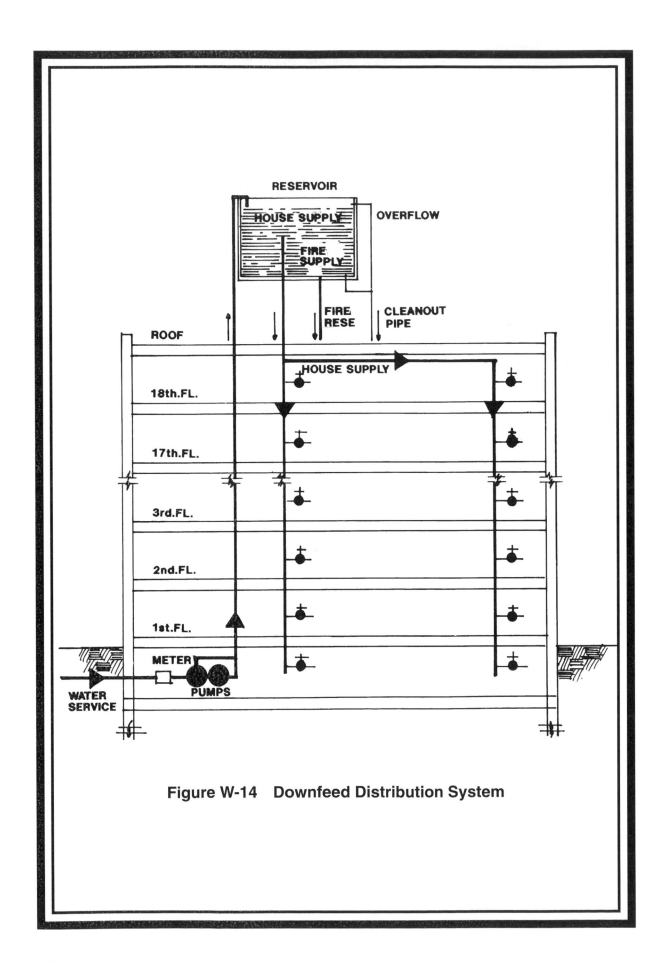

Figure W-14   Downfeed Distribution System

2. ***Using a flush tank.*** Flush tank requires 8 psi (Fig. P-31).

Therefore,   60 psi – 8 psi = 52 psi

52 psi × 2.3 ft/psi = 119.6 ft

119.6 ft ÷ 10 ft/stories = 11.96 ≈ 12 stories

119.6 ft ÷ 12 ft/stories = 9.967 ≈ 10 stories

W-40   DOWNFEED DISTRIBUTION SYSTEM

a.   Water pressure of 60 psi can serve a building of up to 10 stories. For structures with more stories in height, downfeed distribution systems are designed (Fig. W-14). In this system, water from a street main or from a suction tank (which is located in the basement of a building and is filled with water from the street main or private water supply) is pumped to a reservoir on the top of a building. The water from the reservoir serves the floors below by downfeed distribution (gravity) system.

b.   Minimum pressure required on the top floor of the building is usually 15 psi (for flush valve), and maximum pressure on the lowest floor of the building should not exceed 50 psi (pressure above 80 psi will damage the fixtures).

If the pressure on lower floors exceeds 50 psi, pressure-reducing valves are used to reduce the pressure.

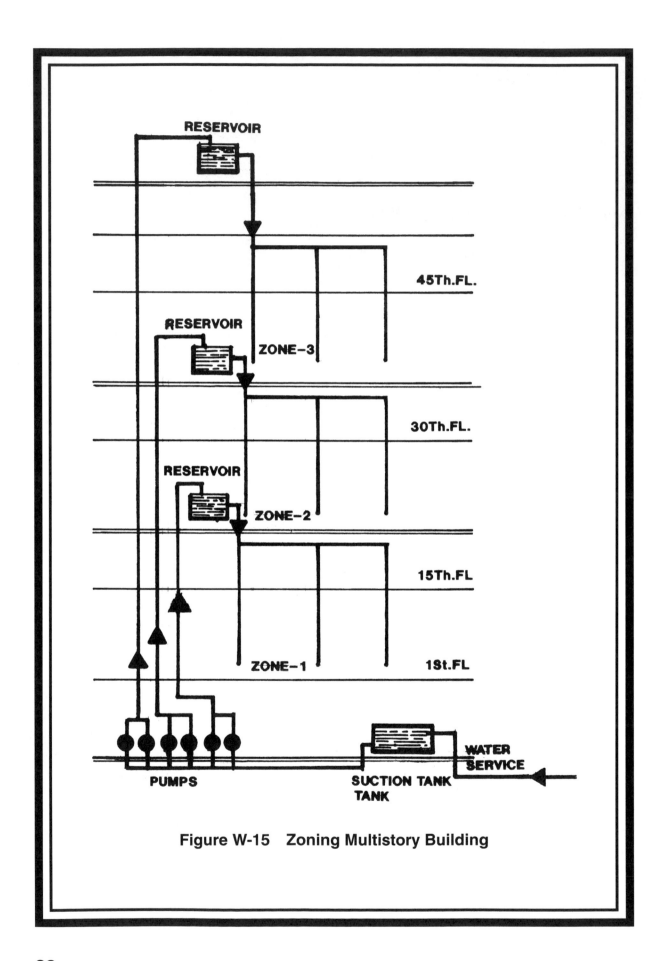

Figure W-15   Zoning Multistory Building

W-41   ZONING MULTISTORY BUILDING

In a multistory building it is logical and economical to limit the height of the water zone to 15 stories each. For example, a 45-story building can be divided into three zones (Fig. W-15):

Zone 1   1st floor to 15th floor, downfeed distribution

Zone 2   15th floor to 30th floor, downfeed distribution

Zone 3   30th floor to 45th floor, downfeed distribution

Each zone is served with a reservoir which is placed approximately 36 ft above the floor of the top level to produce 15.5 psi of pressure necessary to operate a flush valve.

Pressure-reducing valves are placed on the water main approximately every 84 ft in order to reduce the water pressure to 37 psi.

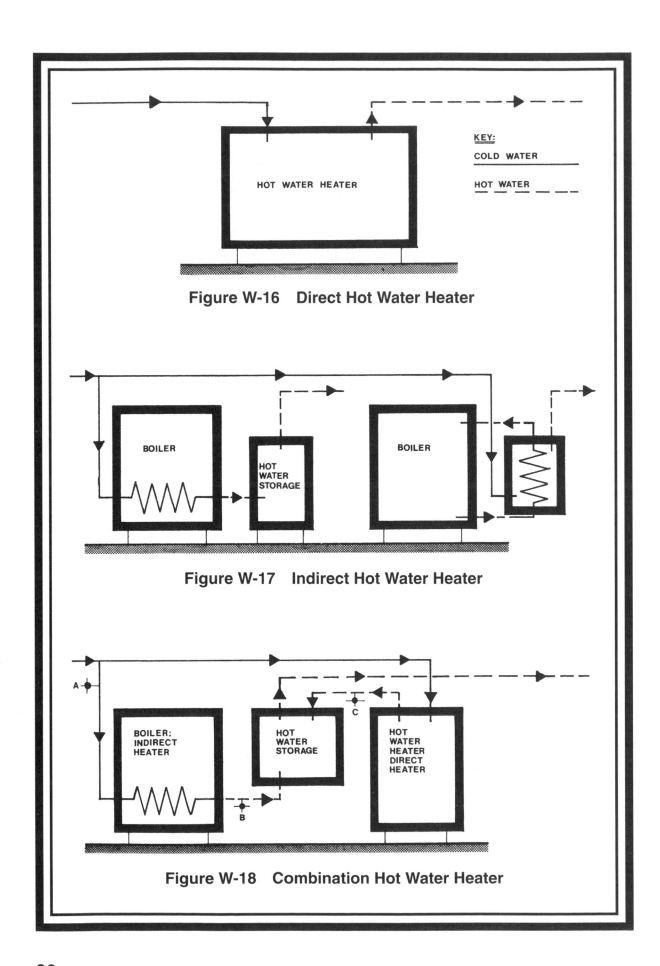

Figure W-16   Direct Hot Water Heater

KEY:

COLD WATER

HOT WATER

Figure W-17   Indirect Hot Water Heater

Figure W-18   Combination Hot Water Heater

HOT WATER SYSTEMS

W-42 SYSTEMS

Hot water is needed within a building for bathing, dishwashing, laundry, and other related services.

There are four types of systems commonly used to obtain hot water for a structure(s):

a. Direct

b. Indirect

c. Direct and indirect (combination)

d. Solar

W-43 DIRECT SYSTEM (Fig. W-16)

The hot water heater solely designed to provide the required domestic hot water for building(s). They are available in a variety of capacities and sizes. This system may be more economical than an indirect hot water heater.

W-44 INDIRECT SYSTEM (Fig. W-17)

A separate coil containing the potable water is fed through the boiler (which is designed for heating system). This type of system is generally used in residential, commercial, and institutional buildings. This method of hot water system is commonly used in cold climate areas, because for 6 to 8 months of the year the boiler is in operation to heat the building. In the other 4 to 6 months of the year, when heating of the building is not required, the boiler has to operate in order to provide domestic hot water. Therefore, it is not an economical solution for obtaining domestic hot water for a structure.

W-45 DIRECT-INDIRECT (COMBINED) SYSTEM (Fig. W-18)

Domestic hot water is obtained from the coils in the boiler in the cold months when the boiler is operational. Valves A and B are open and valve C is closed. In the warm months of the year, when the boiler is shut off, the direct hot water system will become operational. Valves A and B are closed and valve C is open. This is the most economical system to provide domestic hot water for a project in cold-climate areas.

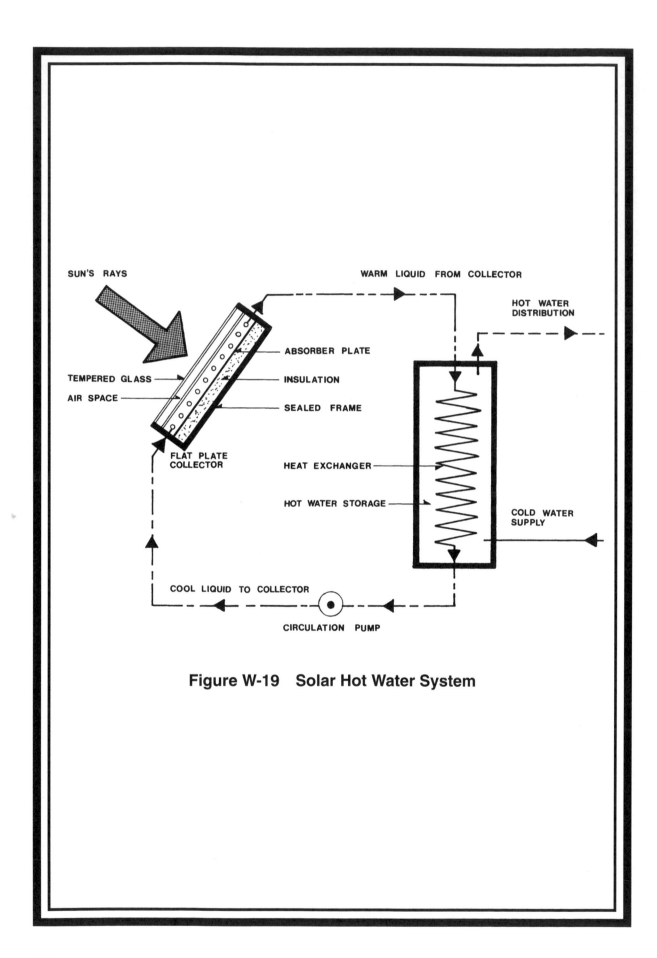

SUN'S RAYS

WARM LIQUID FROM COLLECTOR

HOT WATER
DISTRIBUTION

ABSORBER PLATE

TEMPERED GLASS — INSULATION

AIR SPACE — SEALED FRAME

FLAT PLATE
COLLECTOR

HEAT EXCHANGER

HOT WATER STORAGE

COLD WATER
SUPPLY

COOL LIQUID TO COLLECTOR

CIRCULATION PUMP

Figure W-19   Solar Hot Water System

The solar hot water system has a flat plate facing to the south and east, absorbing heat from the sun and heating the coils of the domestic or service hot water, either directly or indirectly. This system is the most economical way to produce hot water.

a.   In the torrid zone of the earth (Figs. G-9 and G-10) from 23½° north latitude to 23½° south latitude (hot belt), the direct system can be used. The coil of domestic hot water is placed in the plate and connected to the hot water system.

b.   In the north and south temperate zones from 23½ to 66½° north and south latitudes, in the regions where the temperature is above 38°F all year round, the direct system can be used. In areas with a temperature of less than 38°F in the winter months, the indirect system is commonly employed.

c.   In the indirect system, the coils of water inside the plate are a mixture of water and antifreeze to prevent the water from freezing in the winter months. The coil delivers the hot water into a tank installed inside the building containing coils of domestic water to be heated by hot water received from the solar system.

d.   In both cases, in the direct and indirect system, it is a good practice to back up the system with a regular hot water system to operate when necessary to deliver the hot water requirements of the building(s).

Number of Baths →	1 to 1.5			2 to 2.5				3 to 3.5			
Number of Bedrooms →	1	2	3	2	3	4	5	3	4	5	6
Gas[a]											
Storage, gal	20	30	30	30	40	40	50	40	50	50	50
1000 Btu/h input	27	36	36	36	36	38	47	38	38	47	50
1-h draw, gal	43	60	60	60	70	72	90	72	82	90	92
Recovery, gph	23	30	30	30	30	32	40	32	32	40	42
Electric[a]											
Storage, gal	20	30	40	40	50	50	66	50	66	66	80
kW input	2.5	3.5	4.5	4.5	5.5	5.5	5.5	5.5	5.5	5.5	5.5
1-h draw, gal	30	44	58	58	72	72	88	72	88	88	102
Recovery, gph	10	14	18	18	22	22	22	22	22	22	22
Oil[a]											
Storage, gal	30	30	30	30	30	30	30	30	30	30	40
1000 Btu/h input	70	70	70	70	70	70	70	70	70	70	70
1-h draw, gal	89	89	89	89	89	89	89	89	89	89	89
Recovery, gph	59	59	59	59	59	59	59	59	59	59	59
Tank-type indirect[b,c]											
1-W-H rated draw, gal in 3-h, 100 F° rise		40	40		66	66	66	66	66	66	66
Manufacturer-rated draw, gal in 3-h, 100 F° rise		49	66		75	75	75	75	75	75	75
Tank capacity, gal		49	66		66	66	82	66	82	82	82
Tankless-type indirect[c,e]											
1-W-H-rated, gpm 100 F° rise		2.75	2.75		3.25	3.25	3.75	3.25	3.75	3.75	3.75
Manufacturer-rated draw, gal in 5 min, 100 F° rise	15	15	15		25	25	35	25	35	35	35

[a] Storage capacity, input, and recovery requirements indicated in the table are typical and may vary with each individual manufacturer. Any combination of these requirements to produce the stated 1-h draw will be satisfactory.

[b] Boiler-connected water heater capacities [180 F boiler water, internal or external connection].

[c] Heater capacities and inputs are minimum allowable. Variations in tank size are permitted when recovery is based on 4 gph/kW 100 F° rise for electrical. A.G.A. recovery ratings for gas heaters, and IBR ratings for steam and hot water heaters.

[e] Also for 1 to 1.5 baths and 4 bedrooms for indirect water heaters.

Boiler-connected heater capacities [200 F boiler water, internal or external connection].

Figure W-20   Minimum Residential Water Heater Capacities

Source: U.S. HUD-FHA, for one- and two-family living units. Copyright © by the American Society of Heating, Refrigerating and Air Conditioning Engineers, Inc. ASHRAE Systems Handbook, 1984.

DESIGN OF HOT WATER SYSTEM

W-47   ESTIMATING HOT WATER DEMAND FOR RESIDENCES

In a private home consumption of hot water is approximately as follows:

Tub bathing	25 gallons
Showering	6 g/m
Washing machine	36 gallons/wash
Dishwashing	10 gallons/wash

W-48   DESIGN OF WATER HEATER FOR RESIDENCE

Where P = person, B.R. = bedroom, G = gallon, h = hour:

1. For a three-B.R. house with 1½ bath and 4 persons occupancy, use about 15 G/P/h.

    4 P. × 15 G/P/h = 60 G/h water heater is needed.

2. For a four-B.R. house with 2½ baths, 6 persons occupancy, use about 12.5 G/P/h.

    6 P. × 12.5 G/P/h = 75 G/h water heater is needed.

3. For a six B.R. house with 3½ baths, 8 persons occupancy, use about 12.5 G/P/h.

    8 P. × 12.5 G/P/h = 100 G/h water heater is needed

For more accurate calculations, use the table given in Fig. W-20. In this table, the size of the water heater is given as 1-h draw, gal for the number of bedrooms and number of bathrooms.

W-49   ESTIMATING HOT WATER DEMAND FOR BUILDINGS

For small buildings and shops, the design of a hot water system can be similar to residences. For large buildings, use Fig. W-21 for estimating. Under "maximum hours," the size of a water heater is given.

The trade-off between storage tanks and water heaters should be considered in designing the water heater system for large buildings. Under "maximum day," these figures are used to calculate the monthly and yearly energy consumption and cost of operating a hot water heater for the structure.

Type of Building	Maximum Hour	Maximum Day	Average Day
Men's dormitories	3.8 gal/student	22.0 gal/student	13.1 gal/student
Women's dormitories	5.0 gal/student	26.5 gal/student	12.3 gal/student
Motels: No. of units[2]			
20 or less	6.0 gal/unit	35.0 gal/unit	20.0 gal/unit
60	5.0 gal/unit	25.0 gal/unit	14.0 gal/unit
100 or more	4.0 gal/unit	15.0 gal/unit	10.0 gal/unit
Nursing Homes	4.5 gal/bed	30.0 gal/bed	18.4 gal/bed
Office buildings	0.4 gal/person	2.9 gal/person	1.0 gal/person
Food service establishments:			
Type A-full meal Restaurants & Cafeterias	1.5 gal/max meals/h	11.0 gal/max meals/h	2.4 gal/avg meals/day +
Type B-drive-ins, grilles, luncheonettes, sandwich & snack shops	0.7 gal/max meals/h	6.0 gal/max meals/h	0.7 gal/avg meals/day +
Apartment Houses: # of Apartments			
20 or less	12.0 gal/apt.	80.0/gal/apt.	42.0 gal/apt.
50	10.0 gal/apt.	73.0 gal/apt.	40.0 gal/apt.
75	8.5 gal/apt.	66.0 gal/apt.	38.0 gal/apt.
100	7.0 gal/apt.	60.0 gal/apt.	37.0 gal/apt.
200 or more	5.0 gal/apt.	50.0 gal/apt.	35.0 gal/apt.
Elementary Schools	0.6 gal/student	1.5 gal/student	0.6 gal/student +
Junior & Senior High Schools	1.0 gal/student	3.6 gal/student	1.8 gal/student +

+ *Per day of operations.*

Figure W-21   Hot Water Demands and Use for Various Types of Buildings

W-50 DESIGN OF HOT WATER SYSTEM

Example

Design a hot water heater for toilet facilities given in Figs. W-22 and W-23 serving 440 students and 32 faculty members and staff.

Solution

Total number of occupants is 472 persons. From Fig. W-17, using senior high schools (where S = students, G = gallons, h = hour):

$$1.0 \text{ G/h/S}$$

$$472 \text{ P.} \times 1 \text{ G/h/S} = 472 \text{ G/h}$$

Use 500 G/h water heater.

W-51 COST OF PRODUCING HOT WATER

When a hot water heater is designed, the next step is to calculate the cost of operating the heater, which is one of the monthly expenses of the building. The following energy value is needed for the calculation:

$$\text{Energy} = \frac{\text{Btu/month}}{\text{energy value} \times \text{efficiency}} = \text{gallons, therm, or kWh}$$

Heating with oil no. 2.   One gallon of oil no. 2 produces 141,000 Btu (with 75 percent efficiency).

Heating with natural gas.   Natural gas is sold in *therm*. One therm of gas produces 100,000 Btu (with 80 percent efficiency).

Heating with electricity.   One kW of electricity produces 3,413 Btu (with 100 percent efficiency).

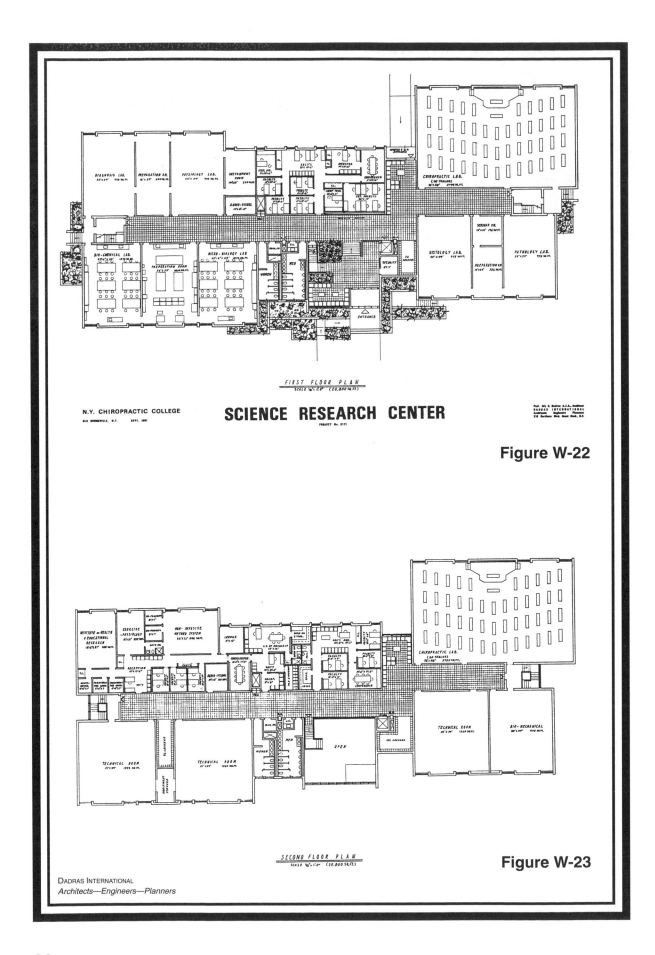

SCIENCE RESEARCH CENTER

N.Y. CHIROPRACTIC COLLEGE

Figure W-22

Figure W-23

DADRAS INTERNATIONAL
Architects—Engineers—Planners

W-52 CALCULATE COST OF HEATING HOT WATER

Example

What is the cost of operating a hot water heater for example W-50 per month for the following energies?

1. Oil no. 2 costs 92 cents per gallon.

2. Natural gas costs 81 cents per therm.

3. Electricity costs 14 cents per kWh.

If the college is open 20 days per month, and 472 persons are using the hot water, then the solution is as follows.

Solution

G = gallon, m = month, P = person, lb = pound, $\blacktriangle°$ = difference in temperature, deg = degree, d = day:

Step 1 From Fig. W-21, maximum use is 3.6 gallons per student per day (using high school figures).

$$472 \text{ P.} \times 3.6 \text{ G/P/d} = 1699.2 \text{ G/P/d}$$

College is open 20 days per month.

$$20 \text{ d/m} \times 1699.2 \text{ G/d} = 33,984 \text{ G/m}$$

Step 2

a. Specific heat of water (W-23) where 1 Btu is required to raise the temperature of 1 pound of water 1°F.

b. Weight of water is 8.33 lb/G (W-17).

c. Cold water temperature is 50°F and has to be raised to 120°F (W-57).

Total Btu = G of water × 8.33 lb/G × 1 Btu/deg × $\blacktriangle°$

$$33,984 \text{ G/m} \times 8.33 \text{ lb/G} \times 1 \text{ Btu/deg} \times (120° - 50°) = 19,816,070 \text{ Btu/m}$$

Step 3

$$\text{Where Energy} = \frac{\text{Btu/m}}{\text{energy value} \times \text{efficiency}}$$

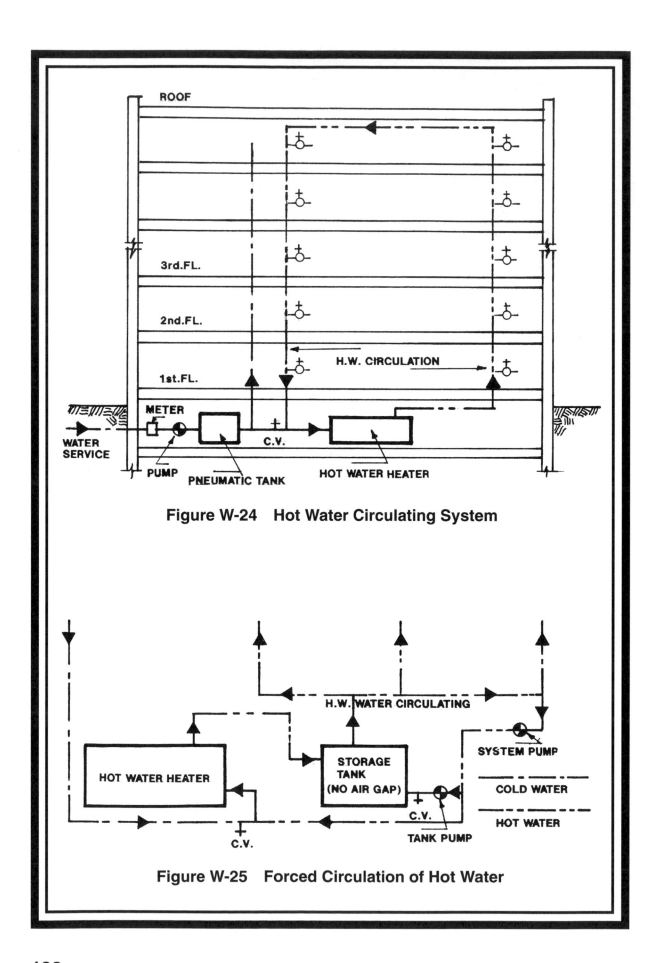

Figure W-24   Hot Water Circulating System

Figure W-25   Forced Circulation of Hot Water

For item 1   Oil no. 2 = $\dfrac{19,816,070 \text{ Btu/m}}{141,000 \times .75}$ = 187.386 G/m

187.386 G/m $\times$ \$0.92/G = \$172.39 cost of oil/m

For item 2   Natural gas = $\dfrac{19,816,070 \text{ Btu/m}}{100,000 \text{ Btu/therm} \times .8}$ = 247.7 therm/m

247.7 therm/m $\times$ \$0.81/therm = \$200.63 cost of gas/m

For item 3   Electricity = $\dfrac{19,816,070 \text{ Btu/m}}{3,413 \text{ Btu/kWh} \times 1 \text{ electricity/m}}$ = 5806 kWh/m

5806 kWh/m $\times$ 0.14 cents = \$812.84 cost of electricity/m

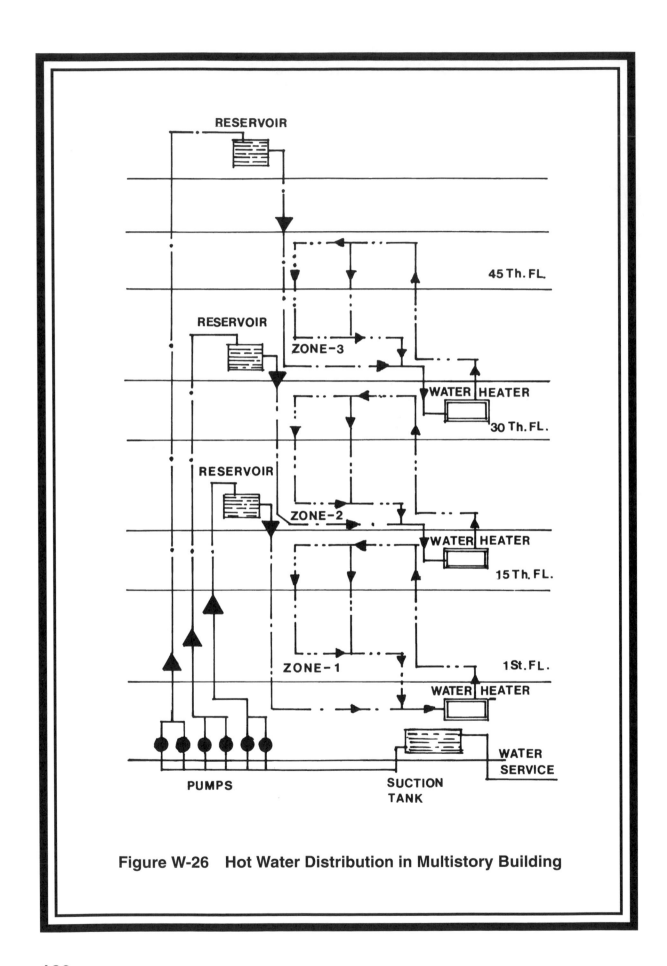

Figure W-26   Hot Water Distribution in Multistory Building

102

HOT WATER DISTRIBUTION

W-53   HOT WATER DISTRIBUTION

The most practical system of distribution is to locate the hot water heater as close as possible to the area which it is serving.

The longer the hot water supply pipe, the less efficient the system will be.

A hot water pipe loses its heat to the surrounding air very quickly, even if it is insulated.

It is a good practice to use two or more water heaters in a structure instead of running a long hot water supply line or to design a hot water circulation system.

W-54   HOT WATER CIRCULATING SYSTEM

In this system hot water continues to the farthest fixture and returns to the hot water heater (Fig. W-24).

In this system only the hot water in the branch piping may cool off.

The hot water circulating system can be used in upfeed, downfeed, or combination of upfeed or downfeed on a horizontal feeding system.

A check valve is used in this system to cause the flow of the water in the proper direction.

W-55   FORCED CIRCULATION OF HOT WATER

Forced circulating hot water system may be used in long structures of a few stories in height. The lack of high pressure in a cold water system and friction loss in the long pipes create low pressure in a hot water system.

This system employs a storage tank with no air gap, and a circulating pump on return pipe of hot water supply (Fig. W-25).

W-56   HOT WATER DISTRIBUTION IN MULTISTORY BUILDINGS

In multistory structures the cold water is taken from the cold water reservoir (tank) and fed into the hot water heater, which is located on the lower floor of the zone. This allows the water to create enough pressure and generate upfeed distribution of hot water to the upper floors (Fig. W-26).

W-57 TEMPERATURES OF DOMESTIC HOT WATER

Domestic hot water with high temperatures allows the use of less hot water mixed with cold water to obtain a desirable temperature.

It limits the growth of bacteria; however, it can cause burns if the user is not careful.

Domestic hot water with lower temperatures allows the water heating unit to be smaller, but the storage tank has to be larger.

It may not limit the growth of bacteria. It is less likely to cause burns.

Normal temperatures of domestic hot water for different types of uses are as follows:

Showers, tubs, lavatories	105 to 120°F
Commercial dishwashing	140 to 155°F
Sanitizing use	180°F
Laundry, residential	130 to 140°F
Laundry, commercial	180°F

CONTENTS

Part 3

SEWAGE DISPOSAL SYSTEMS

S

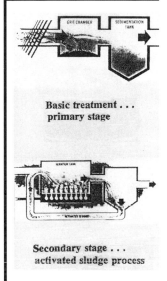

Basic treatment . . . primary stage

Secondary stage . . . activated sludge process

SEWAGE DISPOSAL SYSTEMS

BASIC INFORMATION

S-1 HISTORY AT A GLANCE

One of the earliest known sewers was the *cloaca maxima* in Rome which was built (6th century B.C.) to drain the site of the Forum.

London's drainage system was constructed in the 13th century, and the discharge of sewer into it started in 1815.

In Paris, sewers were constructed in the 13th century, and by 1893 only 5 percent of the buildings in the cities were connected to the system.

In the United States, the city of Boston was the first to construct a drainage system in 1701.

In the mid-19th century sewage disposal systems were widely used in many cities in the United States.

Early in the 20th century, cities began the installation of sewage treatment plants.

In 1928 the Water Pollution Control Federation (WPCF) was established.

In 1949, improvement of the sewage pollution problem standard was based on the Federal Water Pollution Control Act.

S-2 SEWAGE OR WASTE

Gray water.   Wastewater with minor pollution discharged from bathtubs, sinks, lavatories, dishwashers, and washing machines is called *gray water*.

Black water.   Wastewater with major pollution from toilets and urinals is referred to as *black water*.

Sewage or waste.   A combination of gray water and black water is called *sewage* or *waste*.

S-3 USE OF WATER IN BUILDINGS

All fixtures within a building are provided with both water supply and waste pipes.

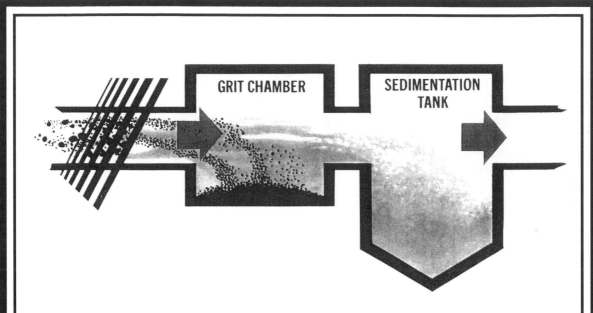

Basic Treatment—Primary Stage

Sedimentation Tank

Figure S-1

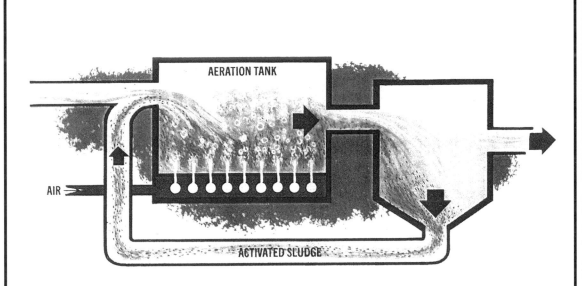

Secondary Stage—Activated Sludge Process

Aeration Tank

Figure S-2

Type of Establishment Add 50% for food disposal units	_Gal. per day per person_
Schools (toilet and lavatories only)	15 Gal. per day per person
Schools (with above plus cafeteria)	25 Gal. per day per person
Schools (with above plus cafeteria and showers)	35 Gal. per day per person
Day workers at schools and offices	15 Gal. per day per person
Day Camps	25 Gal. per day per person
Trailer parks or tourist camps (with built-in bath)	50 Gal. per day per person
Trailer parks or tourist camps (with central bathhouse)	35 Gal. per day per person
Work or construction camps	50 Gal. per day per person
Public picnic parks (toilet wastes only)	5 Gal. per day per person
Public picnic parks (bathhouse, showers and flush toilets)	10 Gal. per day per person
Swimming pools and beaches	10 Gal. per day per person
Country Clubs	25 Gal. per locker
Luxury residences and estates	150 Gal. per day per person
Rooming houses	40 Gal. per day per person
Boarding houses	50 Gal. per day per person
Hotels (with connecting baths)	50 Gal. per day per person
Hotels (with private baths—2 persons per room)	100 Gal. per day per person
Boarding Schools	100 Gal. per day per person
Factories (gallons per person per shift—exclusive of industrial wastes)	25 Gal. per day per person
Nursing Homes	75 Gal. per day per person
General Hospitals	150 Gal. per day per person
Public Institutions (other than hospitals)	100 Gal. per day per person
Restaurants (toilet and kitchen wastes per unit of serving capacity)	25 Gal. per day per person
Kitchen wastes from hotels, camps, boarding houses, etc. Serving three meals per day	10 Gal. per day per person
Motels	50 Gal. per bed space
Motels with bath, toilet, and kitchen wastes	60 Gal. per bed space
Drive-in theaters	5 Gal. per car space
Stores	400 Gal. per toilet room
Service stations	10 Gal. per vehicle served
Airports	3-5 Gal. per passenger
Assembly Halls	2 Gal. per seat
Bowling Alleys	75 Gal. per lane
Churches (small)	3-5 Gal. per sanctuary seat
Churches (large with kitchens)	5.7 Gal. per sanctuary seat
Dance Halls	2 Gal. per day per person
Laundries (coin operated)	400 Gal. per machine
Service Stations	1000 Gal. (First Bay)
	500 Gal. (Each add. Bay)
Subdivisions or individual homes	75 Gal. per day per person
Marinas—Flush toilets	36 Gal. per fixture per hr
Urinals	10 Gal. per fixture per hr
Wash basins	15 Gal. per fixture per hr
Showers	150 Gal. per fixture per hr

Figure S-3   Estimated Sewage Flow Rates

Extracted from the 1988 Supplement to the _1987 National Standard Plumbing Code_ with permission of PHCC.

Conventional water closets (W.C., toilet) use more than 3.5 gallons of water per flush.

New water-saver water closet uses 1.7 to 3.5 gallons per flush.

New low-consumption water closet (ultra-low-flush) uses 1.5 gallons or less per flush.

Shower heads discharge water at the rate of 6 to 12 gallons per minute. In 10 minutes more than 90 gallons of water are consumed.

Lavatory faucet at full flow delivers 4 to 5 gallons of water per minute.

A dishwasher uses 12 to 18 gallons of water per cycle.

A washing machine consumes 40 to 55 gallons of water for a full-size load.

Water used in these fixtures creates sewage or waste which has to be removed from the building and discharged into a sewage main or private sewage treatment system.

Analyzing the aforementioned extensive usage of water, common sense and good practice require and dictate saving as much water as possible in the buildings.

A wide variety of water-saving fixtures, faucets, and equipment are available on the market and their use is required by many codes and regulations.

S-4   COMPOSITION OF SEWAGE

Sewage is composed largely of water and very small amounts of solid material. Only two-tenths of 1 percent of sewage is solid.

Solid material consists of organic and mineral held either in suspension or solution.

S-5   SEWAGE TREATMENT

There are four basic stages in the treatment of sewage and waste:

1. *Primary stage.*   In this stage solids are allowed to settle and are removed from the waste.
2. *Secondary stage.*   The second stage uses biological processes to purify the waste.
3. *Chlorination stage.*   In this stage, chlorine will kill harmful bacteria in an effluent.
4. *Post-aeration stage.* The removal of most of the chlorine from the water.

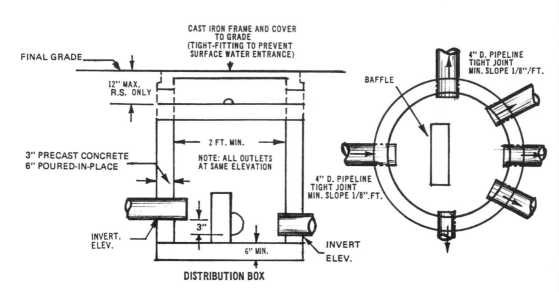

CAST IRON FRAME AND COVER
TO GRADE
(TIGHT-FITTING TO PREVENT
SURFACE WATER ENTRANCE)

FINAL GRADE

12" MAX.
R.S. ONLY

2 FT. MIN.

3" PRECAST CONCRETE
6" POURED-IN-PLACE

NOTE: ALL OUTLETS
AT SAME ELEVATION

4" D. PIPELINE
TIGHT JOINT
MIN. SLOPE 1/8".FT.

INVERT.
ELEV.

3"

6" MIN.

INVERT
ELEV.

DISTRIBUTION BOX

BAFFLE

4" D. PIPELINE
TIGHT JOINT
MIN. SLOPE 1/8"/FT.

Nassau County Department of Health

Distribution Box

Figure S-4a

Type of Soil	Required ft² of Leaching Area/100 Gal	Maximum Absorption Capacity, Gal/ft² of Leaching Area for a 24-h Period	Maximum Septic Tank Size Allowable Gallons
1. Coarse sand or gravel	20	5	7500
2. Fine sand	25	4	7500
3. Sandy loam or sandy clay	40	2.5	5000
4. Clay with considerable sand or gravel	90	1.10	3500
5. Clay with small amount of sand or gravel	120	0.83	3000

Septic Tank and Leaching Area Design Criteria

Figure S-4b

Source: the *Uniform Plumbing Code*, copyright © 1994 by the International Association of Plumbing and Mechanical Officials.

S-6 PRIMARY STAGE (Fig. S-1)

The sewage enters a plant for treatment. First it flows through an inclined screen; then it passes into a *grit chamber* where small stones, sand, cinders, and grit are allowed to settle to the bottom.

The sewage still contains dissolved organic and inorganic matter along with suspended solids when it enters a *sedimentation tank*.

In this tank suspended solids will gradually sink to the bottom. This mass of solids is called *raw sludge*.

S-7 SECONDARY STAGE (Fig. S-2)

The sewage from the sedimentation tank (settling tank) in the primary stage is pumped or flows to an aeration tank where it is mixed with the air's oxygen for several hours. During this time, the bacteria breaks down the organic matter.

The secondary stage of treatment removes 90 percent of the organic matter in sewage.

In order to remove more organic matter from the water, in many treatment plants a tertiary treatment system (a combination of aeration and clarifier) is used to remove an additional 6 to 8 percent of the organic matter for a total of approximately 97 percent.

S-8 CHLORINATION STAGE

In this stage liquid chlorine is converted to gas and injected into the effluent for 15 to 30 minutes.

Chlorination will kill more than 99 percent of the harmful bacteria in an effluent.

S-9 POST-AERATION STAGE

In this stage, air is used to remove the chlorine from the water before it is discharged to streams, bodies of water, recycling, or is used for irrigation.

S-10 BIOCHEMICAL OXYGEN DEMAND

The body of water must maintain a certain amount of dissolved oxygen (DO) in order for fish to breathe and water plants to have life.

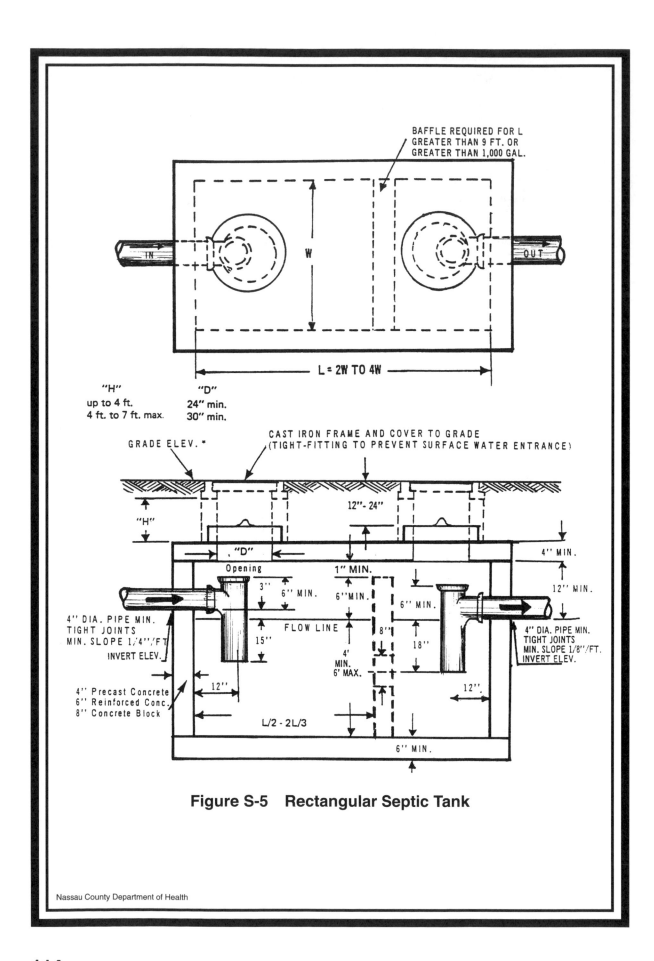

Figure S-5   Rectangular Septic Tank

If treated, sewage discharged to the body of water contains a high percentage of organic matter, which demands oxygen from the water to break down the sewage and, consequently, will leave the water with less oxygen—resulting in the death of fish and plants.

A measuring device called **biochemical oxygen demand** (BOD) is used to measure the end product from a treatment plant to ensure the water discharged to a body of water has a very low percentage of BOD.

S-11   SEWER SYSTEMS

In general there are two types of sewer systems:

1.   Municipal (public) sewer systems
2.   Private sewer systems

S-12   MUNICIPAL (PUBLIC) SEWER SYSTEM

There are three systems in use:

1. **Combined sewer system.**   Carries away both sewage from the buildings and water polluted as it drains off buildings, streets, or land during a storm.

2. **Sewer (sanitary) system.**   Carries only sewage from buildings.

3. **Storm drainage system.**   Used to carry storm water only.

A municipality may have item 1 only, item 2 only, or items 2 and 3.

A sewer system may be owned by local government (public) or may be owned by private enterprise.

If there is a sewer system serving the site of the project, you may use the following steps, given in S-13.

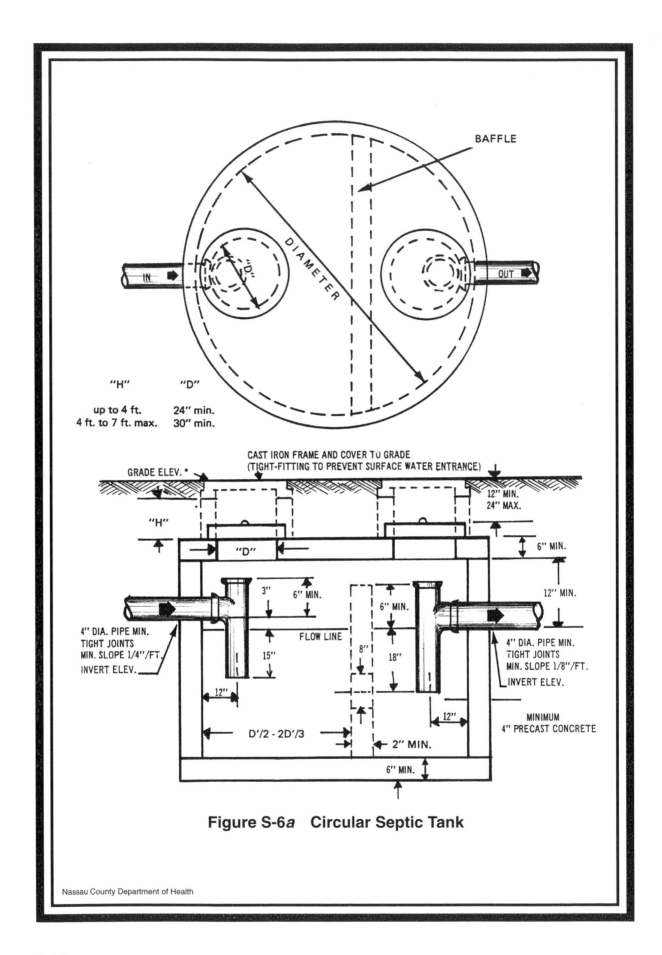

Figure S-6a Circular Septic Tank

S-13   DESIGN PROCEDURE FOR MUNICIPAL SEWER SYSTEM

1. Determine the gallons of sewer your building(s) will discharge per day using Fig. S-3.

   ### Example

   A 15-story office building will house 78 employees. What is the estimated sewage flow rate per day?

   ### Solution

   From Fig. S-3, each employee will produce 20 gallons of sewer per day.

   $$78\ E \times 15\ G/d/E = 1170\ G/d$$

   E = employees, G = gallons, d = day

2. Contact the owner for the sewer system and obtain confirmation *in writing* stating that your project may discharge the required gallons of sewer into the sewer main.

3. Obtain information as to the location, elevation, and requirements for connecting the building sewer to the main sewer line, and the cost required.

4. If there is no public sewer or the public sewer does not have adequate capacity to serve your building(s), then a private sewer system for the building(s) has to be designed. You may use the steps that follow in S 14.

S-14   DESIGN OF PRIVATE SEWER SYSTEMS

In general, there are three types:

1. ***Septic tank with leaching field system.***   Used for residences and small buildings. The design criteria are given in Fig. S-4*b*.

2. ***Seepage pits system (leaching pools).***   Commonly used for residences and other small buildings where maximum discharge of sewer does not exceed 7500 G/d for the site having coarse sand or gravel and 3000 G/d for the site containing clay with small amounts of sand or gravel.

3. ***Private sewer treatment system.***   This system of sewer treatment is generally used for projects producing an excessive amount of sewage (*over* 7500 G/d).

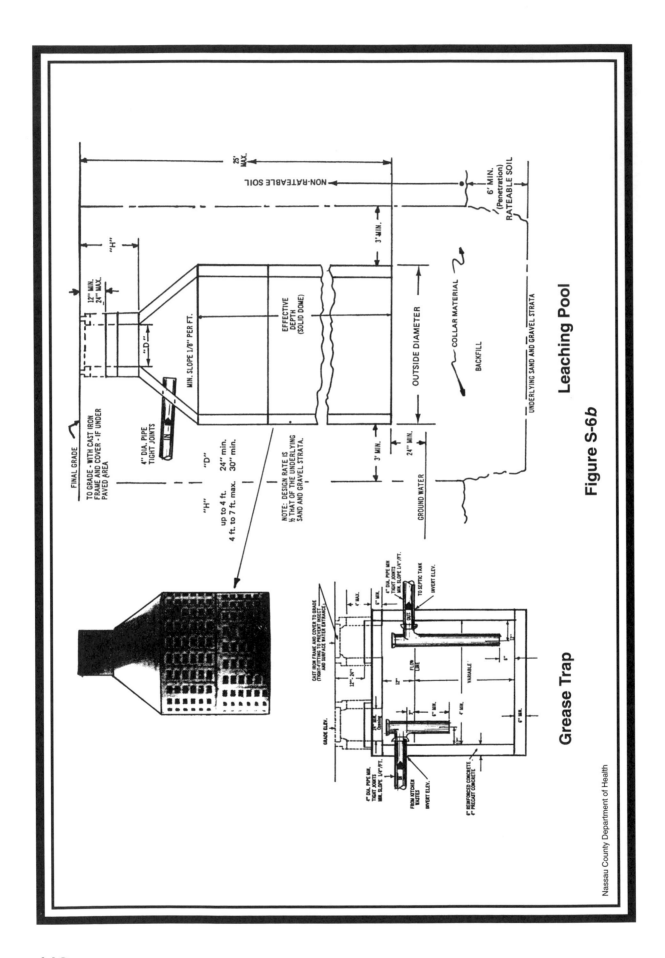

Leaching Pool

Figure S-6*b*

Grease Trap

Nassau County Department of Health

S-15 SEPTIC TANK SYSTEM

Septic tanks have been and still are constructed with brick, stone, concrete blocks, precast concrete, or steel. However, the use of septic tanks constructed with precast concrete is very common.

There are two types of septic tanks:

1. **Rectangular septic tank (Fig. S-5)**
2. **Circular septic tank (Fig. S-6a)**

In principal their performance is identical. Septic tanks have two chambers as shown in Figs. S-5 and S-6a.

A 4-inch pipe (with min. slope of ¼ in/ft) delivers the sewage into the first chamber where all objects and grit are allowed to settle to the bottom.

In this chamber, dissolved organic and inorganic matter, along with suspended solids, gradually sink to the bottom; raw sludge and light sludge and scum form on the top of a flow line.

The wall, which divides the two chambers, has an opening 18 inches below the flow line in order to stop floating sludge and scum from entering the second chamber.

The effluent, approximately 70 percent purified, leaves the second chamber (with a 4-inch-diameter pipe min., ⅛ in/ft slope) to a distribution box (Fig. S-4a) and on to either "leaching pools" (seepage pits) or to "drainage fields" (disposal area) for secondary treatment.

The size and capacity of septic tanks (Fig. S-7) are based on code requirements and Department of Health's regulations. (You must check the code and regulations governing the site of your project before designing a septic system.)

Minimum distance between components of an individual sewage disposal system is given in Figs. S-18 and S-19.

The capacity of a septic tank in general is based on retaining the liquid in the tank for a 24-hour period; however, the longer the sewage stays in the tank the longer the anaerobic composition process will take place. For this reason, oversized septic tanks (although the initial expense is higher) are recommended, because they discharge cleaner effluent; therefore, it prolongs the life of the secondary treatment process (leaching pools or drainage field).

Septic tank sizes all for connection of food waste disposable units

Single family dwellings-number of bedrooms	Multiple dwellings units or apartments-one bedroom each	Other uses; maximum fixture units served	Minimum septic tank capacity in gallons
1-3		20	1000
4	2 units	25	1200
5 or 6	3	33	1500
7 or 8	4	45	2000
	5	55	2250
	6	60	2500
	7	70	2750
	8	80	3000
	9	90	3250
	10	100	3500

Extra bedroom, 150 gallons each.
Extra dwelling units over 10, 250 gallons each.
Extra fixture units over 100, 25 gallons per fixture unit.

Figure S-7   Capacity of Septic Tanks

Time in Minutes for 1-inch Drop	Tile Length for Trench Widths of		
	1-foot	2-feet	3-feet
1	25	13	9
2	30	15	10
3	35	18	12
5	42	21	14
10	59	30	20
15	74	37	25
20	91	46	31
25	105	53	35
30	125	63	42

Figure S-8   Tile Length for Each 100 Gal. of Sewage per Day

Extracted from the 1988 Supplement to the *1987 National Standard Plumbing Code* with permission of PHCC.

Type of Fixture or Group of Fixtures	Drainage Fixture Unit Value (d.f.u.)
Automatic clothes washer 2″ standpipe and trap required—direct connection	3
Bathroom group consisting of a water closet, lavatory and bathtub or shower stall:	6
Bathtub[1] (with or without overhead shower)	2
Bidet	1
Clinic Sink	6
Combination sink-and-tray with food waste grinder	4
Combination sink-and-tray with one $1\text{-}1/2_0$ trap	2
Combination sink-and-tray with separate $1\text{-}1/2_0$ traps	3
Dental unit or cuspidor	1
Dental lavatory	1
Drinking fountain	½
Dishwasher, domestic	2
Floor drains with 2_0 waste	3
Kitchen sink, domestic, with one $1\text{-}\frac{1}{2}_0$ trap	2
Kitchen sink, domestic, with food waste grinder	2
Kitchen sink, domestic, with food waste grinder and dishwaster $1\text{-}\frac{1}{2}_0$ trap	3
Kitchen sink, domestic, with dishwasher $1\text{-}\frac{1}{2}_0$ trap	3
Kitchen sink, domestic, with dishwasher $1\text{-}\frac{1}{2}_0$ trap	3
Lavatory with $1\text{-}\frac{1}{4}_0$ waste	1
Laundry trap (1 or 2 compartments)	2
Shower stall, domestic	2
Showers (group) per head[2]	2
Sinks:	
Surgeon's	3
Flushing rim (with valve)	6
Service (trap standard)	3
Service (P trap)	2
Pot, scullery, etc.[2]	4
Urinal, syphon jet blowout	6
Urinal, wall lip	4
Urinal, stall, washout	4
Urinal trough (each 6-ft. section)	2
Wash sink (circular or multiple) each set of faucets	2
Water closet, private	4
Water closet, public	6
Fixtures not listed above:	
Trap Size 1-¼″ or less	1
Trap Size 1-½″	2
Trap Size 2″	3
Trap Size 2-½″	4
Trap Size 3″	5
Trap Size 4″	6

[1] A shower head over a bathtub does not increase the fixture unit value.

[2] See Section 11.4.2 for method of computing equivalent fixture unit values for devices or equipment which discharge continuous or semi-continuous flows into sanitary drainage systems.

Figure S-9   Drainage Fixture Unit Values
for Various Plumbing Fixtures

Extracted from the *1987 National Standard Plumbing Code* with permission of PHCC.

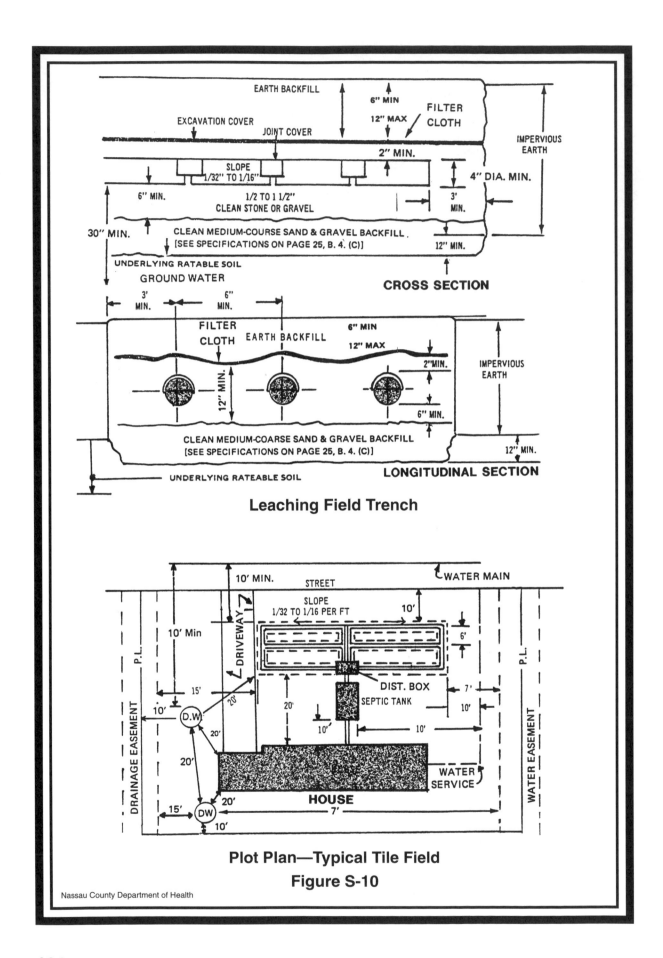

Leaching Field Trench

Plot Plan—Typical Tile Field

Figure S-10

S-16 DESIGN PROCEDURE FOR A SEPTIC TANK

Step 1. Group all fixtures (fix) which are producing waste.

Step 2. By using Fig. S-9, find drainage fixture unit (F.U.) valves for each fixture.

Step 3. Construct a table as follows:

No. of fixtures × fixture unit/fix. = total F.U.

Step 4. Use Fig. S-7 to determine min. septic tank capacity in gallons.

S-17 PERCOLATION TEST

A method for determining the ground allocated for a leaching field's ability to absorb water. This method is acceptable by many codes and by the Department of Health.

How to conduct a percolation test

Step 1. Dig a hole of 1 foot square or round and 18 to 24 inches deep in the area where the leaching field is to be located.

Step 2. Place a steel measuring ruler in the hole and fill the hole with water up to 12 inches from the top of the hole.

Step 3. Record the time in minutes for drop to 1 inch of water.

Step 4. Repeat the test a second time and use the average time in minutes.

Step 5. Use Fig. S-8 to determine the size of the leaching field.

S-18 LEACHING FIELD

Also known as *leaching area, disposable field* (area), and *drainage field* (area).

Leaching field is a method for further oxidizing the effluent discharged from a septic tank for secondary treatment.

The available size of a leaching field dictates the widths of the trench: 1, 2, or 3 ft (Fig. S-8), 4-inch apex joint clay tile or perforated plastic pipe (if permitted) with a maximum slope of ¼ inch to 8 feet of length laid on the top of 12-inch gravel as shown in Fig. S-10.

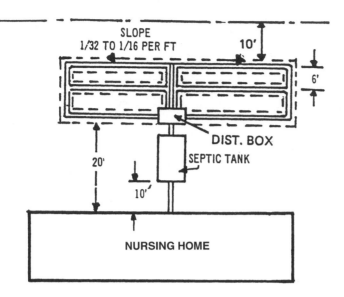
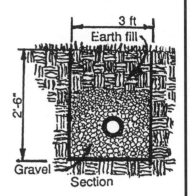

Figure S-11

Width of Trench at Bottom	Recommended Depth of Trench	Spacing Tile Lines[1]	Effective Absorption Area per Lineal Foot of Trench
Inches	Inches	Feet	Square Feet
18	18 to 30	6.0	1.5
24	18 to 30	6.0	2.0
30	18 to 36	7.6	2.5
36	24 to 36	9.0	3.0

Extracted from the 1988 Supplement to the *1987 National Standard Plumbing Code* with permission of PHCC.

Figure S-12   Size and Spacing for Disposal Fields

Diam.	Depth				
	4'	5'	6'	8'	10'
4'	50.2	62.8	75.3	100.4	125.6
5'	62.8	78.5	94.2	125.6	157.0
6'	75.4	94.2	113.0	150.7	188.4
8'	100.4	125.6	150.7	200.9	251.2

**Figure S-13   Absorption Areas of Typical Seepage Pit
(in square feet)**

124

S-19 DESIGN OF A LEACHING FIELD

Example

Design a leaching field for a nursing home (Fig. S-11) with a total population of 25 persons. Percolation test shows time in minutes for 1-inch drop in 10 minutes.

Solution

Step 1. Using Fig. S-3 for a nursing home sewage flow, it is 75 gallons per person per day.

$$75 \text{ G/p/d} \times 25 \text{ p} = 1875 \text{ G/d size of septic tank}$$

Step 2. From Fig. S-8, for 10 minutes drop of 1 inch and trench width of 3 feet, 20 feet of length is required per 100 gallons per day.

$$1875 \text{ G/d} \div 100 \text{ G/d} = 18.75$$

$$18.75 \times 20 \text{ ft.} = 375 \text{ feet of tile field}$$

Step 3. It requires 6 lengths of tile drains (Fig. S-11) 62.5 feet long with a trench 3 feet wide. See Figs. S-18 and S-19 for min. components of disposal system.

S-20 SEEPAGE POOL (PITS)

Also referred to as *leaching pool (pits)* (Figs. S-6*b* and S-16).

Seepage pits have been and are constructed with hollow tile, stone, brick, or concrete block; circular wall laid with open joints without mortar in order for the water to seep through the opening into the surrounding soil.

However, the use of seepage pools constructed with precast concrete is commonly used today, and they are available in 4-, 5-, 6-, and 10-ft diameters, and 4-, 5-, 6-, 8-, and 10-ft depths (Fig. S-13).

The seepage pools are sized by the area of the wall exposed to the soil in square feet. The depth, diameter, and total square feet of seepage pools are given in Fig. S-13. The bottom of seepage pool is not considered in design.

A seepage pool is required to be placed a minimum of 2 feet above the water table. (See W-13.)

Time in Minutes for 1-inch Drop	Effective Absorption Area Square Feet
1	32
2	40
3	45
5	56
10	75
15	96
20	108
25	139
30	167

Note: Minimum 125 s.f. required. Bottom of pit shall not be considered part of the absorption area.

Extracted from the 1988 Supplement to the *1987 National Standard Plumbing Code* with permission of PHCC.

Figure S-14   Effective Absorption Area in Seepage Pits for Each 100 Gal. of Sewage per Day

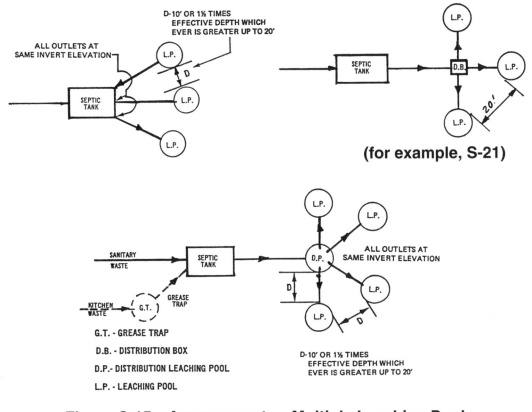

(for example, S-21)

G.T. - GREASE TRAP

D.B. - DISTRIBUTION BOX

D.P.- DISTRIBUTION LEACHING POOL

L.P. - LEACHING POOL

Figure S-15   Arrangements—Multiple Leaching Pools

The percolation test is performed by drilling to the depth where the seepage pit will be placed, and the hole is filled with water and drops of 1 inch in minutes recorded.

Effective absorption area in a seepage pit for each 100 gallons of sewage per day is given in Fig. S-14.

S-21   DESIGN OF SEEPAGE POOLS

Example

Design a seepage pool for a nursing home with a total population of 25 persons.

Perculation test shows time in minutes for 1-inch drop is 10 minutes and water table is 22 ft below grade.

Solution

Step 1. Using Fig. S-3, nursing home sewage flow is 75 gallons per person per day.

$$75 \text{ G/p/d} \times 25 \text{ p} = 1875 \text{ G/d}$$

Step 2. From Fig. S-14, the effective absorption area in seepage pits for each 100 gallons of sewage per day for 10 minutes for 1-inch drop is 75 sq. ft.

$$1875 \text{ G/D} \div 100 \text{ G/d} = 18.75$$

$$18.75 \times 75 \text{ sq. ft.} = 1406 \text{ sq. ft. absorption area}$$

Step 3. Referring to Fig. S-13, seepage pits with an 8-ft diameter and a 6-ft depth has an absorption area of 150.7 sq. ft.

$$1406 \text{ sq. ft.} \div 150.7 \text{ sq. ft./unit} = 9.33 \approx 9 \text{ units}$$

Use three seepage pits 18 feet in height (three units/seepage pits).

Step 4. Spacing of seepage pits outside to outside 10 ft or 1½ times effective depth, whichever is greater up to 20 ft (Fig. S-15).

$$18 \text{ ft} \times 1.5 = 27 \text{ ft}$$

Use 20-ft spacing

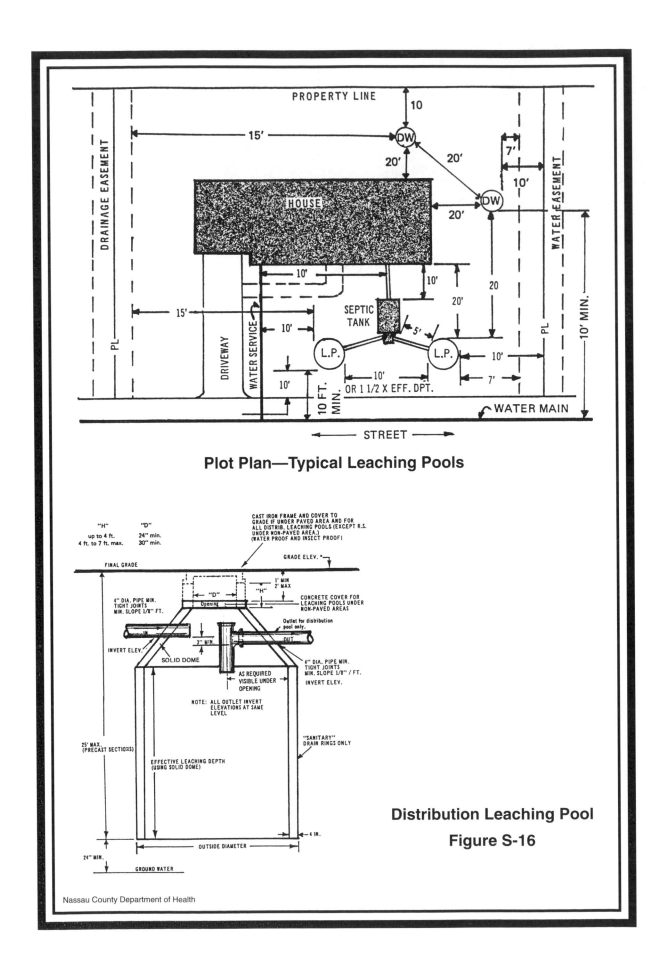

Plot Plan—Typical Leaching Pools

Distribution Leaching Pool

Figure S-16

128

S-22   DESIGN OF SEPTIC SYSTEM FOR A HOUSE

Example

Design a septic tank and leaching field system for the house shown in Fig. S-17 using flush tank (F.T.) water closet.

The percolation for the leaching field for 1-inch drop is 30 minutes.

The water table is 6 feet below the grade.

Solution

G = gallons, P = persons, d = day, B.R. = bedroom, L = lengths

1. **Design of septic tank**

   Step 1. Using the plans of Fig. S-17 and counting the fixtures (fix), and obtaining the fixture unit (F.U.) from Fig. S-9, construct the following table:

Fix	F.U./fix		Total F.U.
2 water closets, private	× 4	=	8
3 lavatories	× 1	=	3
2 shower stalls	× 2	=	4
2 bathtubs	× 2	=	4
1 kitchen sink, domestic	× 2	–	2
1 laundry (trap)	× 2	=	2
1 dishwasher	× 2	=	2
1 auto. clothes washer	× 3	=	_3_
	Total F.U.		28

   Step 2. Select the size of the septic tank from Fig. S-7. For three bedrooms and 20 F.U., the minimum size septic tank is 1000 gallons. However, there are 28 F.U. used in the house. Therefore, the minimum size of the septic tank is 1500 gallons.

2. **Design of leaching field**

   Step 3. From Fig. S-3, sewage flows for subdivision or individual homes is 75 G/p/d, and for luxury residences and estates it is 150 G/p/d, using 100 G/p/d required by N.Y.S. Dept. of Health.

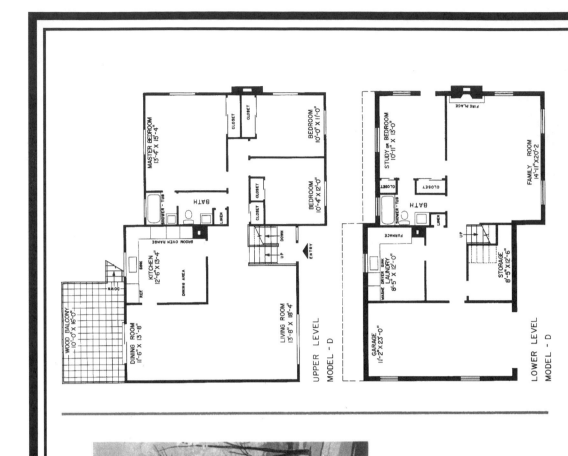

UPPER LEVEL
MODEL - D

LOWER LEVEL
MODEL - D

(Model D) THE CASPIAN BI-LEVEL

3 bedrooms including spacious master bedroom; plus study or den which can also be a 4th bedroom. 2 full baths. Huge luxurious living room, formal dining room, eat-in kitchen with General Electric Appliances*. Oversize family room with Fireplace*. Large open balcony, 1 (or 2)* car garage.

*Optional.

Figure S-17   Design of Septic System for a House

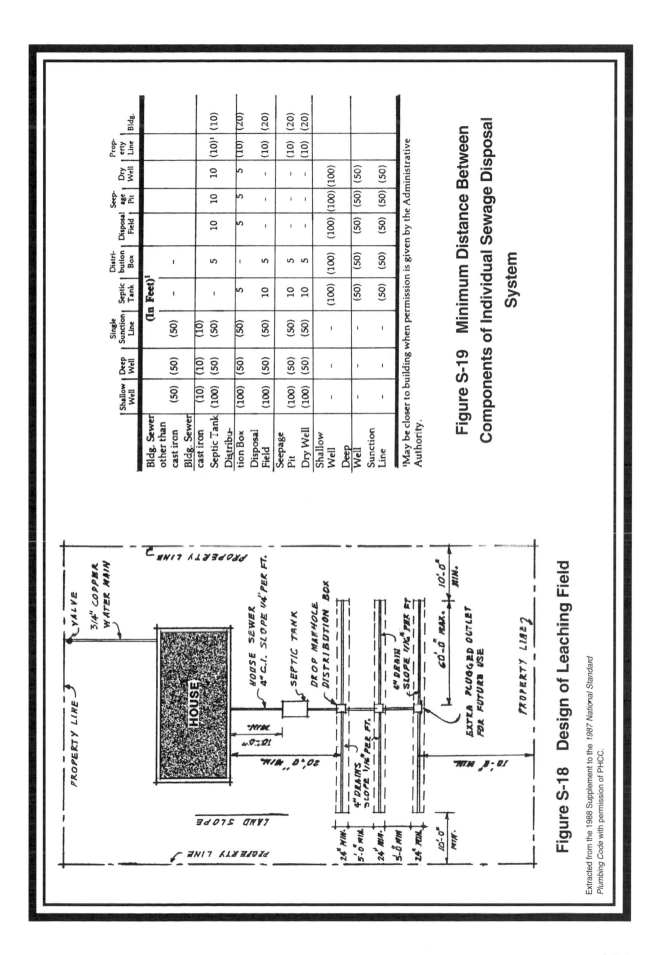

Figure S-19 Minimum Distance Between Components of Individual Sewage Disposal System

¹May be closer to building when permission is given by the Administrative Authority.

Figure S-18 Design of Leaching Field

Extracted from the 1988 Supplement to the *1987 National Standard Plumbing Code* with permission of PHCC.

RIDGEBURY LAKE ACRES

TOWN OF WAWAYANDA NEAR MIDDLETOWN, ORANGE COUNTY, NEW YORK

Architects & Engineers: Dadras International

Figure S-20

132

Step 4. Find total amount of sewage per day

$$3 \text{ B.R.} \times 2 \text{ p/B.R.} = 6 \text{ p}$$

$$6 \text{ p} \times 100 \text{ G/d/p} = 600 \text{ G/d}$$

Step 5. Using Fig. S-8, for 30 minutes drop of 1-inch and trench width of 2 feet, tile length for each 100 gallons is 63 ft.

$$600 \text{ G/d} \div 100 \text{ G/d} = 6$$

$$6 \times 63 \text{ ft} = 378 \text{ ft total length}$$

$$378 \text{ ft} \div 60 \text{ ft/L} = 6.3 \approx 6 \text{ L}$$

Use 6 lengths of 60 ft each (60 ft instead of 63 is OK).

Design of septic system for the house in Fig. S-17 is illustrated in Fig. S-18. The minimum distance between components of a septic system is given in Fig. S-19.

S-23   PRIVATE SEWAGE TREATMENT SYSTEM

Housing project or subdivision

(Design procedure described in the following may be used for any other project.)

If a housing project is planned for more than 50 lots, regardless of the size of the lots, a central water system and a central sewage treatment system are required.

References are to Ridgebury Lake Acres, Middletown, New York (Fig. S-20).

This housing project was planned for more than 50 lots; therefore, the central water system and central sewage treatment plant was designed to serve this community. We discuss the design of a central sewer treatment system in the following (the design of central water system is given in W-29).

The land was 87 acres and was divided into 78 lots: 75 lots for houses, one lot allocated for a park and location of wells (A), one lot designated for a park and location of a reservoir (B), one lot for the location of a sewage treatment plant (C). A natural creek was located on this site. Therefore, a package sewage treatment plant was designed capable of removing approximately 97 percent of the organic matter and was permitted to be discharged to a natural creek.

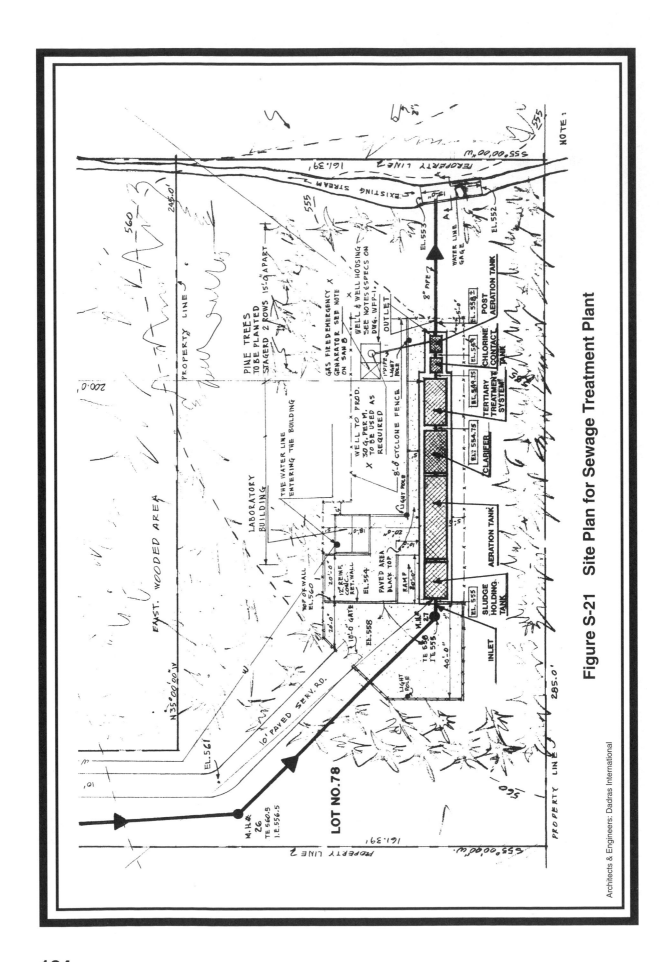

Figure S-21   Site Plan for Sewage Treatment Plant

Architects & Engineers: Dadras International

134

S-24 DESIGN OF PRIVATE SEWAGE TREATMENT PLANT

New York State Department of Health had jurisdiction over the design, installation, and operation of this sewage treatment plant. All their rules, regulations, and criteria were followed.

Find the size of the plant.

H = house, B.R. = bedroom, P = persons, G = gallons, d = day

Step 1. Determine the total population of the project.

$$75 \text{ H} \times 3 \text{ B.R./H} = 225 \text{ B.R.}$$

$$225 \text{ B.R.} \times 2 \text{ p/B.R.} = 450 \text{ p}$$

Step 2. From Fig. S-3, sewage flow from luxury residences and estates is 150 G/d/p and for subdivisions or individual houses is 75 G/d/p, using 100 G/d/p.

$$450 \text{ p} \times 100 \text{ G/d/p} = 45,000 \text{ G/d}$$

Note: 40,000 G/d and 60,000 G/d capacity was available. 40,000 G/d was approved.

Step 3. A package sewage treatment plant with 40,000 G/d was installed in lot no. 78 (shown in Fig. S-20 as "C"). This lot was chosen because it had the lowest elevation in the project (ev. 560), and a creek was located on this lot, which allowed the discharge of clean water from the treatment plant (Fig. S-21).

Step 4. The sewer discharge from houses was delivered to a sewage treatment plant by gravity, except from houses on lots 8 through 17 and lots 74 and 75 (with lower elevation) which were delivered to the corner of lot no. 7(A) to a sewage lift station with two pneumatic ejectors engaged in sending sewage to the main sewage line.
A package sewage treatment plant manufactured by Clow Corp. was used.
(See Fig. S-22.)

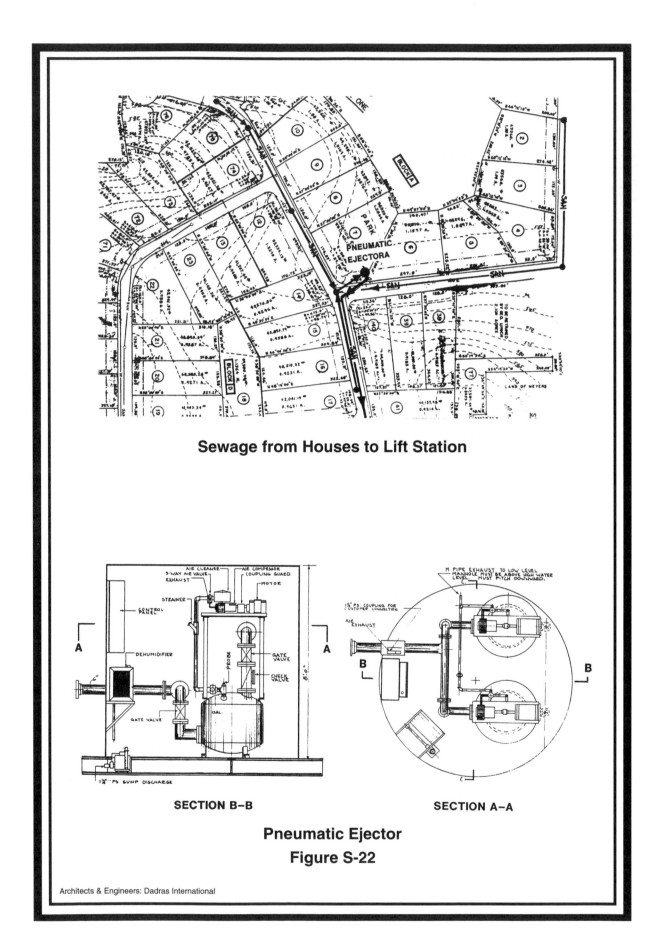

Sewage from Houses to Lift Station

SECTION B–B

SECTION A–A

Pneumatic Ejector

Figure S-22

Architects & Engineers: Dadras International

136

S-25   WHEN NATURAL RUNOFF IS NOT AVAILABLE

If, for a housing project, subdivision, or any other project, no natural creek or body of water is available for discharge of treated water from a sewage treatment plant, then depending on local codes, requirements, and the Department of Health's rules and regulations, there are two ways to design the sewage disposal systems:

1.   Use of primary sewage treatment system and
   Use of leaching pools for secondary treatment

2.   Use of primary sewage treatment system and
   Use of stabilization or oxydation ponds or
   Leaching ponds for discharge of the water

S-26 WASTE TREATMENT TERMINOLOGY

activated sludge A process that removes organic matter from sewage by saturating it with air and adding biologically active sludge.

adsorption An advanced way of treating wastes in which activated carbon removes organic matter from wastewater.

aeration tank Serves as a chamber for injecting air into water.

algae Plants which grow in sunlit water. They are a food for fish and small aquatic animals and, like all plants, put oxygen into the water.

bacteria Small living organisms which often consume the organic constituents of sewage.

BOD Also known as biochemical oxygen demand. The dissolved oxygen required by organisms for the aerobic decomposition of organic matter present in water. It is used as a measure in determining the efficiency of a sewage treatment plant or to determine the potential of an effluent to degrade a stream.

chlorinator A device for adding chlorine gas to sewage to kill infectious germs.

coagulation The clumping together of solids to make them settle out of the sewage faster. Coagulation of solids is brought about with the use of certain chemicals such as lime, alum, and iron salts.

combined sewer Carries both sewage and storm-water runoff.

comminutor A device for the catching and shredding of heavy solid matter in the primary stage of waste treatment.

diffused air A technique by which air under pressure is forced into sewage in an aeration tank. The air is pumped down into the sewage through a pipe and escapes through holes in the side of the pipe.

digestion Digestion of sludge takes place in tanks when the materials decompose, resulting in partial gasification, liquefaction, and mineralization of pollutants.

distillation Distillation in waste treatment consists of heating the effluent and then removing the vapor or steam. When the steam is returned to a liquid it is almost pure water. The pollutants remain in the concentrated residue.

effluent Liquid that comes out of a treatment plant after completion of the treatment process.

eutrophication The normally slow aging process by which a lake evolves into a bog or marsh and ultimately assumes a completely terrestrial state and disappears. During eutrophication the lake becomes so rich in nutritive compounds, especially nitrogen and phosphorus, that algae and other microscopic plant life become superabundant, thereby "choking" the lake, and causing it eventually to dry up. Eutrophication may be accelerated by many human activities.

floc A clump of solids formed in sewage by biological or chemical action.

flocculation The process by which clumps of solids in sewage are made to increase in size by chemical, physical, or biological action.

fungi Small, non-chlorophyll-bearing plants which may play a useful role in trickling filter treatment operations.

groundwater The body of water beneath the surface of the ground. It is made up primarily of the water that has seeped down from the surface.

incineration   Consists of burning the sludge to remove the water and reduce the remaining residues to a safe, nonburnable ash. The ash can be disposed of safely on land, in water, or into caves or other underground locations.

infiltration   The penetration of water through the ground's surface into subsurface soil.

infiltration/percolation   A land application technique where large volumes of wastewater are applied to land and allowed to penetrate the surface and percolate through the underlying soil.

interceptor   Interceptor sewers in a combined system control the flow of the sewage to the treatment plant. In a storm, they allow some of the sewage to flow directly into a receiving stream. This protects the treatment plant from being overloaded in case of a sudden surge of water into the sewers. Interceptors are also used in separate sanitation systems to collect the flows from main and trunk sewers and carry them to the points of treatment.

ion   An electrically charged atom or group of atoms which can be drawn from waste water during the electrodialysis process.

irrigation   A land application technique where wastewater is applied to the land to supply the water and nutrient needs of plants.

land application   The discharge of wastewater onto the ground for treatment or reuse.

lateral   Lateral sewers are the pipes that run under the streets of a city and into which empty the sewers from homes or businesses.

mechanical aeration   Uses mechanical energy to inject air into water, causing the waste stream to absorb oxygen from the atmosphere.

microbes	Minute plants or animal life. Some microbes which may cause disease exist in sewage.
mixed liquor	A mixture of activated sludge and waters containing organic matter undergoing activated sludge treatment in the aeration tank.
nitrogenous wastes	Wastes of animal or plant origin that contain a significant concentration of nitrogen.
nutrients	Elements or compounds essential as raw materials for organism growth and development; for example, carbon, oxygen, nitrogen, and phosphorus.
organic matter	The carbonaceous waste contained in plant or animal matter and originating from domestic or industrial sources.
overland flow	A land application technique that cleanses wastewater by allowing it to flow over a sloped surface. As the water flows over the surface, the contaminants are removed and the water is collected at the bottom of the slope for reuse.
oxidation	The addition of oxygen which breaks down organic wastes or chemicals in sewage by bacterial and chemical means.
oxidation pond	A humanmade lake or body of water in which wastes are consumed by bacteria. It is used most frequently with other waste treatment processes. An oxidation pond is basically the same as a sewage lagoon.
percolation	The movement of water through subsurface soil layers, usually continuing downward to the groundwater.

phosphorus	An element that, while essential to life, contributes to the eutrophication of lakes and other bodies of water.
pollution	Results when animal, vegetable, mineral, or heat wastes or discharges reach water, making it less desirable for domestic, recreation, industry, or wildlife uses.
polyelectrolytes	Synthetic chemicals used to speed the removal of solids from sewage. The chemicals cause the solids to flocculate or clump together more rapidly than chemicals like alum or lime.
primary treatment	The stage in basic treatment that removes the material that floats or will settle in sewage. It is accomplished by using screens to catch the floating objects and tanks for the heavy matter to settle in.
receiving waters	Rivers, lakes, oceans, or other water courses that receive treated or untreated wastewater.
salts	Minerals that water picks up as it passes through the air, over and under the ground, and through household and industrial uses.
sand filters	Remove some suspended solids from sewage. Air and bacteria decompose additional wastes filtering through the sand. Cleaner water drains from the bed. The sludge accumulating at the surface must be removed from the bed periodically.
sanitary sewers	Sanitary sewers, in a separate system, are pipes in a city that carry domestic waste water only. The storm-water runoff is taken care of by a separate system of pipes.
suspended solids	The small particles of solid pollutants that are present in sewage and that resist separation from the water by conventional means.

trickling filter

A support media for bacterial growth, usually a bed of rocks or stones. The sewage is trickled over the bed so the bacteria can break down the organic wastes. The bacteria collect on the stones through repeated use of the filter.

waste treatment plant

A series of tanks, screens, filters, and other processes by which pollutants are removed from water.

virus

The smallest form of microorganism capable of causing disease.

CONTENTS

Part 4

STORM DRAINAGE SYSTEMS

D

Drainage Systems

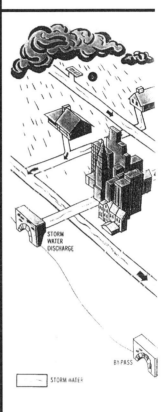

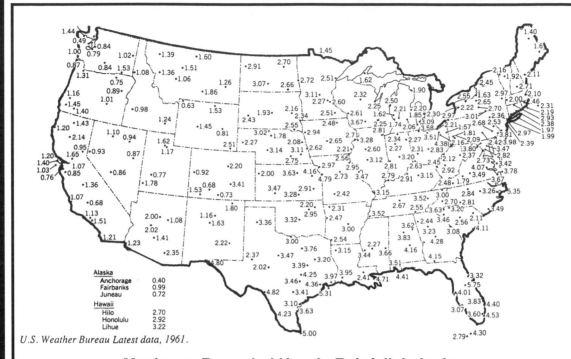

Maximum Recorded Hourly Rainfall, In Inches
(for information only)

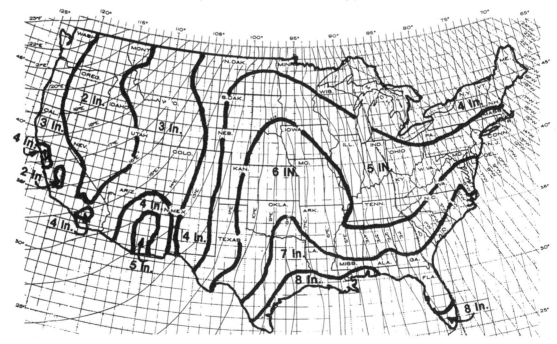

Storm Drainage Precipitation Rate Inches/Hour—
Based on 15-Minute Precipitation
Figure D-1

DRAINAGE SYSTEMS

D-1 RAIN

When the particles of moisture in the clouds are heavy enough, they fall as drops of rain.

Precipitation is formed by further condensation of the moisture in the cloud.

The raindrops formed are enlarged by coalescing with others on impact and by condensing on their colder surfaces the moisture in the air through which they pass.

From the time they leave the bottom of the cloud, evaporation takes place, and, if the air is warm and dry and the cloud is high, the raindrops are small and they fall slowly, or they may evaporate completely before they reach the earth.

Rainfall in the United States ranges from less than 2 in. in Death Valley to more than 100 in. on the coast of Washington state. In the rest of the country, the average rainfall is between 15 and 45 in. annually (Fig. D-1 shows max. rainfall in in/H).

Areas near the sea and ocean receive more rain than inland regions because the winds constantly lose moisture and may be quite dry by the time they reach the interior of a continent.

Rainfall is measured in terms of inches of depth, by means of a simple receptable-and-gauge apparatus or electrical or weighing devices placed where eddies of air will not interfere with the normal fall of the raindrops.

Rainfall is measured on a daily, monthly, and annual total. It is also recorded during a specific period of hours or minutes.

All calculations for roof drains, leader size, and gutter size are based on maximum hourly rainfall in inches.

D-2 STORM DRAINAGE SYSTEMS

Rainfall (also known as **storm water**) on the roof and balconies of the building, paved areas around the structure, and parking areas serving the project has to be collected and discharged to one of the following:

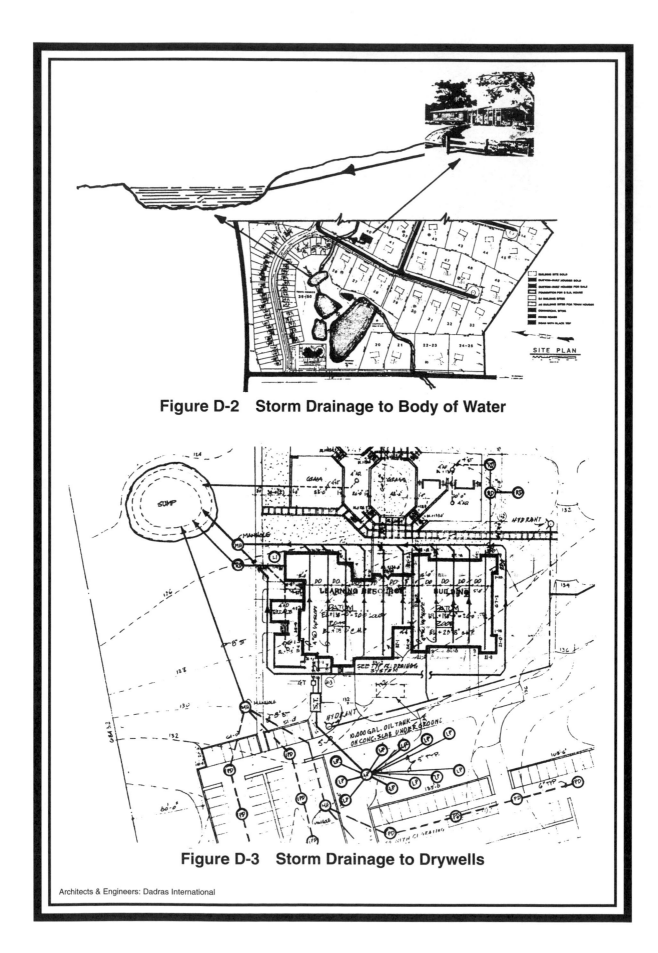

Figure D-2   Storm Drainage to Body of Water

Figure D-3   Storm Drainage to Drywells

Architects & Engineers: Dadras International

1. Municipality storm drainage systems (D-3)

2. Private storm drainage system (D-4)

D-3   MUNICIPAL STORM DRAINAGE SYSTEM

There are two systems in use:

1. Combined sewer system, which carries away both sewage and storm water

2. Storm drainage system, which carries only storm water

If one of the above is available to serve your building(s), the following steps may be followed:

1. Find gallons of rainfall to be discharged to the storm drainage system.

Step 1. Find total areas (*square feet*) in your project which receive rainfall.

Step 2. From Fig. D-1, find the maximum hourly rainfall in inches for the location of the project.

Step 3. Use the following formulas to determine the gallons of rainfall per minute

G = gallons, hr = hour, m = minute, A = area (ft²), R = rainfall (in/h):

1 gallon of water = 231 in³ or 0.123 ft³ (W-17)

$$G/m = \frac{A\ ft^2}{96} \times R\ in/hr$$

$$G/m \times 60\ m/hr = G/hr$$

2. Contact the municipality. Obtain confirmation *in writing* stating that your project can discharge required gallons of runoff rainfall into storm drainage system or combined sewer system.

If none of the above services are available for the project, then a private storm drainage system can be designed (see D-4).

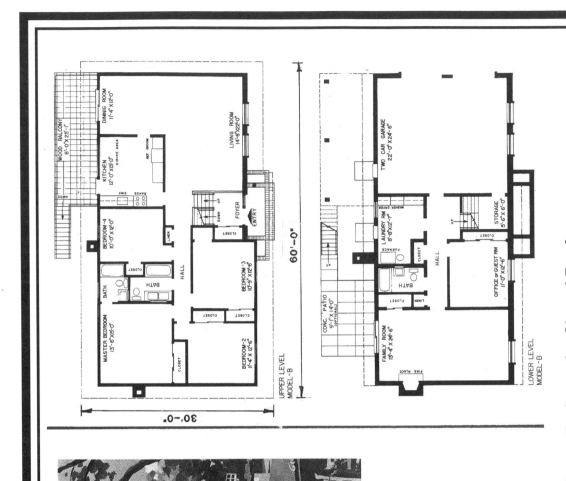

UPPER LEVEL MODEL-B

LOWER LEVEL MODEL-B

(Model B) THE MANCHESTER BI-LEVEL

4 large bedrooms, including an oversize master bedroom. 3 full baths. Spacious luxurious living room, dining room, office or guest room. Huge recreation family room with Fireplace* and sliding patio doors. Eat-in kitchen with General Electric Appliances*, laundry room, storage room, 25 ft. large open balcony, 2 car garage.

*Optional.

Figure D-4   Design of Storm Drainage for Sloped Roof

Architects & Engineers: Dadras International

D-4   PRIVATE STORM DRAINAGE SYSTEM

There are two ways to discharge the storm water from the project:

1. Collected rainfall can be delivered to a stream, river, or body of water, if available (some local codes and ordinances require a permit for discharging storm water to a body of water) (Fig. D-2).

2. Collected rainfall can be discharged to drywell(s) installed for this purpose (Fig. D-3).

Regardless of how the water collected from the project will be discharged, first the storm drainage system has to be designed to collect the rainfall from the building and the site.

D-5   DESIGN OF STORM DRAINAGE SYSTEM

In general, there are two types of roofs from which the rainfall must be collected and directed to a storm drainage system:

1. *Sloped roof,* which normally receives gutters and leaders

2. *Flat roof,* where the collected rainfall runs into horizontal pipes and roof drain

D-6   DESIGN OF STORM DRAINAGE FOR SLOPED ROOF

Example

Design gutters and leaders for the house designed for Ridgebury Lake Acres in Middletown, New York (Fig. D-4).

Solution

Step 1. From Fig. D-1, maximum hourly rainfall for Middletown, New York, is 5 in/hr.

Step 2. Find the area of the roof. For area of the rainfall on the roof horizontal, projected area of the roof is used for calculation:

$$30 \text{ ft} \times 60 \text{ ft} = 1800 \text{ ft}^2 \text{ total area of roof}$$

$$1800 \text{ ft}^2 \div 2 = 900 \text{ ft}^2 \text{ each side of the roof}$$

Note: The length of roof is 60 ft; it is logical to use three leaders; therefore, each leader will carry rainfall from 300 ft^2.

Gutter Sizes

Diameter of Gutter 1/16" Slope	Maximum Rainfall (in./hr)				
	2	3	4	5	6
	Maximum Horizontal Projected Roof Areas, Square Feet				
3	340	226	170	136	113
4	720	480	360	288	240
5	1250	834	625	500	416
6	1920	—	960	768	640
7	2760	1840	1380	1100	918
8	3980	2655	1990	1590	1325
10	7200	4800	3600	2880	2400

Diameter of Gutter 1/8" Slope	Maximum Rainfall (in./hr)				
	2	3	4	5	6
	Maximum Horizontal Projected Roof Areas, Square Feet				
3	480	320	240	192	160
4	1020	681	510	408	340
5	1760	1172	880	704	587
6	2720	1815	1360	1085	905
7	3900	2600	1950	1560	1300
8	5600	3740	2800	2240	1870
10	10200	6800	5100	4080	3400

Diameter of Gutter 1/4" Slope	Maximum Rainfall (in./hr)				
	2	3	4	5	6
	Maximum Horizontal Projected Roof Areas, Square Feet				
3	680	454	340	272	226
4	1440	960	720	576	480
5	2500	1668	1250	1000	834
6	3840	2560	1920	1536	1280
7	5520	3680	2760	2205	1840
8	7960	5310	3980	3180	2655
10	14400	9600	7200	5750	4800

Diameter of Gutter 1/2" Slope	Maximum Rainfall (in./hr)				
	2	3	4	5	6
	Maximum Horizontal Projected Roof Areas, Square Feet				
3	960	640	480	384	320
4	2040	1360	1020	816	680
5	3540	2360	1770	1415	1180
6	5540	3695	2770	2220	1850
7	7800	5200	3900	3120	2600
8	11200	7460	5600	4480	3730
10	20000	13330	10000	8000	6660

Figure D-5   Round, Square, or Rectangular Gutter Sizes

Source: Reprinted by permission from *Uniform Plumbing Code*, copyright © 1994 by the International Association of Plumbing and Mechanical Officials.

Step 3. Find gutter size. From Fig. D-5, use ¹⁄₁₆ in. slope for gutter, 5 in/hr rainfall and 300 ft² projected area of the roof. Diameter of gutter is 5 inches, good for 550 ft².

Therefore, use a 5-inch-diameter gutter with ¹⁄₁₆ in. slope, one on the front side and one on the back side of the house.

Step 4. Find leader size. Use three leaders on the front side and three leaders on the back side of the house:

$$900 \text{ ft}^2 \div 3 \text{ leaders} = 300 \text{ ft}^2/\text{leader}$$

From Fig. D-6, using 5 in. hourly rainfall and 300 ft² projected area of the roof, a 2-in. drain leader is good for 575 ft². (Leaders are available in rectangular shapes 2 × 4 in., 2 × 6 in., etc.)

Therefore, use three 2 × 4 in. leaders on the front side and three 2 × 4 in. leaders on the back side of the house.

D-7   DESIGN OF STORM DRAINAGE FOR FLAT ROOF

Example

Design a storm drainage system for the building shown in Fig. D-7, which is located in New York City.

Solution

Step 1. From Fig. D-1, maximum hourly rainfall for New York City is 5 in/hr.

Step 2. The roof area is 69 by 40 ft. Dividing the roof into three sections, find the area of each section (it can be divided into two).

$$23 \text{ ft} \times 40 \text{ ft} = 920 \text{ ft}^2/\text{section}$$

Step 3. The roof area of each section should be sloped in order to direct the rainfall toward the roof drain by using lightweight concrete or asphalt as shown in Fig. D-7.

Step 4. Find horizontal rainfall piping size from Fig. D-8 using 5 in/hr rainfall ⅛ in. slope and 920 ft² area. Pipe size is 4 in., good for 1504 ft² of area.

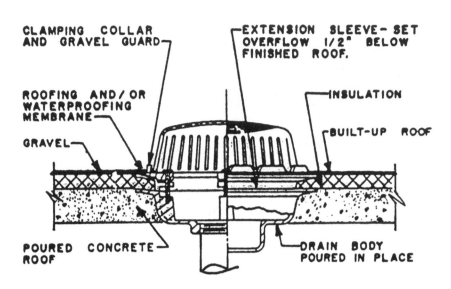

Roof Drain Installation

Max. Hourly Rainfall (in.)	Size of Drain or Leader (in.)					
	2	3	4	5	6	8
	Maximum Horizontal Projected Roof Areas, Square Feet					
1	2880	8800	18400	34600	54000	116000
2	1440	4400	9200	17300	27000	58000
3	960	2930	6130	11530	17995	38660
4	720	2200	4600	8650	13500	29000
5	575	1760	3680	6920	10800	23200
6	480	1470	3070	5765	9000	19315
7	410	1260	2630	4945	7715	16570
8	360	1100	2300	4325	6750	14500
9	320	980	2045	3845	6000	12890
10	290	880	1840	3460	5400	11600
11	260	800	1675	3145	4910	10545
12	240	730	1530	2880	4500	9660

Roof Drain and Leader Sizes

Figure D-6

Source: Reprinted by permission from *Uniform Plumbing Code*, copyright © 1994 by the International Association of Plumbing and Mechanical Officials.

Therefore, use 4 in. horizontal pipe ⅛ in. slope for both sections.

Check: For the drop of horizontal pipe

$$23 \text{ ft} \times \text{⅛ in/ft} = 2.99 \text{ in., which is OK}$$

Note: Check the clearance above the finished ceiling to make sure the horizonatal pipe does not interfere with structural or other systems; if the drop of pipe becomes excessive, then two or more leaders have to be provided in order to reduce the drop.

Step 5. Find leader size. Since one leader is used, it will carry the rainfall from the entire roof area; therefore,

$$69 \text{ ft} \times 40 \text{ ft} = 2760 \text{ ft}^2 \text{ total roof area}$$

Using Fig. D-6 for 5 in/hr rainfall, the size of leader is 4 in., good for 3680 ft².

Therefore, use a 4-in. leader.

Step 6. Find horizontal rainfall pipe size for balconies. All balconies are 6 ft wide and 40 ft long. Rainfall is collected at the center.

$$6 \text{ ft} \times 40 \text{ ft} = 240 \text{ ft}^2 \text{ area of balcony}$$

From Fig. D-8, for 5 in/hr rainfall ⅛-in.-slope horizontal pipe size is 3 in., good for 657 ft².

Therefore, use 3-in. horizontal pipe, ⅛ in. slope.

Step 7. Find leader size for balconies. From Fig. D-6,

$$240 \text{ ft}^2 \times 2 \text{ balconies} = 480 \text{ ft}^2 \text{ total area for 2 balconies}$$

for 5 in/hr rainfall and 480 ft² area. **Use 2-in. leader on each side.**

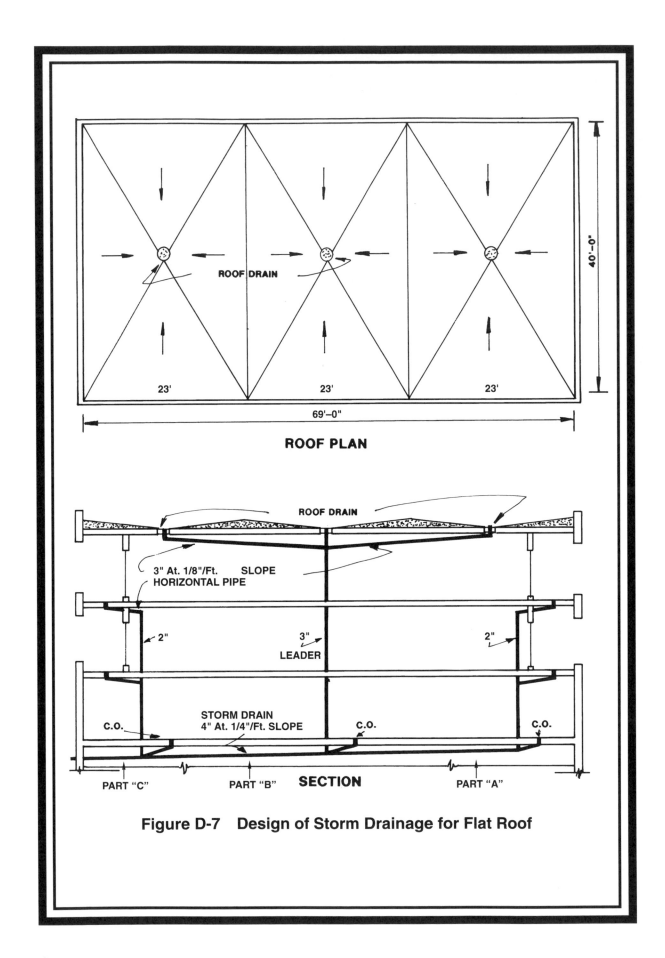

Figure D-7   Design of Storm Drainage for Flat Roof

Step 8. Find size of horizontal storm drain. From Fig. D-8, using ¼ in. slope, 5 in/hr rainfall:

For part "A," 480 ft², **use 3-in. storm drain, ¼ in. slope.**

For part "B," 2760 ft² + 480 ft² = 3240 ft² area, **use 5-in. storm drain, ¼ in. slope.**

For part "C," 3240 ft² + 480 ft² = 3720 ft² area, **use 5-in. storm drain, ¼ in. slope.**

Check: For the drop of horizontal storm drain

69 ft × ¼ in/ft = 17¼ in, which is OK

If the drop is excessive, then design for ⅛-in slope.

D-8   DISCHARGE OF STORM WATER

If there is a community storm drainage system, natural creek, or body of water, the storm drain can be discharged into it (discharge to natural creek or body of water may require a permit). Otherwise, a drywell system should be designed in accordance with the local codes.

D-9   DRYWELL DESIGN PROCEDURES

1.   Storm water should be discharged to drainage area at the same rate at which it is collected.

2.   The required rate of discharge from drywell depends directly on:

   a. Maximum inches of rainfall per hour

   b. Size of the drainage area

   c. Soil absorption (time in minutes for 1-inch drop of water)

3.   Gallons of water collected per inches of rainfall per hours are as follows:

   2 in/hr on 44 ft² area collects 60 G/hr

   3 in/hr on 32 ft² area collects 60 G/hr

   4 in/hr on 24 ft² area collects 60 G/hr

   5 in/hr on 19.2 ft² area collects 60 G/hr

   6 in/hr on 16.8 ft² area collects 60 G/hr

4.   Maximum allowable depth of drywell is 25 ft (Fig. D-9).

   The distance between the sides of the drywells should be minimum 10 ft or 1½ times effective depth, whichever is greater, up to 20 ft.

Size of Pipe (in.), 1/8" Slope	Maximum Rainfall (in./hr)				
	2	3	4	5	6
	Maximum Horizontal Projected Roof Areas, Square Feet				
3	1644	1096	822	657	548
4	3760	2506	1880	1504	1253
5	6680	4453	3340	2672	2227
6	10700	7133	5350	4280	3566
8	23000	15330	11500	9200	7600
10	41400	27600	20700	16580	13800
12	66600	44400	33300	26650	22200
15	109000	72800	59500	47600	39650

Size of Pipe (in.), 1/4" Slope	Maximum Rainfall (in./hr)				
	2	3	4	5	6
	Maximum Horizontal Projected Roof Areas, Square Feet				
3	2320	1546	1160	928	773
4	5300	3533	2650	2120	1766
5	9440	6293	4720	3776	3146
6	15100	10066	7550	6040	5033
8	32600	21733	16300	13040	10866
10	58400	38950	29200	23350	19450
12	94000	62600	47000	37600	31350
15	168000	112000	84000	67250	56000

Size of Pipe (in.), 1/2" Slope	Maximum Rainfall (in./hr)				
	2	3	4	5	6
	Maximum Horizontal Projected Roof Areas, Square Feet				
3	3288	2295	1644	1310	1096
4	7520	5010	3760	3010	2500
5	13360	8900	6680	5320	4450
6	21400	13700	10700	8580	7140
8	46000	30650	23000	18400	15320
10	82800	55200	41400	33150	27600
12	133200	88800	66600	53200	44400
15	238000	158800	119000	95300	79250

Figure D-8   Horizontal Rainwater Piping Sizes

Source: Reprinted by permission from Uniform Plumbing Code, copyright © 1994 by the International Association of Plumbing and Mechanical Officials.

General Notes

1. We have to provide a temporary storage for one hour of rainfall on the site of our project. (Check your local codes; they may require a longer period.)

2. If the site's size and terrain allow the construction of a pond to receive the rainfall from the project, this may be a good and economical solution (see Fig. D-3), or

3. We have to provide underground storage for the rainfall. This can be accomplished by installing an adequate number of precast concrete drywells with a spacing of 1½ times the depth of the drywell, up to 20 feet (see Fig. S-15). The size of the sections for a drywell (seepage pit) are given in Fig. S-13.

4. The construction and installation of a drywell and seepage pool (pit) are identical. However, when designed to receive rainfalls, it is called *drywell;* when used for disposal of sewage effluent, it is called *seepage pool (pit).*

Example

Design drywells for a storm drainage system for the project given in D-7 and Fig. D-7.

The area of the roof is 2760 ft² and the total area of the balconies is 480 ft². The building is located in New York City.

Solution

Step 1. Find the total area receiving rainfall.

$$2760 \text{ ft}^2 + 480 \text{ ft}^2 = 3240 \text{ ft}^2$$

Step 2. Find the hourly rainfall.

From Fig. D-1, 5 in/hr rainfall.

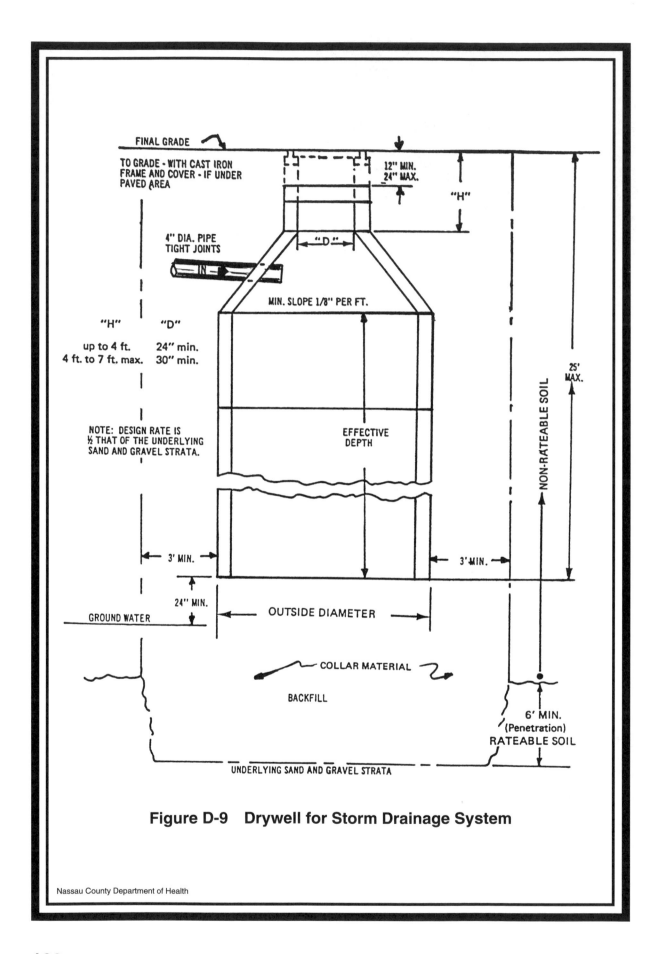

Figure D-9 Drywell for Storm Drainage System

Nassau County Department of Health

160

Step 3. Find the total gallons of water collected using the formula given in D-3.

$$G/m = \frac{A\ ft^2}{96} \times R\ in/hr$$

$$G/m \times 60\ m/hr = total\ G/hr$$

$$G/m = \frac{3240\ ft^2}{96} \times 5\ in/hr = 168.75\ G/m$$

$$168.75\ G/m \times 60\ m/hr = 10{,}125\ G/hr\ rainfall.$$

Step 4. Find cubic feet of rainfall from W-17. One gallon of water is 0.134 ft^3.

$$10{,}125\ G/hr \times 0.134\ ft^3/hr = 1345.75\ ft^3.$$

Step 5. Choose the size of a drywell. Fig. S-13 gives the diameter and the depth of each section of drywell. Let's try a section of 6 ft diameter and 6 ft depth.

Step 6. Find cubic feet of one section.

$$Area\ of\ circle = 0.7854 \times d^2$$
$$Area\ of\ section = 0.7854 \times 6\ ft^2 = 28.20\ ft^2.$$

Step 7. Find cubic feet per section.

$$28.23\ ft^2 \times 6\ ft = 169.68\ ft^3.$$

Step 8. Find out how many sections of precast concrete are needed.

$$1356.75\ ft^3 \div 169.68\ ft^3 = 8\ sections$$

Use 4 drywells 6 ft in diameter and 12 ft in depth (2 sections of 6 ft each).

Step 9. Find the spacing of drywells from Fig. S-15.

$$12\ ft \times 1.5 = 18\ ft\ less\ than\ 20\ ft$$

Use 18-ft spacing for drywells.

CONTENTS

Part 5

PLUMBING SYSTEMS

P

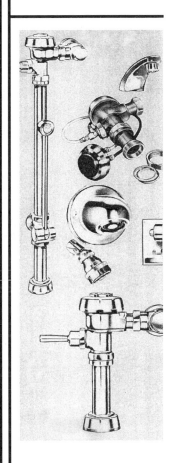

Design of Water Supply Main

Sanitary Drainage System
Drainage, Waste, and Vent (DWV)

Design of Drainage, Waste and Vent (DWV)

DESIGN OF PLUMBING FACILITIES

P-1   DESIGN CRITERIA

Before starting to design the floor plan of any structure, the designer needs to know the following information in regard to the plumbing system.

P-2   RESIDENTIAL BUILDINGS

1.   Size and number of bathrooms required

2.   Size and spacing requirements for fixtures

3.   Size and space requirements for kitchen sink, dishwasher, and garbage disposal

4.   Size and space requirements for washer and drier

Note: If the building or units are used by physically handicapped person(s), then bathrooms, kitchen, and laundry rooms must be designed to conform with the requirements given in P-6.

P-3   PUBLIC BUILDINGS

Includes any structure used by the public.

1.   The number of toilet facilities for men and women on each floor

2.   The size and space requirements for all fixtures

3.   The size and space requirements for kitchen facilities if required

4.   Slop sink for janitors on each floor

5.   Drinking-water fountain(s) on each floor

6.   Toilet facilities and space requirements for physically handicapped persons (minimum of one toilet facility on each floor) (see P-6)

7.   Overall size of the men's and women's rooms and their proper location on each floor

P-4   DESIGN OF PLUMBING FACILITIES FOR RESIDENTIAL BUILDINGS

Schematic design of bathrooms and general spacing of the fixtures are given in Fig. P-1. The arrangements for kitchen and laundry counter and equipment are given in Fig. P-2. These are a few suggested examples given for information; there are many other ways to design these spaces.

1.   Locate all the fixtures and equipment and provide adequate space around them.

167

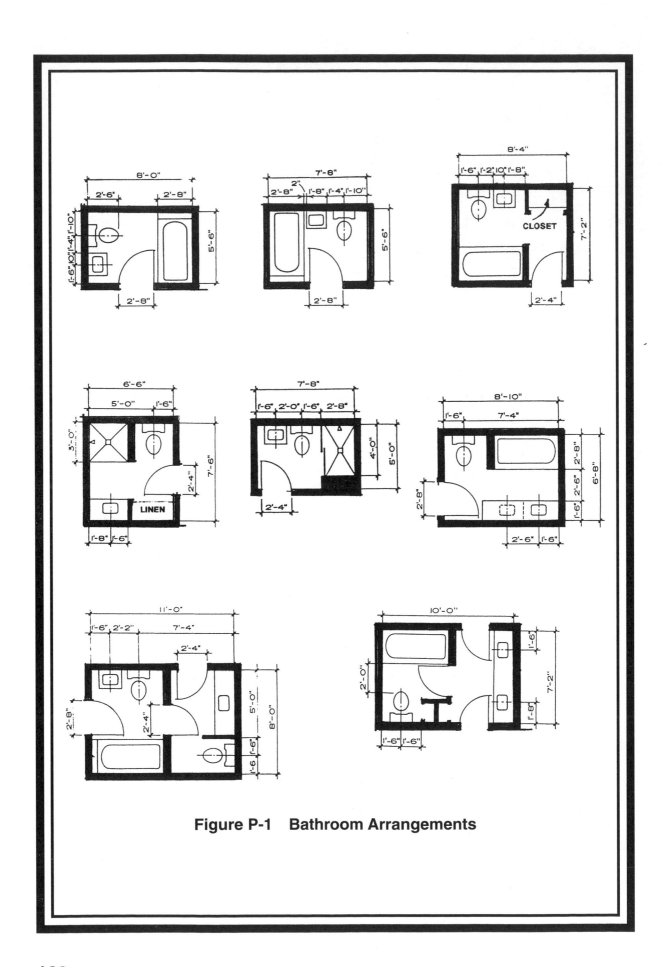

Figure P-1   Bathroom Arrangements

2. Visit the existing facilities which are properly designed and use your judgment as how to do a better design.

3. Avoid repeating mistakes made by others.

P-5   DESIGN OF PLUMBING FACILITIES FOR NONRESIDENTIAL BUILDINGS

Minimum plumbing facilities requirements are given in Fig. P-6, which are accepted and used by many codes.

To design the men's and women's facilities for any nonresidential building:

1. Determine the anticipated number of men and women who will use the building.

2. Using Fig. P-6, choose the minimum number of fixtures required. These numbers can be increased if the design criteria require more facilities.

3. All toilet rooms shall have at least one accessible toilet stall and lavatory for physically handicapped person(s). An example of designing bathroom facilities for a college is given in P-7.

P-6   TOILETS FOR PHYSICALLY HANDICAPPED

It is the law, and essential, to provide an appropriate number of toilet facilities (in accordance with the nature and use of a specific building or facility) accessible to and usable by the physically handicapped.

The toilet rooms shall have space to allow traffic for individuals in wheelchairs.

Dimensions of adult-sized wheelchairs and space needed for a smooth U-turn in a wheelchair are given in Fig. P-3.

Dimensions required for toilet stalls and lavatory clearance are given in Fig. P-4.

Dimensions for clear floor space at bathtubs are given in Fig. P-5.

For more information, use the American National Standard (A117.1, 1980) specifications. For making buildings and facilities accessible to and usable by physically handicapped people.

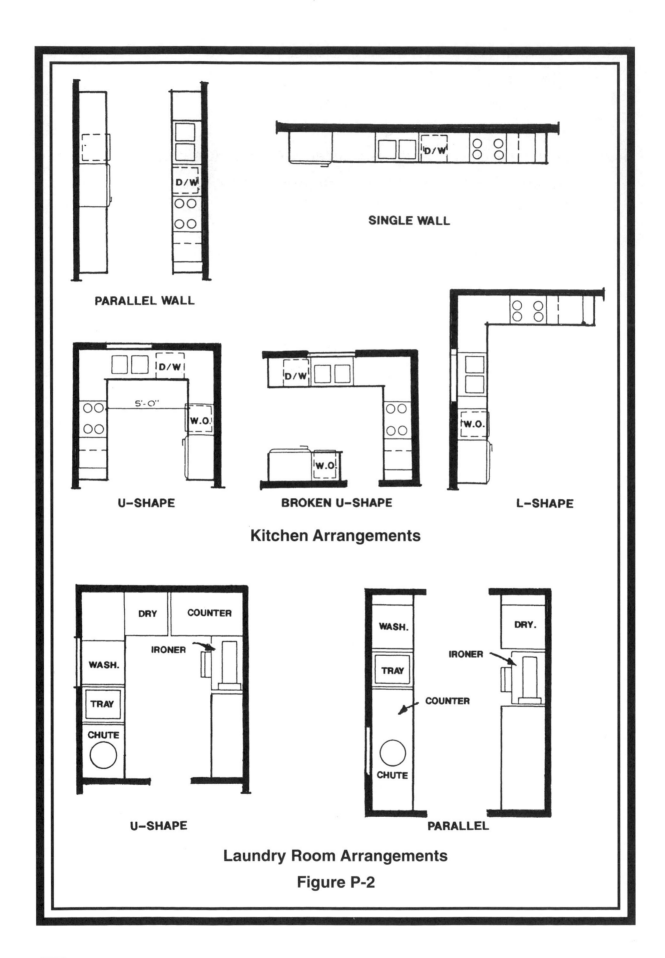

PARALLEL WALL

SINGLE WALL

U–SHAPE

BROKEN U–SHAPE

L–SHAPE

Kitchen Arrangements

U–SHAPE

PARALLEL

Laundry Room Arrangements

Figure P-2

170

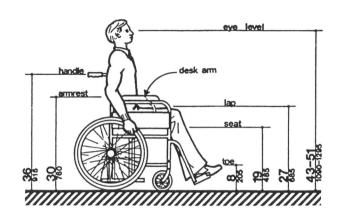

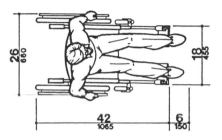

NOTE: Footrests may extend further for very large people.

DIMENSIONS OF ADULT-SIZED WHEELCHAIRS

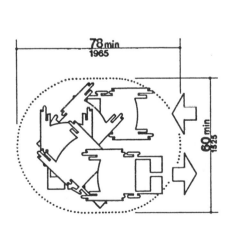

SPACE NEEDED FOR SMOOTH U-TURN IN A WHEELCHAIR

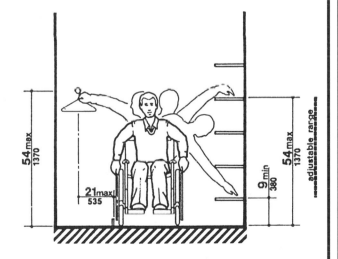

STORAGE SHELVES AND CLOSETS

Figure P-3

AMERICAN NATIONAL STANDARD A117.1-1980

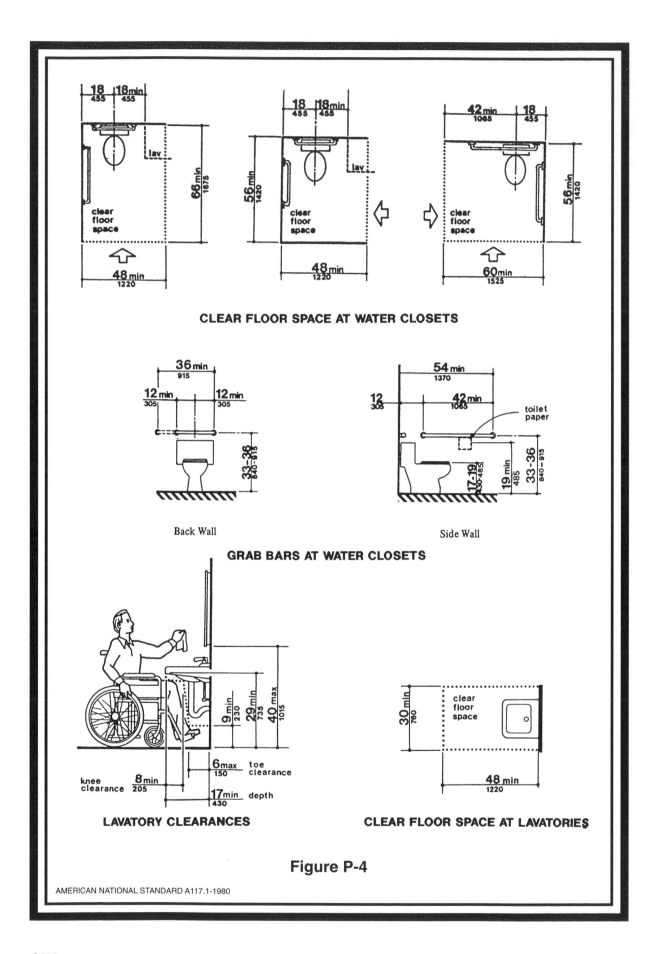

CLEAR FLOOR SPACE AT WATER CLOSETS

Back Wall

Side Wall

GRAB BARS AT WATER CLOSETS

LAVATORY CLEARANCES

CLEAR FLOOR SPACE AT LAVATORIES

Figure P-4

AMERICAN NATIONAL STANDARD A117.1-1980

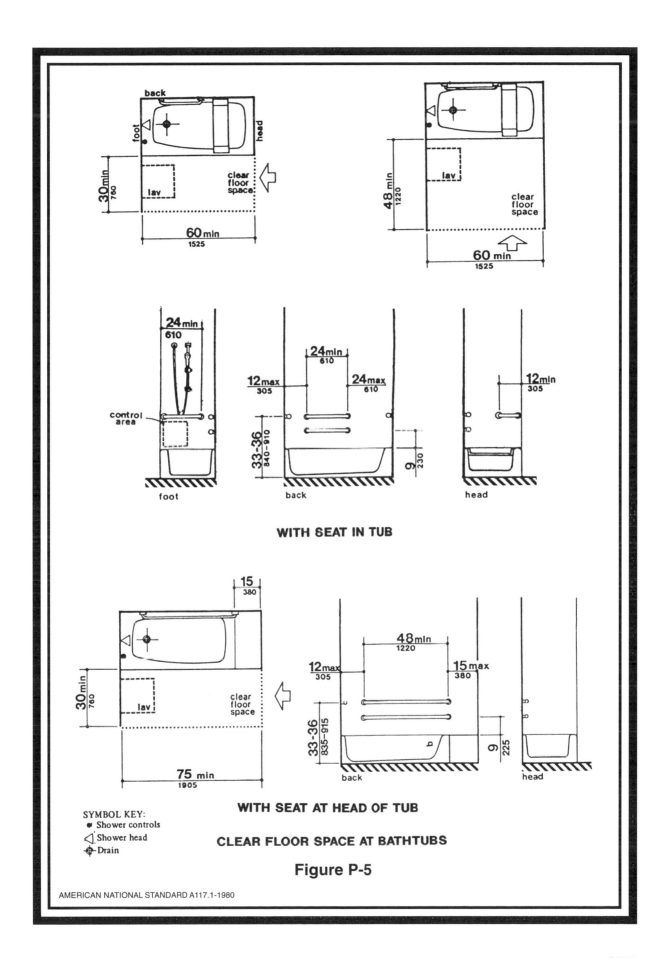

WITH SEAT IN TUB

WITH SEAT AT HEAD OF TUB

SYMBOL KEY:
- Shower controls
- Shower head
- Drain

CLEAR FLOOR SPACE AT BATHTUBS

Figure P-5

AMERICAN NATIONAL STANDARD A117.1-1980

Type of Building or Occupancy[b]	Water Closets (Fixtures per Person)		Urinals[c] (Fixtures per Male)	Lavatories (Fixtures per Person)		Bathtubs or Showers (Fixtures per Person)	Drinking Fountains[d,e] (Fixtures per Person)
Assembly places (theaters, auditoriums, convention halls, etc.)—for permanent employee use	**Male** 1:1–15 2:16–35 3:36–55 Over 55, add 1 fixture for each additional 40 persons	**Female** 1:1–15 2:16–35 3:36–55	1 per 50	**Male** 1 per 40	**Female** 1 per 40	—	—
Assembly places (theaters, auditoriums, convention halls, etc.)—for public use	**Male** 1:1–100 2:101–200 3:201–400 Over 400, add 1 fixture for each additional 500 males and 2 for each 300 females	**Female** 3:1–100 6:101–200 8:201–400	1:1–100 2:101–200 3:201–400 4:401–600 Over 600, add 1 fixture for each additional 300 males	**Male** 1:1–200 2:201–400 3:401–750 Over 750, add 1 fixture for each additional 500 persons	**Female** 1:1–200 2:201–400 3:401–750	—	1 per 75[f]
Dormitories[g]—school or labor	**Male** 1 per 10 Add 1 fixture for each additional 25 males (over 10) and 1 for each additional 20 females (over 8)	**Female** 1 per 8	1 per 25 Over 150, add 1 fixture for each additional 50 males	**Male** 1 per 12 Over 12, add 1 fixture for each additional 20 males and 1 for each 15 females	**Female** 1 per 12	1 per 8 For females, add 1 bathtub per 30; over 150, add 1 per 20	1 per 75[f]
Dormitories—for staff use	**Male** 1:1–15 2:16–35 3:36–55 Over 55, add 1 fixture for each additional 40 persons	**Female** 1:1–15 2:16–35 3:36–55	1 per 50	**Male** 1 per 40	**Female** 1 per 40	—	—
Dwellings[h] Single Multiple or apartment house	1 per dwelling 1 per dwelling or apartment unit		—	1 per dwelling 1 per dwelling or apartment unit		1 per dwelling 1 per dwelling or apartment unit	—
Hospitals Waiting room For employee use	1 per room **Male** 1:1–15 2:16–35 3:36–55 Over 55, add 1 fixture for each additional 40 persons	**Female** 1:1–15 2:16–35 3:36–55	— 1 per 50	1 per room **Male** 1 per 40	**Female** 1 per 40	— —	1 per 75[f]
Hospitals Individual room Ward room	1 per room 1 per 8 patients		— —	1 per room 1 per 10 patients		1 per room 1 per 20 patients	— 1 per 75[f]
Industrial[i] warehouses, workshops, foundries and similar establishments (for employee use)	**Male** 1:1–10 2:11–25 3:26–50 4:51–75 5:76–100 Over 100, add 1 fixture for each additional 30 persons	**Female** 1:1–10 2:11–25 3:26–50 4:51–75 5:76–100		Up to 100, 1 per 10 persons Over 100, 1 per 15 persons[j,k]		1 shower for each 15 persons exposed to excessive heat or to skin contamination with poisonous, infectious, or irritating material.	1 per 75[f]
Institutional (other than hospitals or penal institutions), on each occupied floor	**Male** 1 per 25	**Female** 1 per 20	1 per 50	**Male** 1 per 10	**Female** 1 per 10	1 per 8	1 per 75[f]

Figure P-6   Minimum Number of Plumbing Fixtures

Type of Building or Occupancy[b]	Water Closets (Fixtures per Person)		Urinals[c] (Fixtures per Male)	Lavatories (Fixtures per Person)		Bathtubs or Showers (Fixtures per Person)	Drinking Fountains[d,e] (Fixtures per Person)
Institutional (other than hospitals or penal institutions), on each occupied floor—for employee use	Male 1:1–15 2:16–35 3:36–55 Over 55, add 1 fixture for each additional 40 persons	Female 1:1–15 2:16–35 3:36–55	1 per 50	Male 1 per 40	Female 1 per 40	—	—
Office or public building	Male 1:1–15 2:16–35 3:36–55 4:56–80 5:81–110 6:111–150 Over 150, add 1 fixture for each additional 40 persons	Female 1:1–15 2:16–35 3:36–55 4:56–80 5:81–110 6:111–150		Male 1:1–15 2:16–35 3:36–60 4:61–90 5:91–125 Over 125, add 1 fixture for each additional 45 persons	Female 1:1–15 2:16–35 3:36–60 4:61–90 5:91–125	—	1 per 75[f]
Office or public building—for employee use	Male 1:1–15 2:16–35 3:36–55 Over 55, add 1 fixture for each additional 40 persons	Female 1:1–15 2:16–35 3:36–55	1 per 50	Male 1 per 40	Female 1 per 40	—	—
Penal institutions—for employee use	Male 1:1–15 2:16–35 3:36–55 Over 55, add 1 fixture for each additional 40 persons	Female 1:1–15 2:16–35 3:36–55	1 per 50	Male 1 per 40	Female 1 per 40	—	1 per 75[f]
Penal institutions—for prisoner use Cell	1 per cell		—	1 per cell		—	1 per cell block floor
Exercise room	1 per exercise room		1 per exercise room	1 per exercise room		—	1 per exercise room
Restaurants, pubs and lounges	Male 1:1–50 2:51–150 3:151–300 Over 300, add 1 fixture for each additional 200 persons	Female 1:1–50 2:51–150 3:151–300	1:1–150 Over 150, add 1 fixture for each additional 150 males	Male 1:1–150 2:151–200 3:201–400 Over 400, add 1 fixture for each additional 400 persons	Female 1:1–150 2:151–200 3:201–400		
Schools—for staff use	Male 1:1–15 2:16–35 3:36–55 Over 55, add 1 fixture for each additional 40 persons	Female 1:1–15 2:16–35 3:36–55	1 per 50	Male 1 per 40	Female 1 per 40	—	—

Figure P-6 (*cont'd*)   Minimum Number of Plumbing Fixtures

Type of Building or Occupancy[b]	Water Closets (Fixtures per Person)		Urinals[c] (Fixtures per Male)	Lavatories (Fixtures per Person)		Bathtubs or Showers (Fixtures per Person)	Drinking Fountains[d,e] (Fixtures per Person)
Schools[m]—for student use Nursery	Male 1:1–20 2:21–50 Over 50, add 1 fixture for each additional 50 persons	Female 1:1–20 2:21–50	—	Male 1:1–25 2:26–50 Over 50, add 1 fixture for each additional 50 persons	Female 1:1–25 2:26–50	—	1 per 75[f]
Elementary	Male 1 per 30	Female 1 per 25	1 per 75	Male 1 per 35	Female 1 per 35	—	1 per 75[f]
Secondary	Male 1 per 40	Female 1 per 30	1 per 35	Male 1 per 40	Female 1 per 40	—	1 per 75[f]
Others (colleges, universities, adult centers, etc.)	Male 1 per 40	Female 1 per 30	1 per 35	Male 1 per 40	Female 1 per 40	—	1 per 75[f]
Worship places—educational and activities unit	Male 1 per 250	Female 1 per 125	1 per 250	1 per toilet room		—	1 per 75[f]
Worship places—principal assembly place	Male 1 per 300	Female 1 per 150	1 per 300	1 per toilet room		—	1 per 75[f]

Whenever urinals are provided, one (1) water closet less than the number specified may be provided for each urinal installed, except that the number of water closets in such cases shall not be reduced to less than two-thirds (⅔) of the minimum specified.

[a]The figures shown are based upon one (1) fixture being the minimum required for the number of persons indicated or any fraction thereof.

[b]Building categories not shown on this table shall be considered separately by the Administrative Authority.

[c]In applying this schedule of facilities, consideration must be given to the accessibility of the fixtures. Conformity purely on a numerical basis may not result in an installation suited to the needs of the individual establishment. For example, schools should be provided with toilet facilities on each floor having classrooms. Temporary workingmen facilities: one (1) water closet and one (1) urinal for each thirty (30) workmen.
  a. Surrounding materials: wall and floor space to a point two (2) feet in front of urinal lip and four (4) feet above the floor, and at least two (2) feet to each side of the urinal shall be lined with nonabsorbent material.
  b. Trough urinals are prohibited.

[d]Drinking fountains shall not be installed in toilet rooms.

[e]There shall be a minimum of one (1) drinking fountain per occupied floor in schools, theaters, auditoriums, dormitories, offices or public buildings.

[f]Where food is consumed indoors, water stations may be substituted for drinking fountains. Theaters, auditoriums, dormitories, offices, or public buildings for use by more than six (6) persons shall have one (1) drinking fountain for the first seventy-five (75) persons and one (1) additional fountain for each one hundred and fifty (150) persons thereafter.

[g]Laundry trays: one (1) for each fifty (50) persons. Slop sinks: one (1) for each hundred (100) persons.

[h]Laundry trays: one (1) laundry tray or one (1) automatic washer standpipe for each dwelling unit or two (2) laundry trays or two (2) automatic washer standpipes, or combination thereof, for each ten (10) apartments. Kitchen sinks: one (1) for each dwelling or apartment unit.

[i]As required by ANSI Z4.1–1968, Sanitation in Places of Employment.

[j]Where there is exposure to skin contamination with poisonous, infectious, or irritating materials, provide one (1) lavatory for each five (5) persons.

[k]Twenty-four (24) lineal inches of wash sink or eighteen (18) inches of a circular basin, when provided with water outlets for such space, shall be considered equivalent to one (1) lavatory.

[l]A restaurant is defined as a business that sells food to be consumed on the premises.
  a. The number of occupants for a drive-in restaurant shall be considered as equal to the number of parking stalls.
  b. Employee toilet facilities are not to be included in the above restaurant requirements. Hand washing facilities must be available in the kitchen for employees.

[m]This schedule has been adopted by the National Council on Schoolhouse Construction.

Figure P-6 (cont'd)   Minimum Number of Plumbing Fixtures

Source: The National Standard Plumbing Code.

P-7   DESIGN OF TOILET FACILITIES FOR NONRESIDENTIAL BUILDINGS

The following examples and solutions are given to demonstrate the design of toilet facilities.

Example

Design toilet facilities for the Science and Research Center given in Fig. P-7 to serve the following occupancy:

	Male	Female
Students	320	120
Faculties	8	6
Administration	12	6
Total Persons	340	132

Solution

Step 1. Use the National Standard Plumbing code, which outlines minimum plumbing facilities required given in Fig. P-6.

Note: Taking into consideration that the break period between classes is only 10 minutes, the minimum requirements in men's toilets have been increased for urinals and lavatories and in women's toilets for W.C. and lavatories.

Step 2. Find the number of water closets required for men's toilets.

From Fig. 6 (colleges and universities), one water closet (W.C.) is required for every 40 persons (P).

$$340 \text{ P} \div 40 \text{ P/W.C.} = 8.5 \approx 8 \text{ W.C.}$$

Use eight W.C., four W.C. per floor; one W.C. should be designed for handicapped persons.

Step 3. Find the number of urinals required for men's toilets.

From Fig. P-6, one urinal (U) is required for every 35 persons (P).

$$340 \text{ P} \div 35 \text{ P/U} = 9.72 \approx 10 \text{ U}$$

Use 16 urinals, 8 per each floor (see note above).

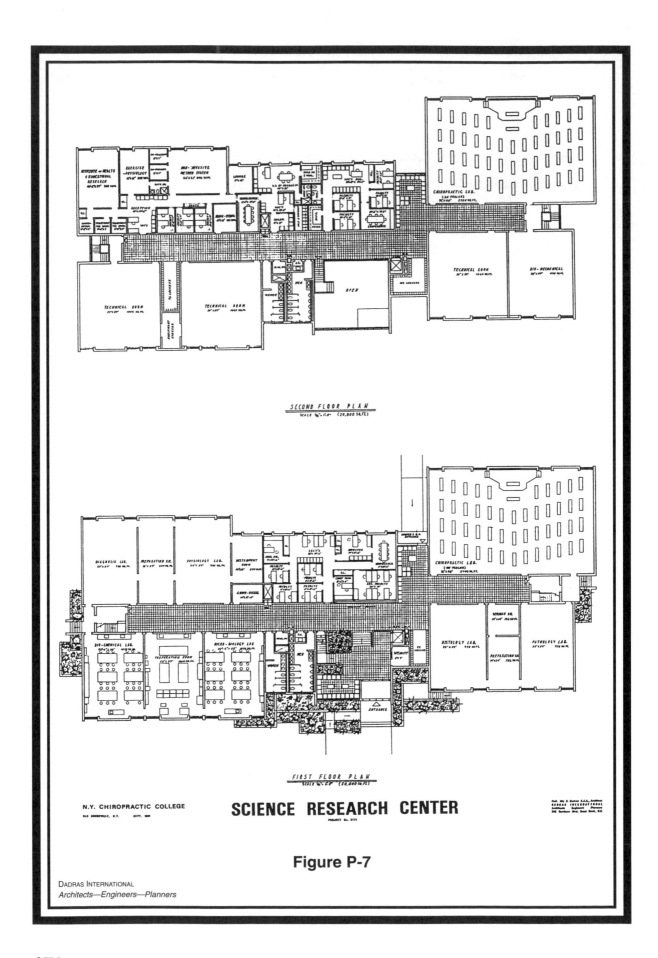

SECOND FLOOR PLAN
SCALE 1/16"=1'-0" (20,800 SQ.FT.)

FIRST FLOOR PLAN
SCALE 1/16"=1'-0" (20,800 SQ.FT.)

N.Y. CHIROPRACTIC COLLEGE
OLD BROOKVILLE, N.Y.   SEPT. 1981

SCIENCE RESEARCH CENTER
PROJECT No. 8171

Figure P-7

DADRAS INTERNATIONAL
Architects—Engineers—Planners

Step 4. Find the number of lavatories required for men's toilets.

From Fig. P-6, one lavatory (lav) is required for every 40 persons (P).

$$340 \text{ P} \div 40 \text{ P/lav} = 8.3 \approx 9 \text{ lav}$$

Use 12 lavatories, 6 per each floor (see note above).

One lavatory should be designed for handicapped person(s).

Step 5. Find the number of water closets required for women's toilets.

From Fig. P-6, one water closet (W.C.) is required for every 30 persons (P).

$$132 \text{ P} \div 30 \text{ P/W.C.} = 4.4 \approx 5 \text{ W.C.}$$

Use eight W.C., four W.C. per floor (see note above). One W.C. should be designed for handicapped person(s).

Step 6. Find the number of lavatories required for women's toilets.

From Fig. P-6, one lavatory (lav) is required for every 40 persons (P).

$$132 \text{ P} \div 40 \text{ P/lav} = 3.3 \approx 4 \text{ lav}$$

Use eight lavatories, four lavatories per floor (see note above), one of which should be designed for handicapped person(s).

Step 7. Summarize the number of fixtures found supra.

a. **Men's toilets**

Design two toilets, one on each floor. Each toilet shall contain three W.C. plus one W.C. for handicapped person(s), eight urinals, five lavatories plus one lavatory for handicapped person(s).

b. **Women's toilets**

Design two toilets, one on each floor. Each toilet shall contain three W.C. plus one W.C. for handicapped person(s), three lavatories plus one lavatory for handicapped person(s). (See Figs. P-8 and P-9.)

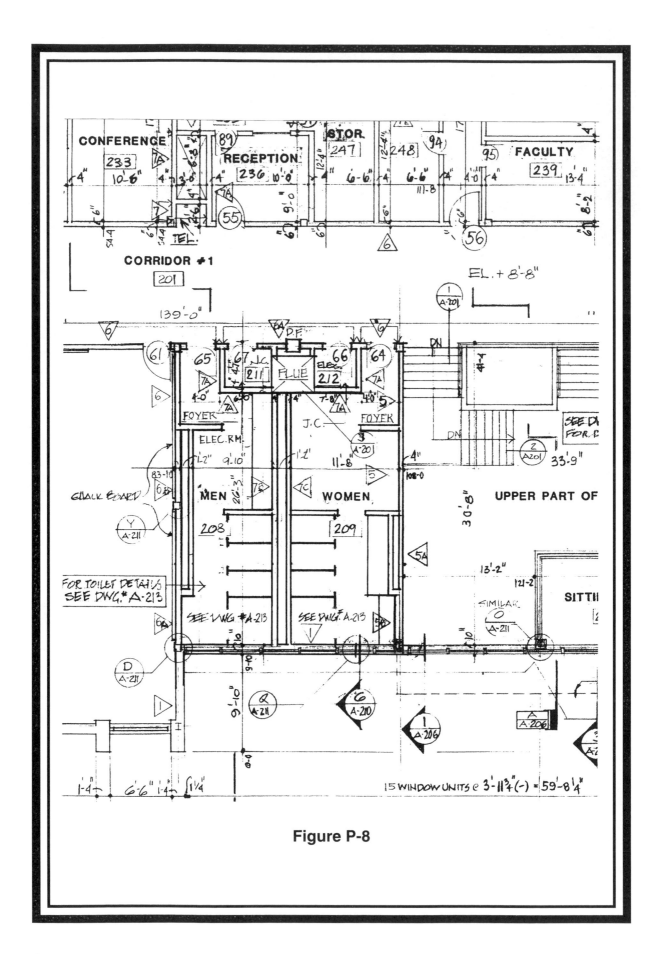

Figure P-8

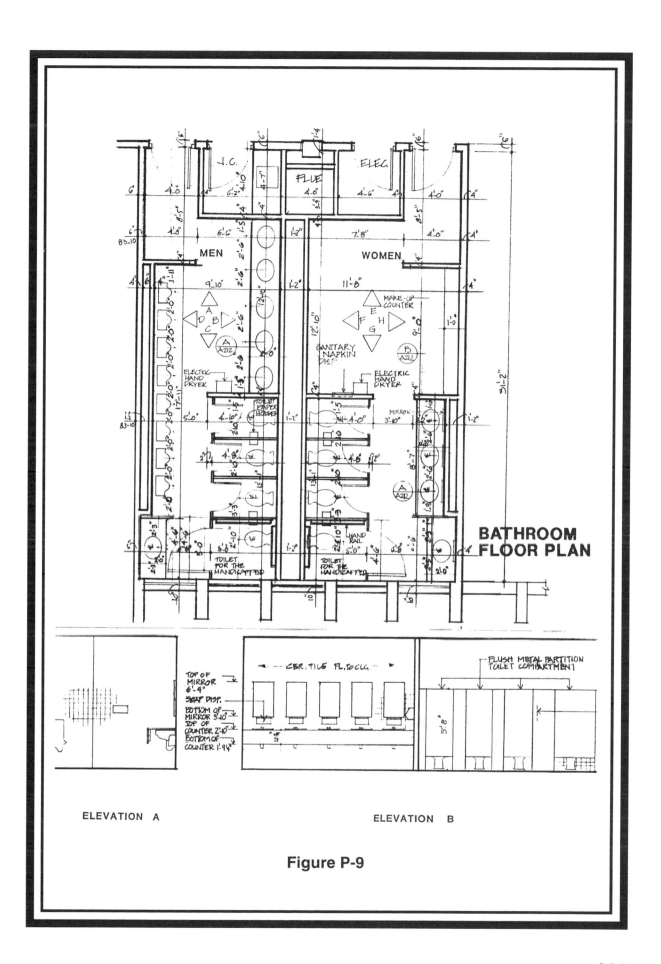

ELEVATION A   ELEVATION B

Figure P-9

Figure P-10

PLUMBING SYSTEMS FOR WATER SUPPLY AND DWV IN BUILDINGS

P-8   HISTORY AT A GLANCE

The earliest pipes were probably those made of bamboo used by the Chinese to carry water about 5000 B.C.

The Egyptians made the first copper pipes in 3000 B.C.

The cast-iron pipe was made and used in Germany in the mid-16th century.

In the mid-18th century, production of cast iron became relatively cheap in comparison to the pipes which were made of clay, lead, copper, bronze, or bored wood or stone.

Cast-iron pipes appeared in the United States in the early 19th century.

In the early 20th century plastic pipe was used to deliver water.

During the Second World War (1945) plastic pipes were further developed to replace the metals that were in short supply and were expensive.

P-9   CODES

The national codes commonly specify the type of materials allowed to be used for delivering water and drainage, waste and vents, DWV in the building. These are called ***model codes,*** which are used by local jurisdiction, either directly or adapted and modified to satisfy the localities' needs.

The model codes include:

> ***B.O.C.A. Basic Plumbing Code Administration,*** prepared by Building officials and Code Administrations International.

> ***N.S.P.C. National Standard Plumbing Code,*** prepared by National Association of Plumbing, Heating, Cooling Contractors.

> ***S.S.P.C. Southern Standard Plumbing Code,*** prepared by Southern Building Code Congress.

> ***U.P.C. Uniform Plumbing Code,*** prepared by International Association of Plumbing and Mechanical officials.

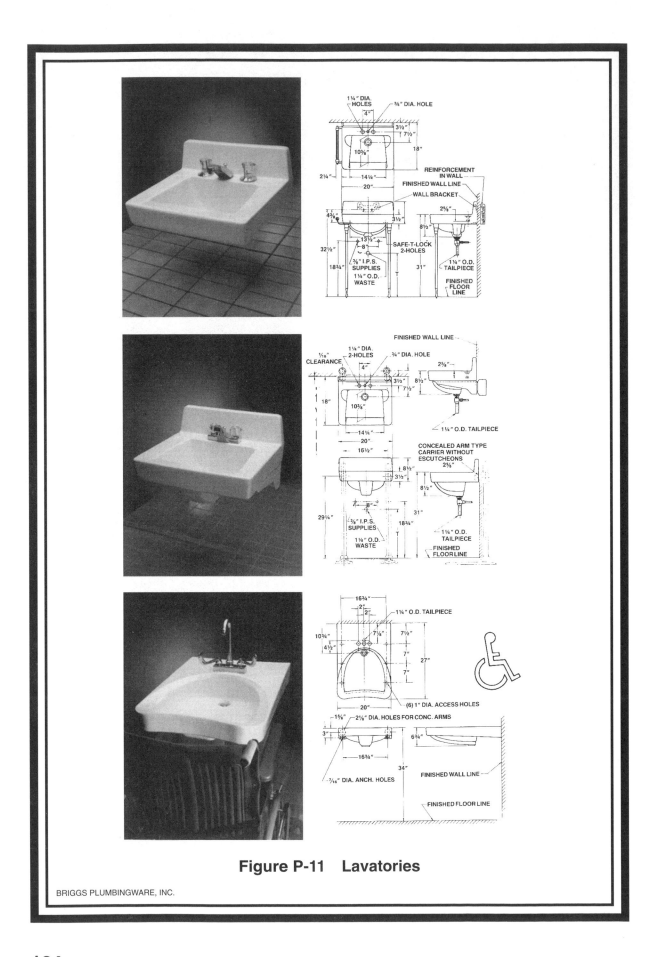

Figure P-11 Lavatories

P-10 PLUMBING FIXTURES AND APPLIANCES

The plumbing fixtures and appliances are the only portion of plumbing systems which are visible in the building. All fixtures should be selected carefully, keeping in mind the budget limitations and code and regulations requirements.

The taste and preference of the owners and occupants of a building for colors, shapes, and appearances of the fixtures and appliances should be seriously considered.

The following samples of various fixtures and appliances are given to be used for approximate dimensioning and their appearance:

Men's rooms	Fig. P-10
Lavatories	Fig. P-11
Toilet bowls	Fig. P-12
Urinals	Fig. P-13
Water coolers	Fig. P-14
Water cooler features	Fig. P-15
Toilet partitions and utility sinks	Fig. P-16
Bathtubs and showers	Fig. P-17
Faucets and valves	Fig. P-18
Washers and dishwashers	Fig. P-19

Latest manufacturer's catalogues for cost and availability should be reviewed before selections are made.

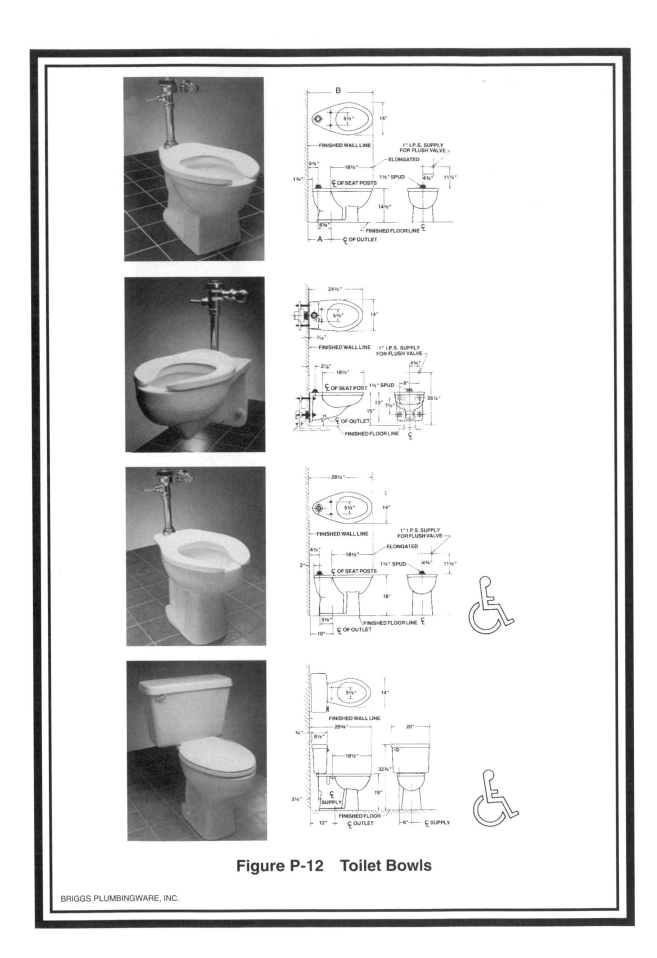

Figure P-12 Toilet Bowls

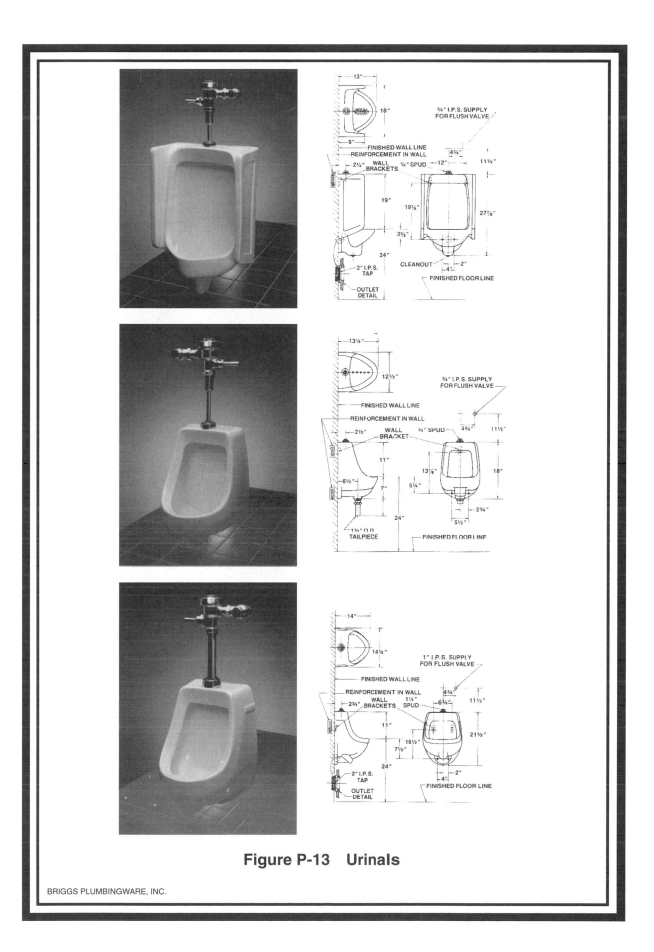

Figure P-13   Urinals

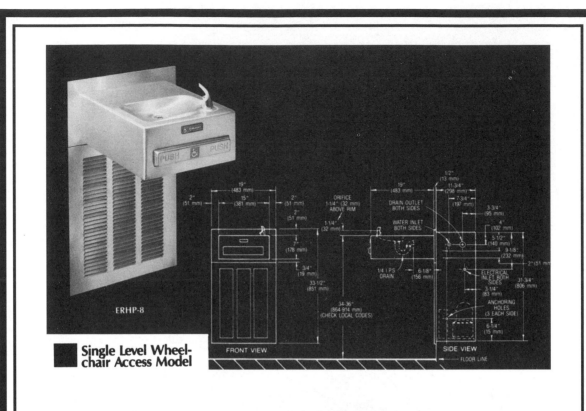

Single Level Wheel-chair Access Model

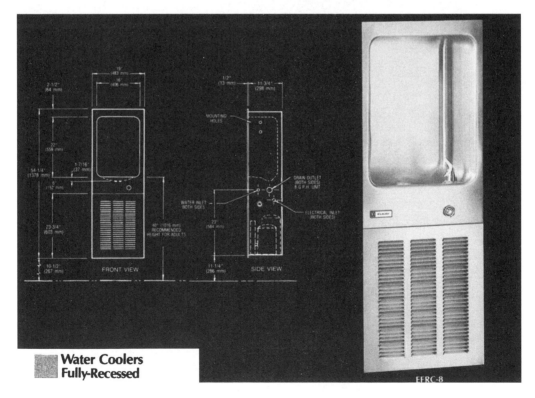

Water Coolers Fully-Recessed

Figure P-14   Water Coolers

ELKAY CORP.

1. **Flexi-Guard.®** Exclusive safety bubbler. Standard on all models with separate pushbutton controls. Available in four colors.

2. **Cascade® Basin.** Splash-resistant. Multi-level deck design. One-piece nickel-bearing stainless steel.

3. **Separate Pushbutton Control.** Positioned to be sanitary and easily accessible.

4. **In-Line Flow Regulator.** Automatically maintains constant stream height at line pressures of 20 to 105 psi.

5. **Water System.** Manufactured of copper components or other lead-free materials. Waterways are free of lead because all leaded materials such as leaded brass have been removed. All brazed joints use silver solder only. No lead solder is permitted.

6. **Compressor and Motor.** Hermetically sealed. Permanently lubricated. Factory tested.

7. **Non-Pressurized Cooling Tank.** Combination tube-type. Tube and tank are constructed of copper. Fully insulated with polyurethane foam which meets Underwriters Laboratories requirements for self-extinguishing plastic foam (U.L.-94HBF).

    Storage tank is subject to line pressure only when regulator button is pressed. In the unlikely event of a burst tank, only stored water would be released.

8. **Fan Motor and Blade.** Heavy duty. Permanently sealed and lubricated.

9. **Condenser Coil.** Fin and tube type.

10. **Dryer.** Prevents internal moisture from contaminating refrigeration system.

11. **Drain Outlet.** 1 1/4-inch clip joint fitting. Unobstructed for easy installation.

12. **Preset Cooler Control.** Requires altitude adjustment only.

13. **Water Inlet Connection.** (Not shown.) Accepts 3/8-inch O.D. tubing for hookup to incoming water line. Unobstructed for easy installation.

14. **Filtrex "Y-Strainer."** (Not shown.) **No Lead Coolers only.** Easily cleanable screen traps waterborne particulates of 140 microns in diameter or larger prior to their entry into the water cooler.

15. **WaterSentry Lead Removal System.** DESIGN 2000 coolers come with a long-life lead removal filter

16. **Optional Glass Filler.** (Not shown.) Requires factory preparation. Models equipped for glass filler require pressurized cooling tank.

17. **Optional Hot Water Dispenser and Tank.** (Not shown.) Storage tank heats and serves up to 40 cups (6 oz.) of 165°F water per hour. Lever-activated dispenser. Accessible on/off switch for hot water dispenser.

18. **HFC-134a Refrigerant.** (Not shown.) This refrigerant is proven to be safer for the environment, protecting it from harmful CFCs. And while it's environmentally friendly, HFC-134a refrigerant has also been tested to be as, or more, effective than previous refrigerants.

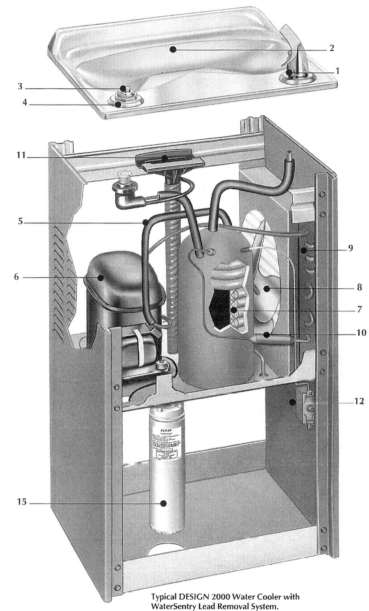

Typical DESIGN 2000 Water Cooler with WaterSentry Lead Removal System.

Figure P-15   Water Cooler Features

ELKAY CORP.

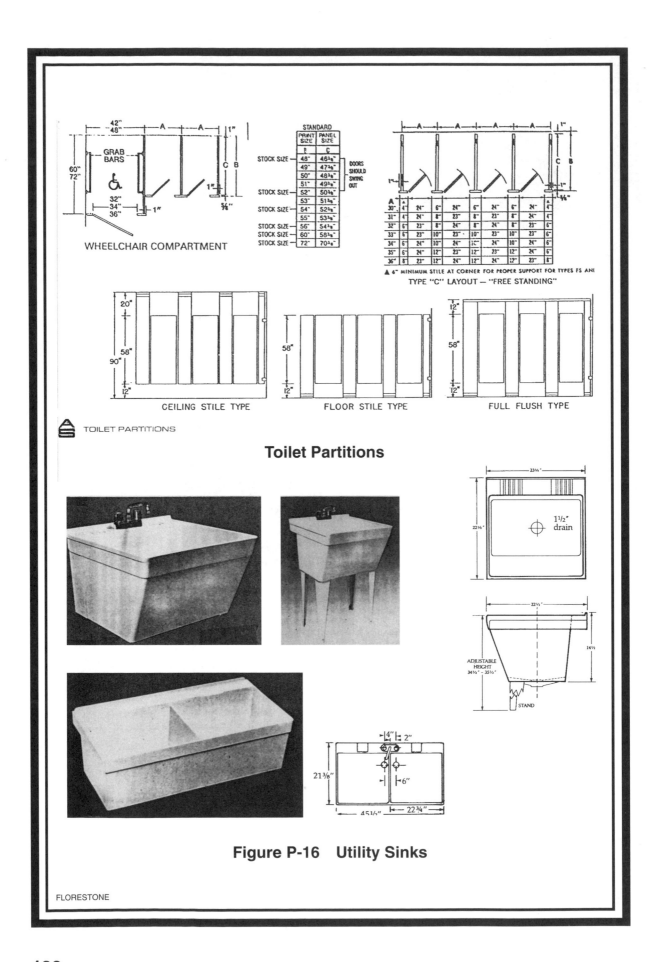

Toilet Partitions

Figure P-16   Utility Sinks

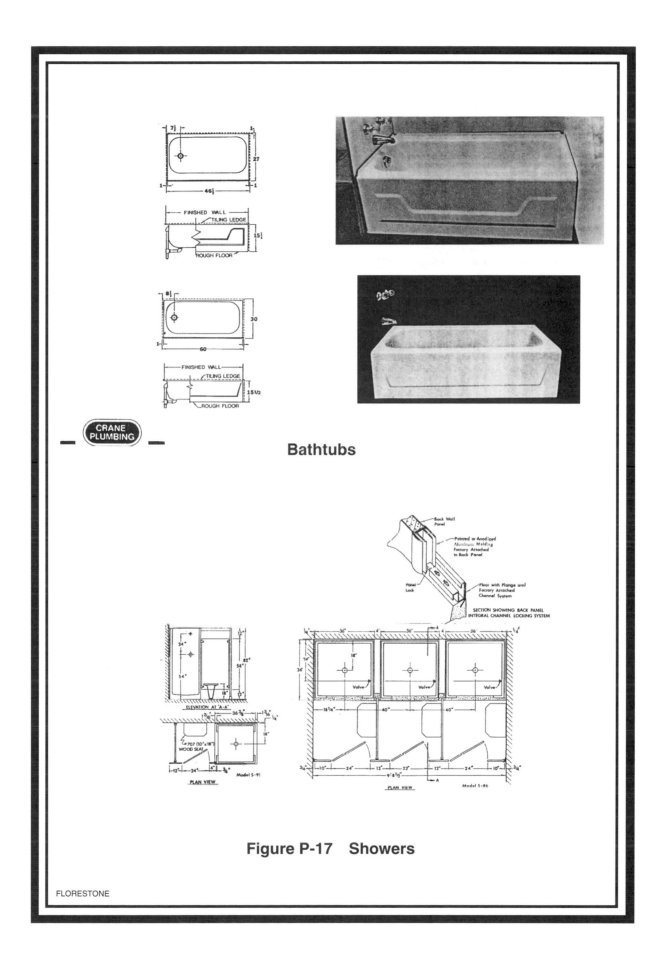

Bathtubs

Figure P-17   Showers

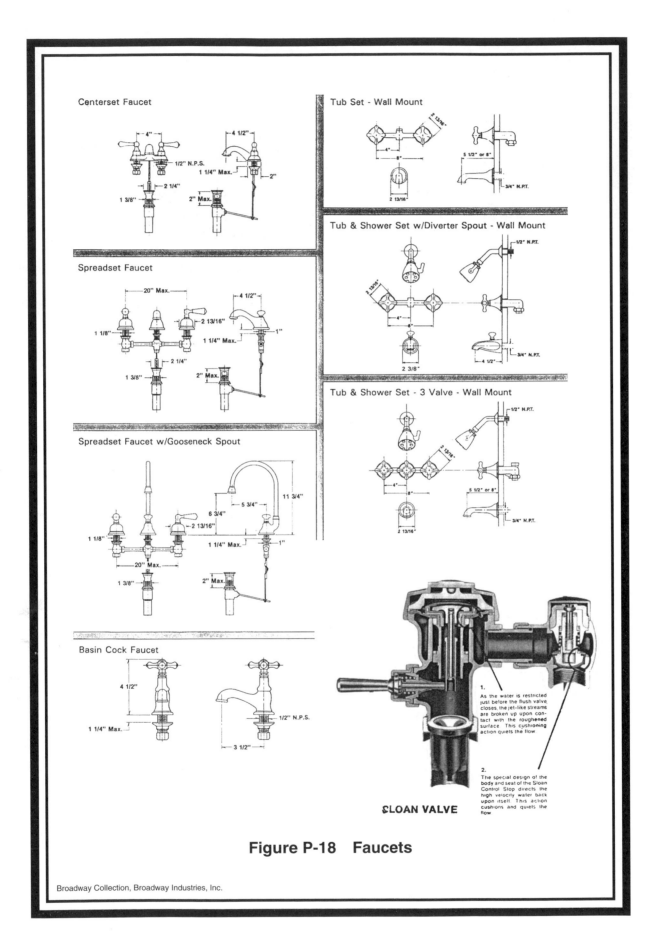

Figure P-18   Faucets

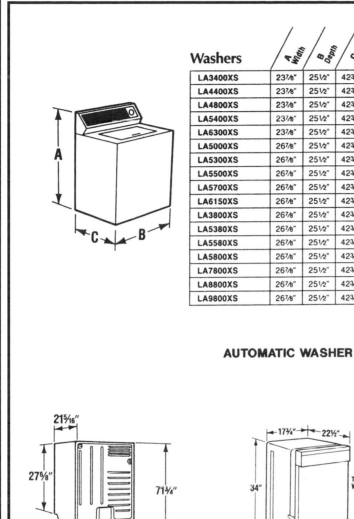

Washers	A Width	B Depth	C Maximum	D Top Height
LA3400XS	23⅞"	25½"	42⅜"	36"
LA4400XS	23⅞"	25½"	42⅜"	36"
LA4800XS	23⅞"	25½"	42⅜"	36"
LA5400XS	23⅞"	25½"	42⅜"	36"
LA6300XS	23⅞"	25½"	42⅜"	36"
LA5000XS	26⅞"	25½"	42⅜"	36"
LA5300XS	26⅞"	25½"	42⅜"	36"
LA5500XS	26⅞"	25½"	42⅜"	36"
LA5700XS	26⅞"	25½"	42⅜"	36"
LA6150XS	26⅞"	25½"	42⅜"	36"
LA3800XS	26⅞"	25½"	42⅜"	36"
LA5380XS	26⅞"	25½"	42⅜"	36"
LA5580XS	26⅞"	25½"	42⅜"	36"
LA5800XS	26⅞"	25½"	42⅜"	36"
LA7800XS	26⅞"	25½"	42⅜"	36"
LA8800XS	26⅞"	25½"	42⅜"	36"
LA9800XS	26⅞"	25½"	42⅜"	36"

AUTOMATIC WASHER

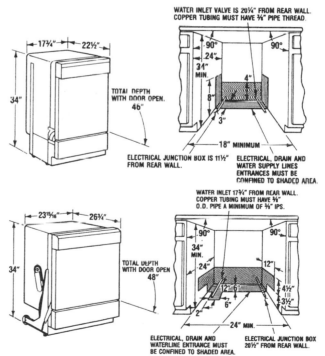

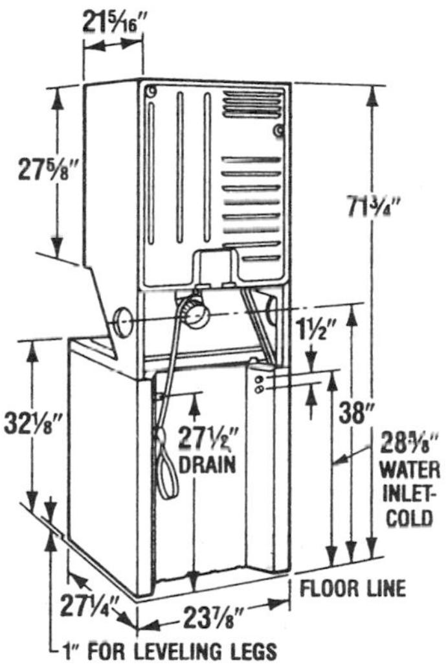

TWIN LAUNDRY SYSTEM

DISHWASHER

Figure P-19

Whirlpool

193

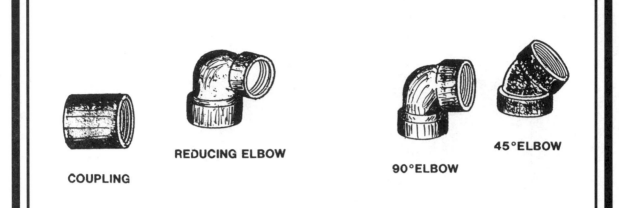

COUPLING

REDUCING ELBOW

90°ELBOW

45°ELBOW

CROSS

UNION

TEE

CLOSE NIPPLE   **SHORT NIPPLE**   **LONG NIPPLE**

PIPE PLUG

**SLOTTED HEAD
PIPE PLUG**

CAP

BUSHING

Figure P-20   Threaded Fittings

PIPES AND TUBINGS USED FOR WATER DISTRIBUTION SYSTEMS

P-11 PIPING, TUBING, FITTINGS, AND CONTROLS

Copper pipes are often referred to as *tubing;* all other materials used for piping are called *pipe.*

Materials used for drainage, waste, and vent are referred to as *DWV.*

Fittings are used to connect the pipe or tubing to each other.

Controls are employed for controlling the flow of water in the pipe or tubing.

P-12 PIPES AND TUBINGS

There are two groups of pipes and tubings used for water distribution systems in the buildings.

Group A. Not commonly used; includes:

1. *Steel pipe.* Threaded, and its use is limited to water which is not corrosive. Many codes do not allow the use of steel pipes.

2. *Brass (red).* It is made of 85 percent copper and 15 percent zinc, threaded (very expensive).

3. *Brass (yellow).* It is a combination of 67 percent copper and 33 percent zinc, threaded (very expensive).

4. *Nickel, silver, and chrome.* The materials used to manufacture these pipes are copper, nickel, zinc, and steel. They are threaded and used when pipes are exposed for decorative purposes.

Group B. Commonly used for water services and distributions:

1. *Galvanized steel pipes* (P-13)

2. *Copper pipes and tubings* (P-15)

3. *Plastic pipes* (P-20)

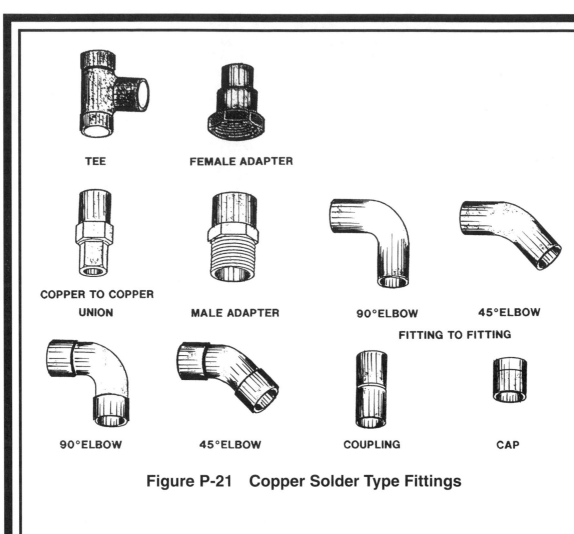

TEE FEMALE ADAPTER

COPPER TO COPPER UNION MALE ADAPTER 90°ELBOW 45°ELBOW

FITTING TO FITTING

90°ELBOW 45°ELBOW COUPLING CAP

Figure P-21   Copper Solder Type Fittings

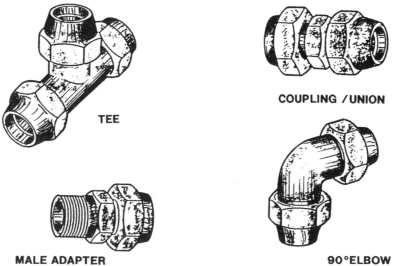

TEE COUPLING / UNION

MALE ADAPTER 90°ELBOW

Figure P-22   Copper Flare Type Fittings

P-13   GALVANIZED STEEL PIPE

This is steel pipe coated with zinc inside and outside.

Size, strength, and use.   It is manufactured in 21-foot lengths with an inside diameter of ⅛ inch and larger. It is available in three strengths: **standard, extra strong,** and **double extra strong.**

Standard weight pipe is used in most plumbing jobs.

Galvanized steel pipe is used in plumbing systems more than any other kind of pipe or tubing.

Advantages

It can be used for hot and cold water; it is strong, durable and has resistance to trench loads.

It is desirable for outside use and gives many years of service.

Disadvantages

It is subject to corrosion; water with a high acid content will rust the inside of the pipe.

Water which carries a large amount of calcium and magnesium, **"hard water,"** builds deposits inside the pipe and causes the reduction of water pressure and, finally, can close the pipe completely.

P-14   FITTINGS FOR GALVANIZED STEEL PIPES

Galvanized steel pipes are connected to each other with threaded fittings. The name of the fitting usually describes its use and shape (Fig. P-20):

Tees (Ts).	Used to connect a branch pipe at a right angle to the supply pipe.
Elbows (Ls).	Angles of 90 or 45° used to change the direction of the pipeline.
Unlons.	Used to permit removing a section of piping system without distancing the other existing pipes or fittings.
Couplings.	Used to connect two lengths of the same size pipe in the same direction.
Plug.	Used to close the opening of the fittings.
Cap.	Used to close the end of the threaded pipe.

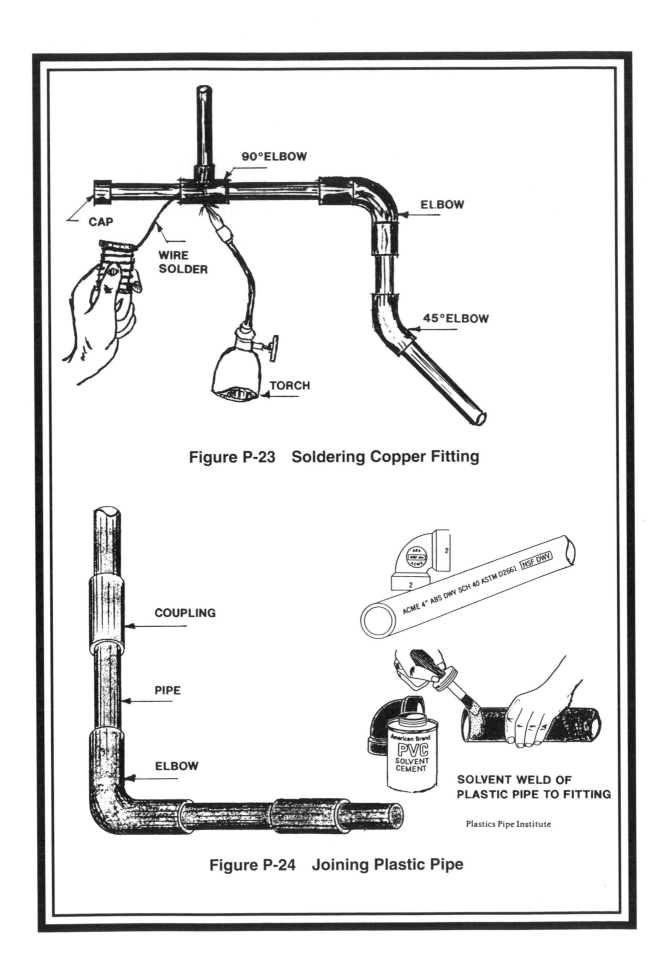

Figure P-23 Soldering Copper Fitting

Figure P-24 Joining Plastic Pipe

Nipples.	Used to connect two fittings together.
Bushing.	Comes with female thread on the inside and male thread on the outside, it is used for reducing the size of pipes.
Cross.	Used for a piping system going four ways.

P-15   COPPER PIPES AND TUBING

There are two kinds:

1.   *Copper pipe,* rigid and hard tempered

2.   *Copper tubing,* flexible and soft tempered

They are both used for hot and cold water distribution systems.

They are light in weight (in comparison with galvanized steel pipe), have strong resistance to corrosion, are easily put together and dismantled, and are used for interior piping and underground installation.

P-16   COPPER PIPE

It is manufactured rigid and hard-tempered. It does not bend; therefore, to change directions, fittings are employed similar to galvanized steel, except the joints are soldered (Figs. P-21 and Fig. P-23). They are available in 20-foot lengths, ⅛ inch in diameter and larger.

P-17   COPPER TUBING

It is flexible, soft-tempered, and easily bent by hand. Therefore, many fittings used for rigid pipe can be eliminated, except for 90°, tees, and cross turns. Copper tubing is available in coils of 50 to 100 feet long, ⅛ inch in diameter or larger.

P-18   TYPES OF COPPER PIPE AND TUBING

Copper pipe and tubing are manufactured in three types:

| **Type K** | Has the thickest wall and is available in rigid-tempered pipe or flexible soft-tempered coil. It is usually used for underground work. |
| **Type L** | The same as Type K except that it has a medium wall thickness and is commonly used for water service to the building. Some codes require its use for interior water-distribution systems. |

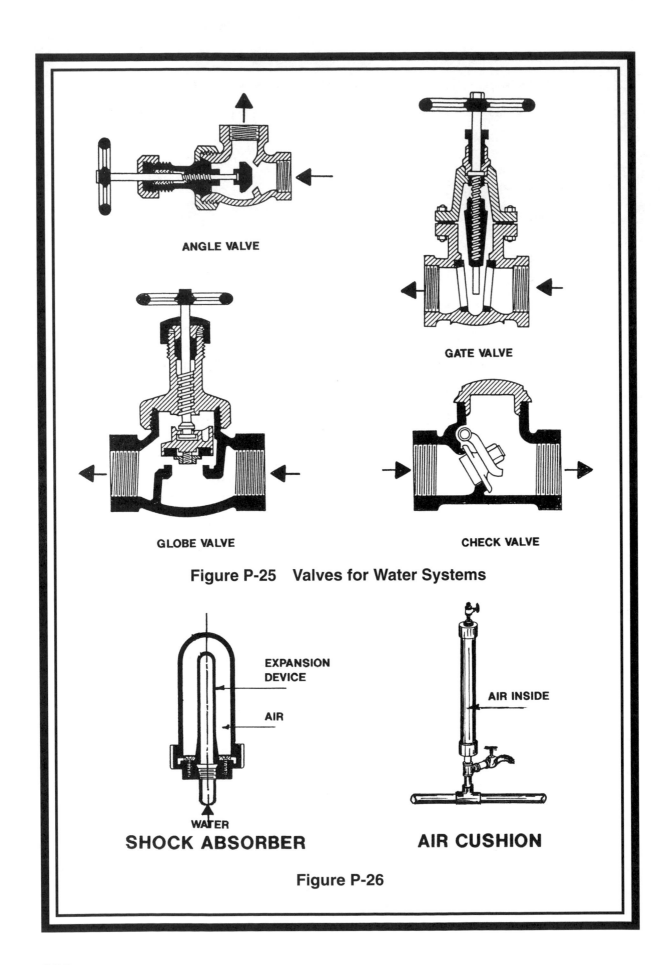

ANGLE VALVE

GATE VALVE

GLOBE VALVE

CHECK VALVE

Figure P-25   Valves for Water Systems

EXPANSION
DEVICE

AIR

AIR INSIDE

WATER

SHOCK ABSORBER

AIR CUSHION

Figure P-26

Type M   Has a thin wall and is available only in rigid hard temper; available in 20-foot lengths. Many codes permit the use of Type M for a general water-distribution system.

Note: Before specifying any of the preceding types of copper pipes or tubings, check with local authorities for restrictions, especially for Type M.

P-19   FITTINGS FOR COPPER PIPES AND TUBINGS

There are two types of copper fittings:

1. *Solder-type.*   Used for both rigid copper pipes and soft copper tubings. The fittings are similar to the galvanized steel pipe patterns such as tees, elbows, couplings, union, etc. (Figs. P-21 and P-23).
2. *Flare-type.*   Used only with soft copper tubing and only when copper tubing is subject to vibration. Flare-type fittings are used only when the copper tubing is exposed (Fig. P-22).

P-20   PLASTIC PIPES

The plastic pipes and fittings are made of synthetic resins produced from coal and petroleum.

They are manufactured in a great variety of types and sizes, as follows:

C.P.V.C.	Chlorinated polyvinyl chloride
P.V.C.	Polyvinyl chloride
A.B.C.	Acrylonitrile budadience styrene
P.B.	Polybutylane
P.E.	Polyethylene
P.P.	Polypropylene

Plastic pipes are rigid and commonly available in 8-, 12-, and 20-foot lengths, ⅛ inch in diameter and larger.

Plastic pipes interiors are smooth; therefore, friction loss is minimal, and they have resistance to corrosion.

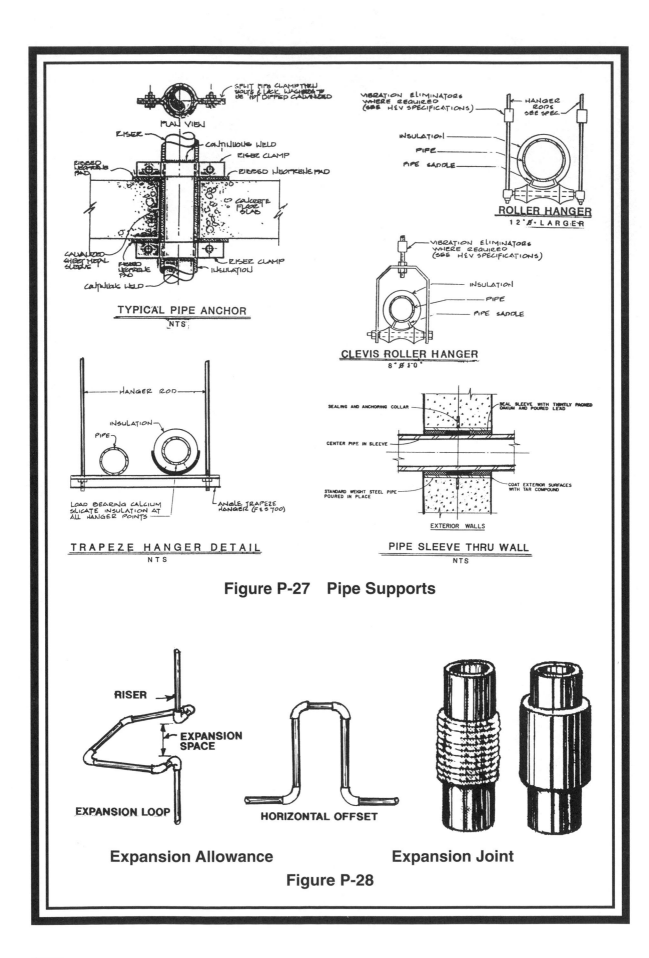

Figure P-27   Pipe Supports

Expansion Allowance

Expansion Joint

Figure P-28

202

The only plastic pipes and fittings permitted to be used inside the structures for cold and hot water distributions are C.P.V.C., which can withstand pressures up to 100 psi and a temperature of 180°F.

All plastic pipes and fittings used for delivering water outside of buildings must withstand a pressure of 160 psi.

All plastic pipes and fittings used in buildings must carry the "ASTM" (American Society for Testing Materials) identification number (Fig. P-24).

Before designing a plastic pipe system for a structure, the local codes must be checked to see if the use is permitted.

For more information you may contact the Plastic Pipe Institute (PPI), a division of the Society of Plastic Industry.

P-21   FITTINGS FOR PLASTIC PIPES

The fittings are similar to the galvanized steel pipe patterns, such as tees, elbows, couplings, unions, etc.

They are solvent-welded to the pipe using liquid cement (Fig. P-24).

P-22   VALVES FOR WATER SYSTEMS

Valves of different types and sizes (Fig. P-25) are made of steel, copper, bronze, etc., and are used to control the flow of water in the system as follows:

a.   *Gate valve.*   A compression-type valve, used where it is to be left open or closed most of the time. This valve has the lowest friction loss value in comparison with other valves.

b.   *Globe valve.*   Also a compression-type valve, it is used for periodic or occasional control of water. It has the highest friction loss value in comparison to other valves.

c.   *Check valve.*   Used to direct the flow of water in one direction only.

d.   *Angle valve.*   A compression-type valve used when a valve is needed at a 90° turn on the system. Its friction loss value is approximately 20 times more than the gate valve and half of the globe valve.

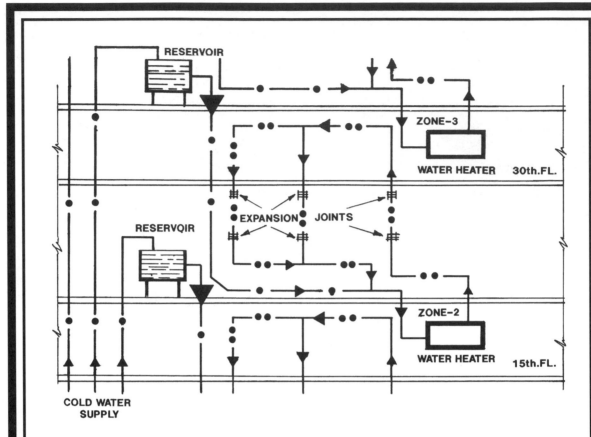

Figure P-29   Design of Expansion Joints

Increase in Temperature (F)	Steel Pipe	Copper Tubing
20	0.00149	0.00222
40	0.00299	0.00444
60	0.00449	0.00668
80	0.00601	0.00893
100	0.00755	0.01119
120	0.00909	0.01346
140	0.01066	0.01575
160	0.01224	0.01805
180	0.01384	0.02035
200	0.01545	0.0268

Expansion of plastic pipe is approximately 5 times of copper tubing.

Figure P-30   Thermal Expansion of Pipe and Tubing (per Foot)

P-23 WATER HAMMER

This is also referred to as *water shock.* Closing the valve quickly in a system causes fast-flowing water to stop. This causes the pipe to rattle and creates a noise (bang) at the top of the pipe in a system. This situation can be corrected by using a shock absorber or air cushion at the end of a pipe in the system (Fig. P-26).

P-24 CONDENSATION

This is also referred to as *sweating pipe.* Pipe carrying domestic cold water normally has a surface temperature of 60°F.

When the temperature of air surrounding the pipe reaches 85°F and the relative humidity exceeds 40 percent, condensation will occur on the surface of the pipe. The higher the relative humidity and temperature, the more condensation.

To prevent condensation, all domestic cold water pipes should be covered with glass-fiber pipe insulation ½ to 1 inch thick.

P-25 HEAT CONSERVATION FOR HOT WATER PIPE

Pipes carrying domestic hot water should be separated from domestic cold water pipes by a minimum of 6 inches in order to prevent heat interchange.

Domestic hot water pipes should be insulated with ½ to 1 inch of glass fiber in order to prevent loss of heat to surrounding air.

P-26 PIPE SUPPORT

Every gallon of water in the pipe weighs 8.33 pounds.

Pipes loaded with water become excessively heavy; therefore, they need to be supported by hangers spaced according to the size of the pipe in order to prevent collapsing of the pipe.

A few methods of pipe support are shown in Fig. P-27.

P-27 PIPE AND TUBE EXPANSION

In a domestic hot water system the heat of the water causes the elongation of the pipe and tubing, which allows the pipe and tubing to buckle laterally.

To prevent this condition from occurring, the expansion joint (Fig. P-28) is used.

Fixture	Flow Pressure[a]	Flow gpm
Ordinary basin faucet	8	3.0
Self-closing basin faucet	12	2.5
Sink faucet—$\frac{3}{8}$ in.	10	4.5
Sink faucet—$\frac{1}{2}$ in.	5	4.5
Bathtub faucet	5	6.0
Laundry tub cock—$\frac{1}{4}$ in.	5	5.0
Shower	12	5.0
Ball cock for closet	15	3.0
Flush valve for closet	10–20	15–40[b]
Flush valve for urinal	15	15.0
Garden hose, 50 ft, and sill cock	30	5.0

[a]Flow pressure is the pressure psig in the pipe at the entrance to the particular fixture considered.

[b]Wide range due to variation in design and type of flush-valve closets.

Figure P-31　Proper Flow and Pressure Required During Flow for Different Fixtures

P-28 DESIGN OF PIPE AND TUBING EXPANSION

Example

A 45-story building is divided into 30 zones of 15 stories each. Using copper tubing for domestic hot water, assume the height of each zone is 180 ft, hot water temperature is 170°F, and inside air temperature is 70°F (Fig. P-29). Design an expansion joint for the copper tubing.

Solution

Using Fig. P-30,

Step 1. Find the increase in temperature

$$170°F - 70°F = 100°F \text{ increase in temperature}$$

Step 2. Find the total expansion of copper tubing.

From Fig. P-30, for increase in temperature of 100°F, the thermal expansion for copper tubing is 0.01119 per foot.

$$180 \text{ ft} \times 0.01119 \text{ in/ft} = 2.0142 \approx 3 \text{ in of expansion}$$

Use two 1½-in or three 1-in expansion joints in each zone.

Note: Use the same steps to determine the thermal expansion for *steel pipe.*

For thermal expansion of *plastic pipe* use the value given for copper tubing and multiply this value by 5.

P-29 DESIGN OF WATER SUPPLY MAIN

All fixtures in the system require adequate pressure of water for proper operation. Proper flow in gallons per minute (gpm) and pressure in pounds per square inch (psi) required for different fixtures in the system are given in Fig. P-31.

P-30 DESIGN PROCEDURE FOR WATER SUPPLY MAIN

Available pressure from a street main or in a private water supply from a pressurized tank, **pneumatic tank** (see W-32 and W-33), is usually 35 to 50 psi (check the pressure available for your project).

Fitting or valve	Equivalent feet of pipe for various sizes							
	½ in.	¾ in.	1 in.	1¼ in.	1½ in.	2 in.	2½ in.	3 in.
45° elbow	1.2	1.5	1.8	2.4	3.0	4.0	5.0	6.0
90° elbow	2.0	2.5	3.0	4.0	5.0	7.0	8.0	10.0
Tee, run	0.6	0.8	0.9	1.2	1.5	2.0	2.5	3.0
Tee, branch	3.0	4.0	5.0	6.0	7.0	10.0	12.0	15.0
Gate valve	0.4	0.5	0.6	0.8	1.0	1.3	1.6	2.0
Balancing valve	0.8	1.1	1.5	1.9	2.2	3.0	3.7	4.5
Plug-type cock	0.8	1.1	1.5	1.9	2.2	3.0	3.7	4.5
Check valve, swing	5.6	8.4	11.2	14.0	16.8	22.4	28.0	33.6
Globe valve	15.0	20.0	25.0	35.0	45.0	55.0	65.0	80.0
Angle valve	8.0	12.0	15.0	18.0	22.0	28.0	34.0	40.0

Allowance in Equivalent Length of Pipe for Friction Loss in *Valves* and *Threaded Fittings*

Fitting or valve	Equivalent feet of tube for various sizes							
	½ in.	¾ in.	1 in.	1¼ in.	1½ in.	2 in.	2½ in.	3 in.
45° elbow (wrought)	0.5	0.5	1.0	1.0	2.0	2.0	3.0	4.0
90° elbow (wrought)	0.5	1.0	1.0	2.0	2.0	2.0	2.0	3.0
Tee, run (wrought)	0.5	0.5	0.5	0.5	1.0	1.0	2.0	-
Tee, branch (wrought)	1.0	2.0	3.0	4.0	5.0	7.0	9.0	-
45° elbow (cast)	0.5	1.0	2.0	2.0	3.0	5.0	8.0	11.0
90° elbow (cast)	1.0	2.0	4.0	5 0	8.0	11.0	14.0	18.0
Tee, run (cast)	0.5	0.5	0.5	1.0	1.0	2.0	2.0	2.0
Tee, branch (cast)	2.0	3.0	5.0	7.0	9.0	12.0	16.0	20.0
Compression Stop	13.0	21.0	30.0	-	-	.	-	.
Globe Valve	-	-	-	53.0	66.0	90.0	-	.
Gate Valve	-	-	1.0	1.0	2.0	2.0	2.0	2.0

'From "Copper Tube Handbook" 1965, by Copper Development Association, Inc.

Allowance in Equivalent Length of Tube for Friction Loss in *Valves* and *Fittings* (*Copper Water Tube*)

Figure P-32

This available pressure is used in a piping system as follows:

1. ***Pressure required for fixture (F.P.).*** Pressure needed to operate the furthest fixture on the highest floor in an upfeed distribution system is usually 8 psi for a water closet with a flush tank and 15 psi when the water closet has a flush valve.

2. ***Pressure lost by static head (S.H.).*** The vertical pipe in a system carries water which weighs 8.33 lb/G. The total weight of this water at the bottom of a pipe creates a static head, which has to be overcome by available pressure (W-19).

3. ***Pressure needed for friction loss in head (F.L.H.).*** When the water moves inside the pipe it rubs against the wall of the piping and creates a friction loss.

   Various fittings and valves are used to complete the piping system. Each one adds an additional friction loss to the piping system as shown in Fig. P-32. This is called ***total equivalent length*** **(E.L.).**

Note

   a. E.L. is commonly estimated at 50 percent of the "developed length of the piping" (D.L.).

   b. D.L. is the length of piping from the meter to the most remote fixture.

   c. Total equivalent length of a piping system (T.E.L.) is the sum of E.L. and D.L.

4. ***Pressure lost in meter (P.L.M.).*** In order to determine the pressure loss in the meter, the size of the meter is needed, which we don't have; therefore, the size of a meter has to be estimated.

   a. For small buildings and residences a 2-in. meter is commonly estimated.

   b. For large buildings a larger-size meter is estimated.

Note. When the actual size of the pipe is determined, then the friction loss in the meter has to be checked and, if necessary, recalculation should be made.

5. The remaining pressure is used to determine the size of a water supply main.

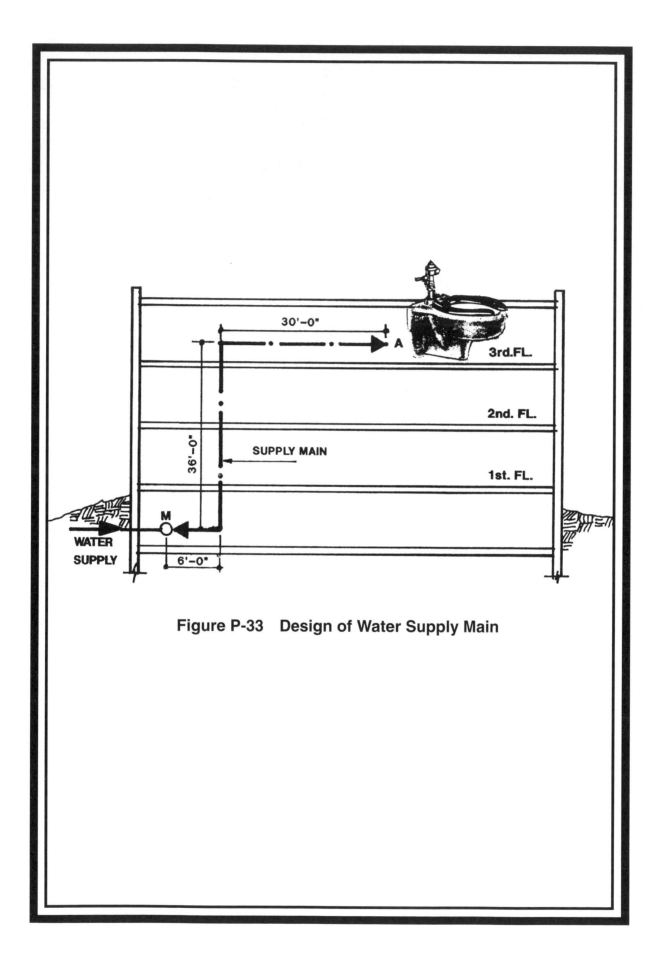

Figure P-33   Design of Water Supply Main

DESIGN OF WATER SUPPLY MAIN

Example

Find the size of copper tubing for the water supply main of a three-story public building (Fig. P-33).

a. Each floor has two water closets, two lavatories, two bath tubs, two shower heads, and two kitchen sinks.

b. Pressure from the street main is 50 psi.

c. The height of the supply main is 36 feet.

d. The water closet on the top floor uses a flush valve.

Solution

Step 1. Find developed length of the piping (DL). The length from meter "M" to the most remote water closet "A" is

$$6 \text{ ft} + 36 \text{ ft} + 30 \text{ ft} = 72 \text{ ft (DL)}$$

Step 2. Find pipe length equivalent to fittings (EL). It is usually estimated at 50 percent of (DL); or use values given in Fig. P-32.

$$72 \text{ ft} \times 0.5 = 36 \text{ ft (EL)}$$

Step 3. Find total equivalent length (TEL).

$$72 \text{ ft (DL)} + 36 \text{ ft (EL)} = 108 \text{ ft (TEL)}$$

Step 4. Find static head (SH). From W-19, static pressure is 0.433 psi; therefore,

$$36 \text{ ft} \times 0.433 \text{ psi/ft} = 15.59 \text{ psi (SH)}$$

Step 5. Find total fixture unit (F.U.).   Using Fig. P-34:

Fixtures		F.U./F		Total F.U.
2 water closets	×	10	=	20
2 lavatories	×	2	=	4
2 bath tubs	×	4	=	8
2 shower heads	×	4	=	8
2 kitchen sinks	×	4	=	8
Total F.U. per floor			=	48

Fixture	Occupancy	Type of Supply Control	Load Values, in Water Supply Fixture Units		
			Cold	Hot	Total
Water closet	Public	Flush valve	10.		10.
Water closet	Public	Flush tank	5.		5.
Urinal	Public	1" flush valve	10.		10.
Urinal	Public	¾" flush valve	5.		5.
Urinal	Public	Flush tank	3.		3.
Lavatory	Public	Faucet	1.5	1.5	2.
Bathtub	Public	Faucet	3.	3.	4.
Shower head	Public	Mixing valve	3.	3.	4.
Service sink	Offices, etc.	Faucet	2.25	2.25	3.
Kitchen sink	Hotel, restaurant	Faucet	3.	3.	4.
Drinking fountain	Offices, etc.	3/8" valve	0.25		0.25
Laundry machine (8 lbs.)	Public or General	Automatic	2.25	2.25	3.
Laundry machine (16 lbs.)	Public or General	Automatic	3.	3.	4.
Water closet	Private	Flush valve	6.		6.
Water closet	Private	Flush tank	3.		3.0
Lavatory	Private	Faucet	0.75	0.75	1.
Bathtub	Private	Faucet	1.5	1.5	2.
Shower stall	Private	Mixing valve	1.5	1.5	2.
Kitchen sink	Private	Faucet	1.5	1.5	2.
Laundry trays (1 to 3)	Private	Faucet	2.25	2.25	3.
Combination fixture	Private	Faucet	2.25	2.25	3.
Dishwashing machine	Private	Automatic		1.	1.
Laundry machine (8 lbs.)	Private	Automatic	1.5	1.5	2.

NOTE: For fixtures not listed, loads should be assumed by comparing the fixture to one listed using water in similar quantities and at similar rates. The assigned loads for fixtures with both hot and cold water supplies are given for separate hot and cold water loads and for total load, the separate hot and cold water loads being three-fourths of the total load for the fixture in each case.

Figure P-34   Load Values Assigned to Fixtures

We have three floors; therefore,

$$48 \text{ F.U./Fl.} \times 3 \text{ Fl.} = 144 \text{ total F.U.}$$

Step 6. Find water demand-flow, gpm (WD). Using Fig. P-36 for total (F.U.) 144 and using curve (1) for flush valve:

$$WD = 80 \text{ gpm}$$

Step 7. Find pressure loss in meter (PLM). Using Fig. P-35 and assuming meter size "M" of 2 inches and WD of 80 gpm (for small buildings you may assume 2 in. "M" and large buildings 4 in. "M"):

Pressure loss in meters = 6.5 psi (PLM)

Step 8. Find pressure needed in fixture (FP). The water closet uses a flush valve. From Fig. P-31, the valve given is 10–20 psi.

Use average 15 psi (FP).

Step 9. Find total pressure loss (TPL).

$$(\text{Step 4}) + (\text{Step 7}) + (\text{Step 8}) = TPL$$

$$15.59 \text{ psi (SH)} + 6.5 \text{ psi (PLM)} + 15 \text{ psi (FP)} = 37 \text{ psi (TPL)}$$

Step 10. Find pressure available for friction loss (PAFL). Street main pressure is 50 psi.

$$(\text{Available pressure}) - (\text{TPL}) = PAFL$$

$$50 \text{ psi} - 37 \text{ psi (TPL)} - 13 \text{ psi (PAFL)}$$

Step 11. Find friction loss in head in psi (F.L.H.).

$$(\text{PAFL}) \times \frac{100^*}{(\text{T.E.L.})} = (\text{F.L.H.})$$

$$13 \text{ psi} \times \frac{100 \text{ ft}}{108 \text{ ft}} = 12.09 \text{ psi (F.L.H.)}$$

*In Figs. P-37, P-38, and P-39, friction loss is given for each 100 feet of pipe.

213

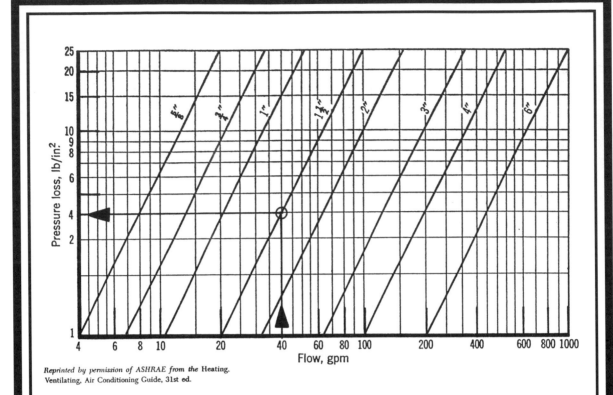

Figure P-35   Pressure Losses in Water Meters

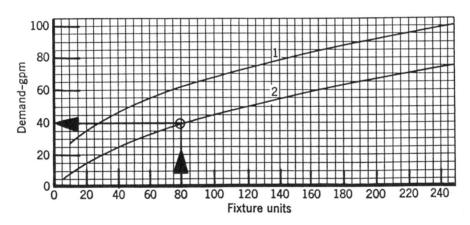

No. 1 for system predominantly flush valves.
No. 2 for system predominantly flush tanks.

Figure P-36   Estimate Curves for Demand Load

Step 12. Find size of water supply main. Using Fig. P-37 for copper tubing (F.L.H.) is 12.09 psi and (WD) flow in gallons per minute is 80 gpm (Step-6).

Use a 2-in. pipe for supply main.

Note

a. Since the assumed meter size was 2 in., checking the pressure in the meter is not necessary. If the size of the supply main is above or below the assumed meter size, then Steps 7, 9, 10, 11, and 12 should be recalculated.

b. For copper tubing and smooth pipe, use Fig. P-37.

c. For threaded piping with few fittings and valves (fairly rough), use Fig. P-38.

d. For threaded piping with many fittings and valves (rough), use Fig. P-39.

e. Usually the same-size pipe is used in a small building for domestic hot water supply main.

P-32   MINIMUM SIZE OF BRANCH PIPING

The minimum size of fixture branch piping is given in Fig. P-40.

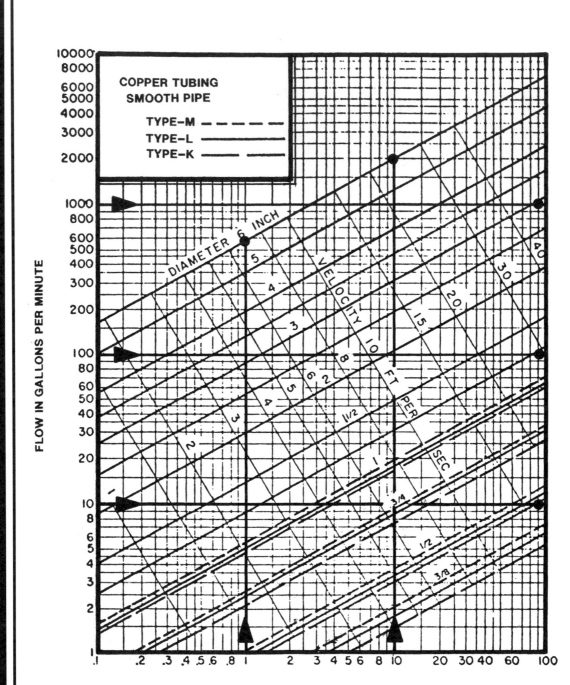

Figure P-37   Friction Loss for Smooth Pipe

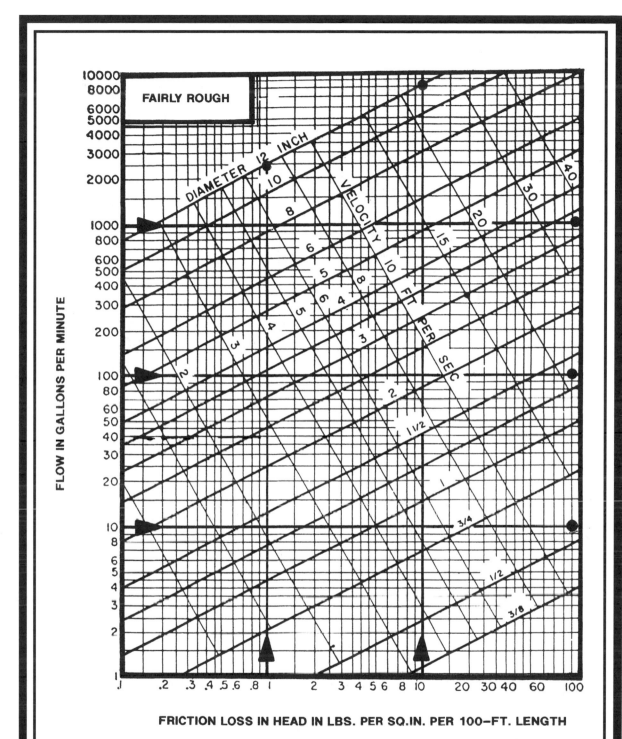

FAIRLY ROUGH

FLOW IN GALLONS PER MINUTE

FRICTION LOSS IN HEAD IN LBS. PER SQ.IN. PER 100–FT. LENGTH

Figure P-38   Friction Loss for Fairly Rough Pipe

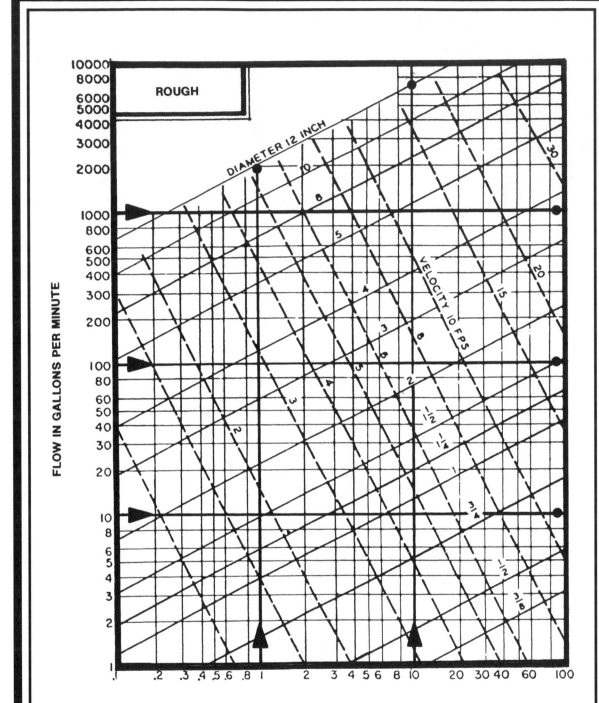

FLOW IN GALLONS PER MINUTE

ROUGH

DIAMETER 12 INCH

VELOCITY 10 FPS

FRICTION LOSS IN HEAD IN LBS. PER SQ.IN. PER 100-FT. LENGTH

Figure P-39   Friction Loss for Rough Pipe

Fixture or Device	Size, (in.)
Bathtub	½
Combination sink and laundry tray	½
Drinking fountain	⅜
Dishwashing machine (domestic)	½
Kitchen sink (domestic)	½
Kitchen sink (commercial)	¾
Lavatory	⅜
Laundry tray (1, 2, or 3 compartments)	½
Shower (single head)	½
Sink (service, slop)	½
Sink (flushing rim)	¾
Urinal (1″ flush valve)	1
Urinal (¾″ flush valve)	¾
Urinal (flush tank)	½
Water closet (flush tank)	⅜*
Water closet (flush valve)	1
Hose bib	½
Wall hydrant or still cock	½

*Fixtures may require larger sizes—see manufacturer's instructions.

Figure P-40   Minimum Size of Fixture Branch Piping

Extracted from the *1987 National Standard Plumbing Code* with permission of PHCC

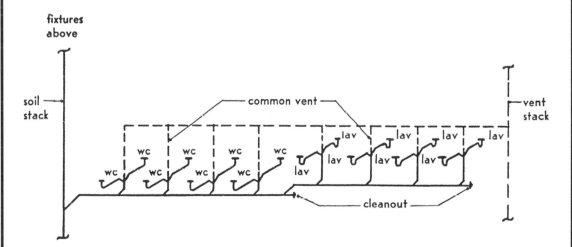

Figure P-41*a*   Venting for Batteries of Fixtures

Extracted from the New York State Building Code.

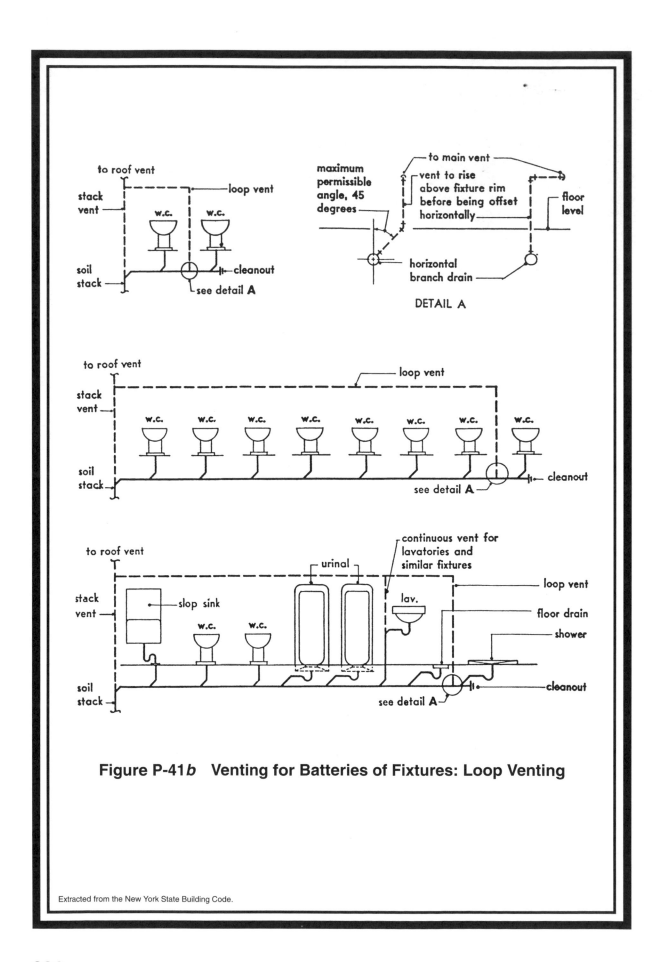

Figure P-41*b*   Venting for Batteries of Fixtures: Loop Venting

SANITARY DRAINAGE SYSTEM
DRAINAGE, WASTE, AND VENT (DWV)

P-33 CODES

All codes require that a plumbing system be designed in such a way as to protect and ensure the health, safety, and welfare of the public. The code requirements govern the design, materials, installation, and maintenance of the plumbing systems. Before designing the plumbing system, the local codes and regulations must be reviewed and followed.

P-34 SOIL STACK OR WASTE STACK

All fixtures receiving domestic water must discharge the used water to a sewage system by a drainage pipe called *soil stack* or *waste stack* (Figs. P-41*a, b,* and *c*).

The pipe sizes for a waste stack are determined by a drainage fixture unit (F.U.) valve, given in Fig. P-48.

The minimum sizes required by the local code should be used.

P-35 VENTS (VENT STACK)

Vent pipes are used in the system to:

a.   Allow gases in the waste stack to discharge to the outside air.

b.   Provide sufficient air to enter into waste stack in order to reduce the air turbulence.

c.   Prevent back pressure or siphoning action from damaging the trap seal of the fixtures.

P-36 WET VENTING

Wet venting is used for a single piping system and serves to vent several adjoining fixtures on the same floor. This system of venting is used commonly and is accepted by many codes (Fig. P-42).

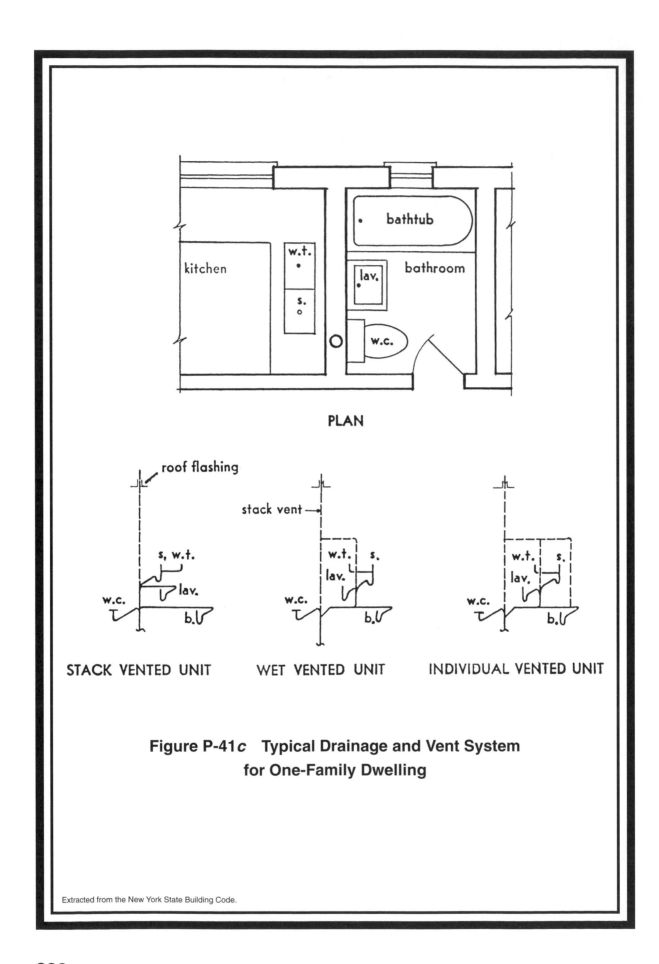

PLAN

roof flashing

s, w.t.

lav.

w.c.

b.

STACK VENTED UNIT

stack vent

w.t.

s.

lav.

w.c.

b.

WET VENTED UNIT

w.t.

s.

lav.

w.c.

b.

INDIVIDUAL VENTED UNIT

**Figure P-41*c*   Typical Drainage and Vent System
for One-Family Dwelling**

P-37   STACK VENTING

A single pipe receives the wastewater and also vents a group of fixtures. It is also known as **double unit stack venting.** This type of venting is used in either of the following situations:

a.   Fixtures are located on the same wall.

b.   Fixtures are located back to back.

In this system each fixture drain must connect directly to the vent stack (Fig. P-43).

P-38   COMBINATION VENTING

A combination waste and vent stack is a one-pipe system which vents and receives waste from fixtures.

It is used generally in high-rise buildings and residential buildings which have three or more stories (Fig. P-44).

P-39   TRAP

Traps are designed to catch and hold wastewater. This acts as a liquid seal which prevents gases resulting from sewage decomposition to enter into the building. All fixtures must be equipped with a water seal trap (Fig. P-45*a*).

P-40   BUILDING TRAP

Also known as *house trap,* these are used at the end of building drains and the beginning of building sewers (Fig. P-45*b*).

They are used as a safeguard to prevent sewer gases, odors, and rats, etc., from entering into a building drain.

Minimum size of nonintegral traps and maximum length of a trap arm are given in Fig. P-47.

P-41   CLEANOUTS (C.O.)

Cleanouts are designated on plumbing drawings as C.O. and are the essential part of the drainage system. They are required to be installed:

a.   After the building trap and before the building sewer (Fig. P-45*b*).

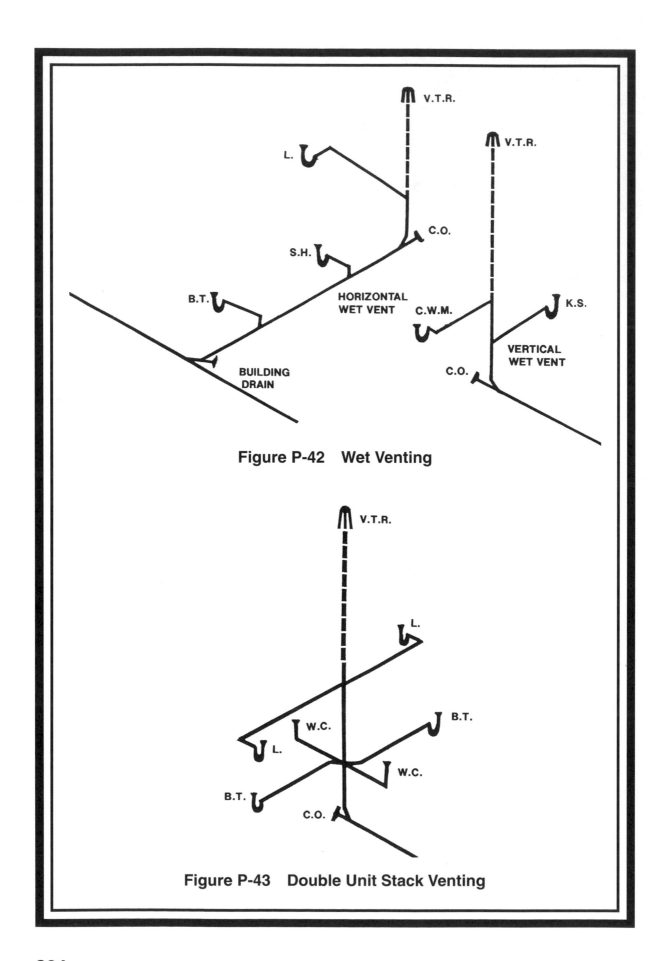

Figure P-42   Wet Venting

Figure P-43   Double Unit Stack Venting

b.   Where vertical waste stacks meet the building drain (Fig. P-41*a* and *b*).

c.   When vertical waste stacks are very long (Fig. P-46).

P-42   MATERIALS USED IN DWV

All materials and installation for DWV are regulated by the national and local plumbing code. The most commonly used materials for DWV are:

1. ***Tar-coated cast-iron pipe and fittings, non-hub-type.***   They are **extra heavy** or **centrifugally spun service weight.** They must not be mixed in the same system. Elastomeric sealing sleeves and stainless steel clamps are used on the joint.

2. ***Tar-coated cast-iron pipe and fittings with hub-and-spigot ends.***   Oakum with hot poured lead are used on the joints.

3. ***Plastic pipe and fittings.***   Plastic pipe and fittings type PVC or 40 ABS with cemented joint. They must not be mixed in the same system.

4. ***Galvanized steel pipe.***   Galvanized steel pipes with recessed drainage fittings are used for fixture branches, *drams,* in cast-iron systems.

5. ***Copper pipe.***   Copper pipe type M is used for extension of a vent through the roof.

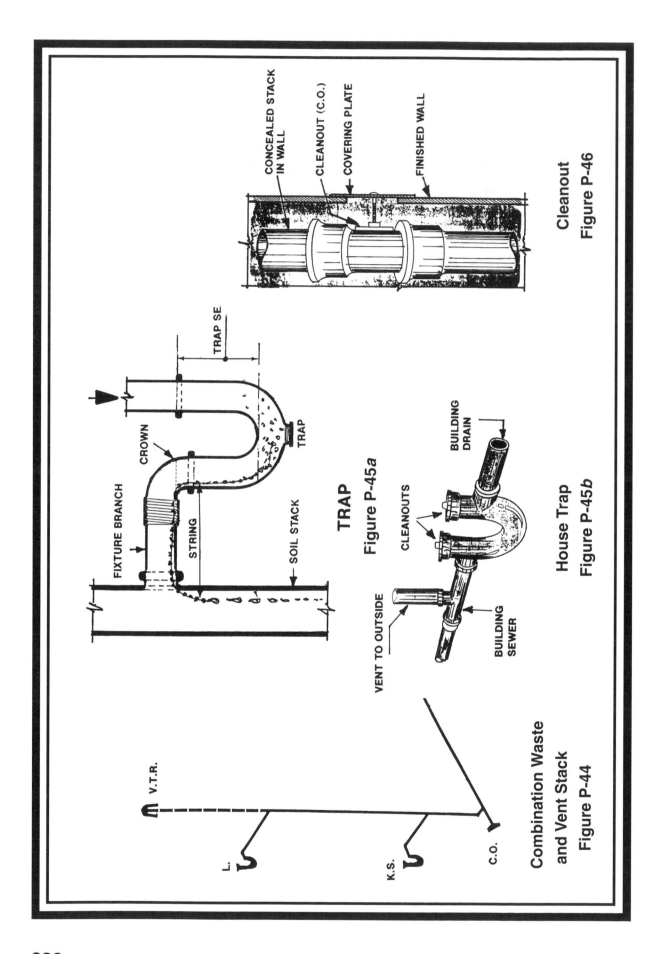

CONCEALED STACK IN WALL

CLEANOUT (C.O.)

COVERING PLATE

FINISHED WALL

Cleanout
Figure P-46

TRAP SE

CROWN

TRAP

FIXTURE BRANCH

STRING

SOIL STACK

TRAP
Figure P-45a

BUILDING DRAIN

CLEANOUTS

VENT TO OUTSIDE

BUILDING SEWER

House Trap
Figure P-45b

V.T.R.

L.

K.S.

C.O.

Combination Waste
and Vent Stack
Figure P-44

226

Plumbing Fixture	Trap Size in Inches
Bathtub (with or without overhead shower)	1-1/2
Bidet	1-1/4
Combination sink and wash (laundry) tray	1-1/2
Combination sink and wash (laundry) tray with food waste grinder unit	1-1/2*
Combination kitchen sink, domestic, dishwasher, and food waste grinder	1-1/2
Dental unit or cuspidor	1-1/4
Dental lavatory	1-1/4
Drinking fountain	1-1/4
Dishwasher, commercial	2
Dishwasher, domestic (non-integral trap)	1-1/2
Floor drain	2
Food waste grinder—Commercial Use	2
Food waste grinder—Domestic-Use	1-1/2
Kitchen sink, domestic, with food waste grinder unit	1-1/2
Kitchen sink, domestic	1-1/2
Kitchen sink, domestic, with dishwasher	1-1/2
Lavatory, common	1-1/4
Lavatory (barber shop, beauty parlor or surgeon's)	1-1/2
Lavatory, multiple type (wash fountain or wash sink)	1-1/2
Laundry tray (1 or 2 compartments)	1-1/2
Shower stall or drain	2
Sink (surgeon's)	1-1/2
Sink flushing rim type, flush valve supplied)	3
Sink (service type with floor outlet trap standard)	3
Sink (service trap with P trap)	2
Sink, commercial (pot, scullery, or similar type)	2
Sink, commercial (with food grinder unit)	2

*Separate trap required for wash tray and separate trap required for sink compartment with food waste grinder unit.

Minimum Size of Nonintegral Traps

Diameter of Trap Arm Inches	Distance — Trap to Vent
1¼	3' 6''
1½	5'
2	8'
3	10'
4	12'

NOTE: THIS TABLE HAS BEEN EXPANDED IN THE "LENGTH" REQUIREMENTS TO REFLECT EXPANDED APPLICATION OF THE WET VENTING PRINCIPLES. SLOPE SHALL NOT EXCEED ¼" PER FOOT.

Maximum Length of Trap Arm
Figure P-47

Extracted from the *1987 National Standard Plumbing Code* with permission of PHCC.

Type of Fixture or Group of Fixtures	Drainage Fixture Unit Value (d.f.u.)
Automatic clothes washer 2" standpipe and trap required—direct connection	3
Bathroom group consisting of a water closet, lavatory and bathtub or shower stall:	6
Bathtub[1] (with or without overhead shower)	2
Bidet	1
Clinic Sink	6
Combination sink-and-tray with food waste grinder	4
Combination sink-and-tray with one $1\text{-}1/2_0$ trap	2
Combination sink-and-tray with separate $1\text{-}1/2_0$ traps	3
Dental unit or cuspidor	1
Dental lavatory	1
Drinking fountain	½
Dishwasher, domestic	2
Floor drains with 2_0 waste	3
Kitchen sink, domestic, with one $1\text{-}\frac{1}{2}_0$ trap	2
Kitchen sink, domestic, with food waste grinder	2
Kitchen sink, domestic, with food waste grinder and dishwaster $1\text{-}\frac{1}{2}_0$ trap	3
Kitchen sink, domestic, with dishwasher $1\text{-}\frac{1}{2}_0$ trap	3
Kitchen sink, domestic, with dishwasher $1\text{-}\frac{1}{2}_0$ trap	3
Lavatory with $1\text{-}\frac{1}{4}_0$ waste	1
Laundry trap (1 or 2 compartments)	2
Shower stall, domestic	2
Showers (group) per head[2]	2
Sinks:	
Surgeon's	3
Flushing rim (with valve)	6
Service (trap standard)	3
Service (P trap)	2
Pot, scullery, etc.[2]	4
Urinal, syphon jet blowout	6
Urinal, wall lip	4
Urinal, stall, washout	4
Urinal trough (each 6-ft. section)	2
Wash sink (circular or multiple) each set of faucets	2
Water closet, private	4
Water closet, public	6
Fixtures not listed above:	
Trap Size 1-¼" or less	1
Trap Size 1-½"	2
Trap Size 2"	3
Trap Size 2-½"	4
Trap Size 3"	5
Trap Size 4"	6

[1]A shower head over a bathtub does not increase the fixture unit value.

[2]See Section 11.4.2 for method of computing equivalent fixture unit values for devices or equipment which discharge continuous or semi-continuous flows into sanitary drainage systems.

Figure P-48   Drainage Fixture Unit Values
for Various Plumbing Fixtures

Maximum Number of Fixture Units that may be Connected to:

Diameter of Pipe	Any Horizontal Fixture Branch[1]	One Stack of Three Branch Intervals or Less	Stacks with More Than Three Branch Intervals	
			Total for Stack	Total at One Branch Interval
Inches	dfu	dfu	dfu	dfu
1½	3	4	8	2
2	6	10	24	6
2½	12	20	42	9
3	20[2]	48[2]	72[2]	20[2]
4	160	240	500	90
5	360	540	1,100	200
6	620	960	1,900	350
8	1,400	2,200	3,600	600
10	2,500	3,800	5,600	1,000
12	3,900	6,000	8,400	1,500
15	7,000	Total Fixture Units (F.U.)		

[1]Does not include branches of the building drain.

[2]Not more than 2 water closets or bathroom groups within each branch interval nor more than 6 water closets or bathroom groups on the stack.

[3]Stacks shall be sized according to the total accumulated connected load at each story or branch interval and may be reduced in size as this load decreases to a minimum diameter of ½ of the largest size required.

Figure P-49   Horizontal Fixture Branches and Stacks

Diameter of Pipe	Maximum Number of Fixture Units That May Be Connected to Any Portion of the Building Drain or the Building Sewer.			
	Slope Per Foot			
	1/16-Inch	1/8-Inch	1/4-Inch	1/2-Inch
Inches	Total Fixture Units (F.U.)			
2			21	26
2½			24	31
3			42[2]	50[2]
4		180	216	250
5		390	480	575
6		700	840	1,000
8	1,400	1,600	1,920	2,300
10	2,500	2,900	3,500	4,200
12	2,900	4,600	5,600	6,700
15	7,000	8,300	10,000	12,000

[1]On site sewers that serve more than one building may be sized according to the current standards and specifications of the Adminstrative Authority for public sewers.

[2]Not over two water closets or two bathroom groups, except that in single family dwellings, not over three water closets or three bathroom groups may be installed.

Figure P-50   Building Drains and Sewers

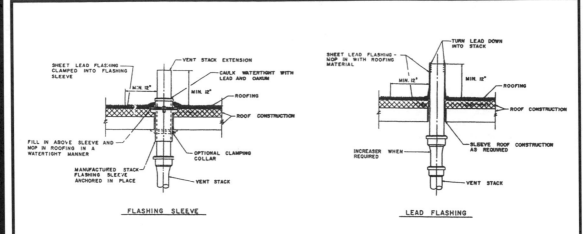

Vents Thru Roof

Dadras International
Architects—Engineers—Planners

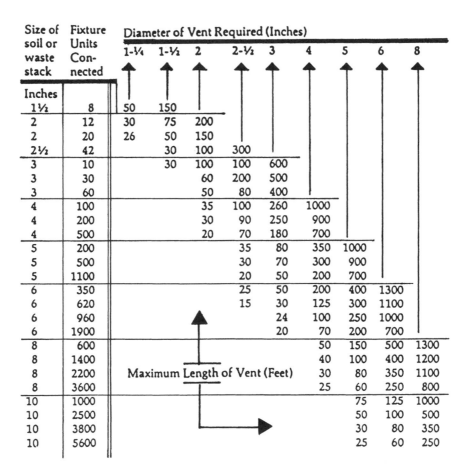

Size of soil or waste stack	Fixture Units Con-nected	Diameter of Vent Required (Inches)								
		1-¼	1-½	2	2-½	3	4	5	6	8
Inches										
1½	8	50	150							
2	12	30	75	200						
2	20	26	50	150						
2½	42		30	100	300					
3	10		30	100	100	600				
3	30			60	200	500				
3	60			50	80	400				
4	100			35	100	260	1000			
4	200			30	90	250	900			
4	500			20	70	180	700			
5	200				35	80	350	1000		
5	500				30	70	300	900		
5	1100				20	50	200	700		
6	350				25	50	200	400	1300	
6	620				15	30	125	300	1100	
6	960					24	100	250	1000	
6	1900					20	70	200	700	
8	600						50	150	500	1300
8	1400						40	100	400	1200
8	2200						30	80	350	1100
8	3600						25	60	250	800
10	1000							75	125	1000
10	2500							50	100	500
10	3800							30	80	350
10	5600							25	60	250

Maximum Length of Vent (Feet)

Figure P-51   Size and Length of Vents

DESIGN OF DRAINAGE, WASTE, AND VENT (DWV)

P-43   DESIGN PROCEDURE FOR DWV

Use the floor plan(s) and section(s) to identify the fixtures using domestic cold or hot and cold water and show where soil drains and vents must be provided.

1.   Check your local plumbing code which has to be followed in the design.

2.   The size of all pipes to be used for DWV are given in the following figures:

    a.   Drainage fixture unit (F.U.) valve (Fig. P-48)

    b.   Horizontal fixture branch and stacks (Fig. P-49)

    c.   Building drains and sewers (Fig. P-50)

    d.   Size and length of vents (Fig. P-51)

3.   Fixture trap and runouts from a fixture should be the same size.

4.   No more than two water closets should be installed on a 3-in. branch pipe. It is a common practice to use a 4-in. runout for even one water closet.

5.   A water closet should have a minimum 2-in. vent.

6.   The size of vertical vents penetrating the roof should be minimum 4 in.

7.   A house drain must not be less than 4 in.

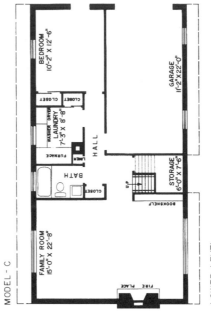

UPPER LEVEL
MODEL - C

LOWER LEVEL
MODEL - C

(Model C) THE RIVIERA BI-LEVEL

4 nice sized bedrooms, 2 full baths, large living room, dining room, spacious family room with Fireplace* and sliding patio doors. Luxurious kitchen with dining area and General Electric Appliances*. Large open balcony, laundry center, storage and 1 (or 2)* car garage.

*Optional.

Figure P-52   Design of "DWV" for Residence

Architects & Engineers: Dadras International

232

Example

Design drainage, waste, and vent for the "Model C" house at Ridgebury Lake Acres, Middletown, New York (Fig. P-52).

Solution

The plumbing system for DWV has been divided into three branches of "A," "B," and "C" (as shown in Fig. P-53).

All horizontal and vertical soil drains are shown with solid lines, and horizontal and vertical vent stacks are shown with dotted lines.

1. Design of DWV for branch "A"

Step 1. Find total fixture units (F.U.).

Construct a chart as follows and use Fig. P-48 for F.U. values.

No.	Fixtures	F.U./F
1	Kitchen sink w/dishwasher	3
2	Lavatory trap (lav.)	2
1	Bathtub (tub)	2
	Total F.U.	7

Step 2. Find soil drains, soil and vent stacks.

Because of the limited number of fixtures, all dimensions are minimum (min.). (See Figs. P-49, P-50, and P-51.)

a. All horizontal soil drains are 2 in. (min.) except for water closet, which should be 4 in.

b. All horizontal soil drains should have ¼ in. per foot pitch.

c. All soil stacks are 1½ in. (min.) except for water closet which is 4 in.

d. All vent stacks are 1¼ in. (min.) except for lavatory and water closet which are 1½ and 2 in. (min.), respectively.

e. Horizontal and main vent stacks are 2 in. (min.).

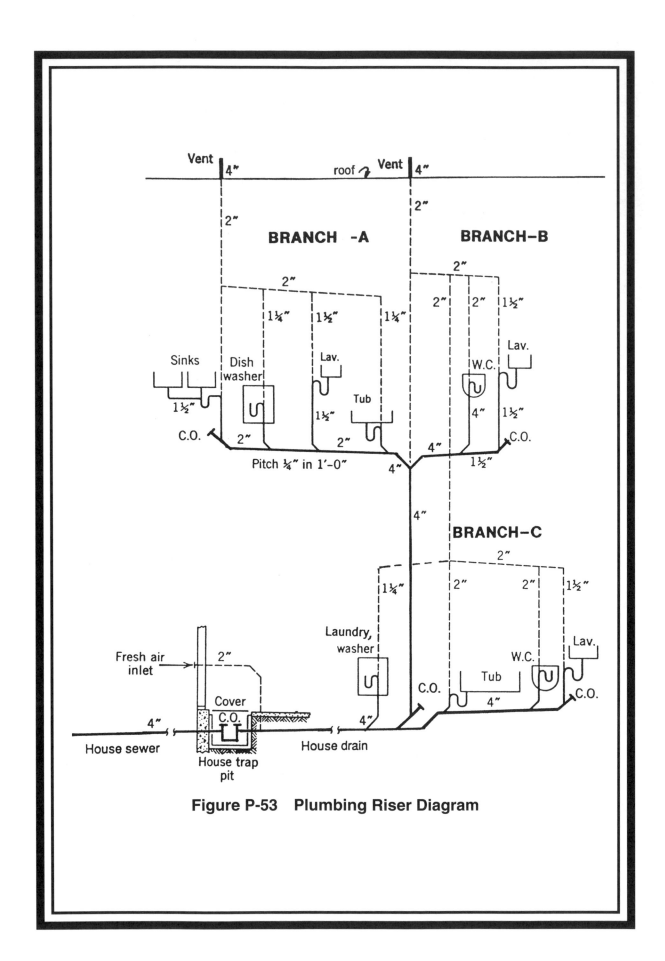

Figure P-53   Plumbing Riser Diagram

2. Design of DWV for branches "B" and "C"

Follow Steps 1 and 2 supra to design DWV for branches "B" and "C."

Note:

a. House drain and house sewer should be 4 in. (min.) with ¼ in. per foot pitch (min.).

b. House trap should be 4 in. (min.).

c. Fresh air inlet before house trap should be 2 in. (min.).

d. Soil stack from the first floor to the second floor should be 4 in. (min.)

e. Vent stack from the first floor to inside the roof should be 2 in. (min.). The size of the vent stack should be increased to 4 in., penetrating through and above the roof.

f. Use cleanouts (C.O.) as shown in Fig. P-53.

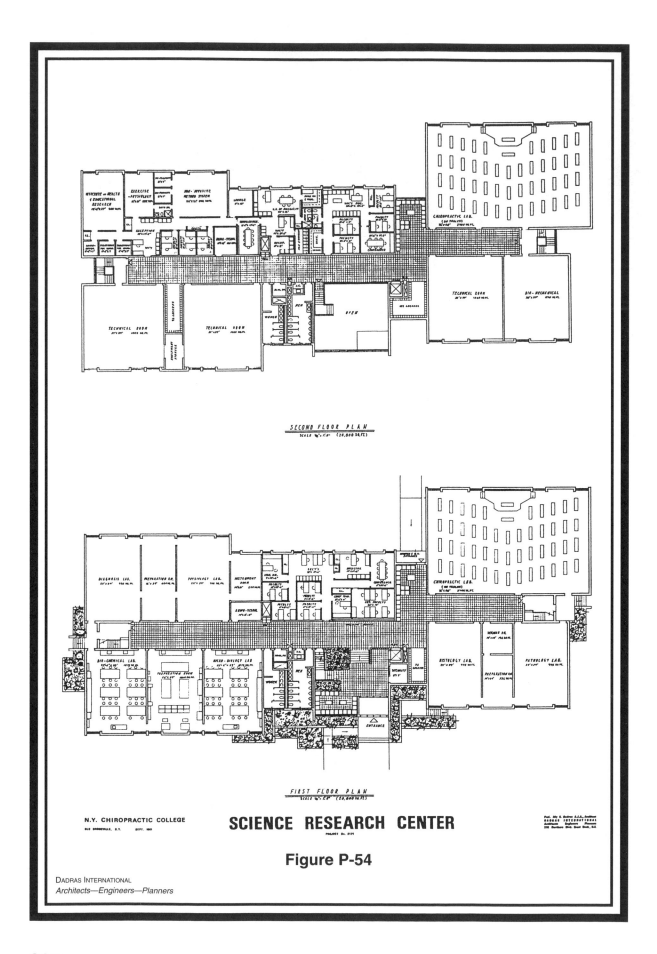

SECOND FLOOR PLAN

FIRST FLOOR PLAN

N.Y. CHIROPRACTIC COLLEGE

SCIENCE RESEARCH CENTER

Figure P-54

DADRAS INTERNATIONAL
Architects—Engineers—Planners

Example

Design DWV for Science Research Center, New York Chiropractic College (Fig. P-54).

Solution

Men's bathroom and women's bathroom *are identical* on the first and second floor (Figs. P-55 and P-56). The fixtures are divided into three groups "A," "B," and "C" (Figs. P-56 and P-57).

1. Design of DWV for group "A" as shown in Fig. P-56:

Step 1. Find total fixture unit (F.U.) for the first-floor bathroom using Fig. P-48.

Fixture (F)	No. of F		F.U./F		Total
Urinals S.J.B.	8	×	6	=	48
Lavatory trap	1	×	1	=	1
			Total F.U. =		49

Step 2. Find the size of horizontal branch, soil stack, and vent stack

    a.   Using Figs. P-49 and P-50, the horizontal branch is 4 in. with 1⅛ in/ft pitch (good for 180 F.U.).

    b.   Using Fig. P-49, the soil stack for each urinal is 2 in. (min.) (good for 10 F.U.).

    c.   Using Fig. P-51, the vent stack for each urinal and lavatory is 1¼ in. (min.); use 1½ in.

    d.   Horizontal vent for eight urinals and lavatory is 1½ in. (min.); use 2 in.

Step 3. Use the same sizes for the second-floor fixtures.

Step 4. Using Fig. P-49,

    a.   Soil stack from second floor to first floor is 4 in. (good for 240 F.U.).

    b.   Vent stack from first floor to the horizontal vent stack of the second floor using Fig. P-51 is 2 in. (min.); use 2½ in.

    c.   Use 4-in. vent stack from horizontal vent stack of the second floor to and above the roof.

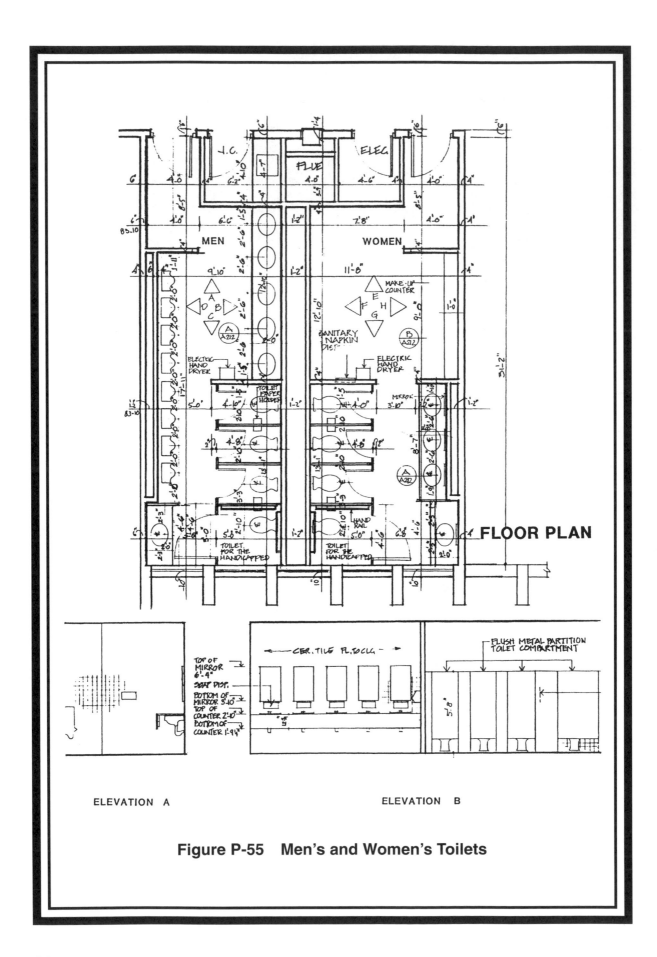

FLOOR PLAN

ELEVATION A

ELEVATION B

Figure P-55 Men's and Women's Toilets

2. Design of DWV for group "B" (Fig. P-57):

Step 1. Find total fixture unit (F.U.) for the first-floor bathroom using Fig. P-48.

Fixture (F)	No. of F		F.U./F		Total
Drinking fountain	1	×	½	=	½
Service sink (T.S.)	1	×	3	=	3
Lavatory trap	5	×	2	=	10
Water closet, public	8	×	6	=	48
			Total F.U. =		61½

Step 2. Find the size of the horizontal fixture branch by using Figs. P-49 and P-50.

The horizontal branch for 61½ F.U. is 4 in. with ⅛ in/ft pitch (good for 180 F.U.).

Step 3. Find the size of the fixtures, soil stack using Fig. P-49, and vent stack using Fig. P-51.

  a. The soil stack for the drinking fountain is 1½ in. (min.), use 2 in. The vent stack is 1½ in.

  b. The soil stack for the slop sink is 1½ in. (min.), use 3 in. The vent stack is 1½ in.

  c. The soil stack for lavatories is 1½ in. (min.) The vent stack is 1½ in.

  d. The soil stack for the water closets is 4 in. (min.). The vent stack is 2 in. min.)

  e. The horizontal vent stack is 3 in.

3. Design of DWV for group "C" (Fig. P-57)

Use the same steps given for group "B."

Note:

  1. Building drain and building sewer are 4 in. (min.) with ¼ in. pitch per foot (min.).

  2. Building trap should be 4 in. (min.).

  3. Fresh air inlet before house trap should be 3 in.

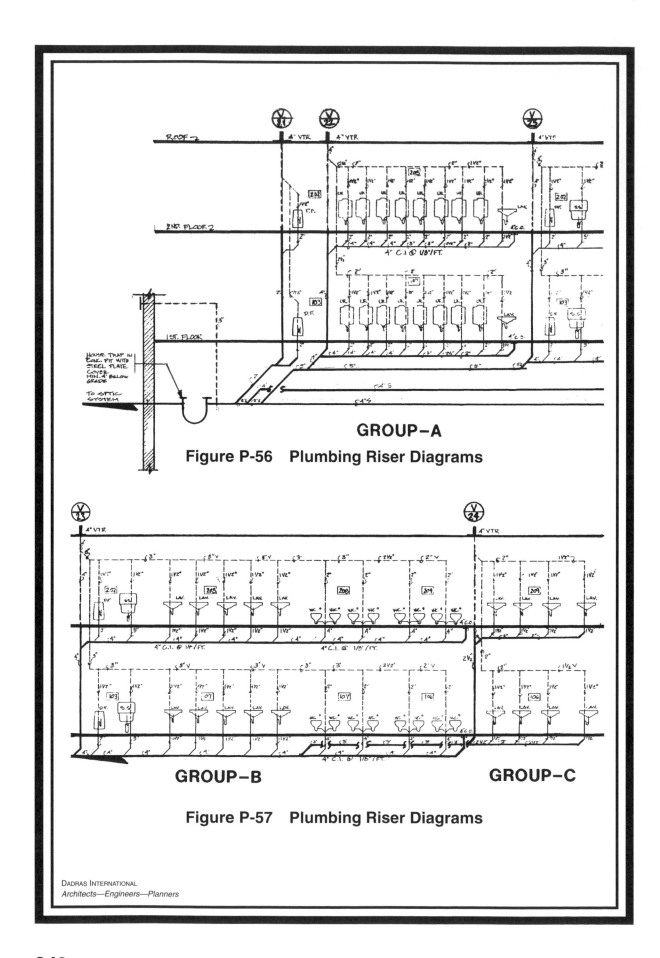

GROUP-A

Figure P-56   Plumbing Riser Diagrams

GROUP-B

GROUP-C

Figure P-57   Plumbing Riser Diagrams

CONTENTS

Part 6

LIGHTNING PROTECTION

L

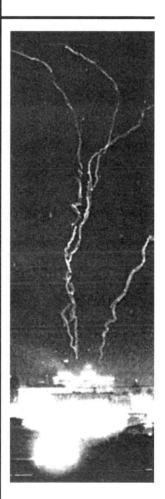

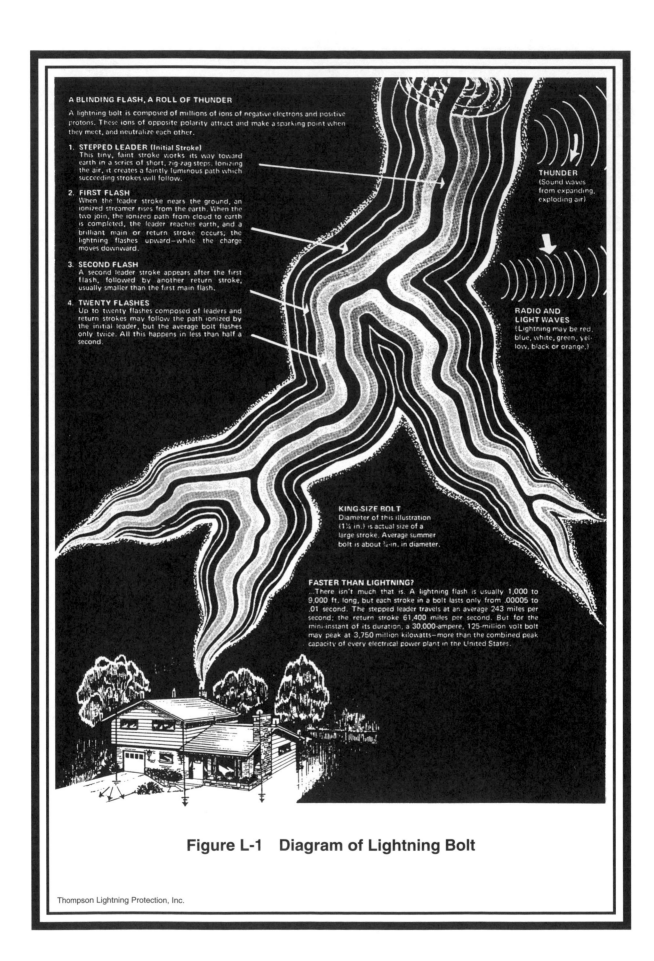

A BLINDING FLASH, A ROLL OF THUNDER

A lightning bolt is composed of millions of ions of negative electrons and positive protons. These ions of opposite polarity attract and make a sparking point when they meet, and neutralize each other.

1. STEPPED LEADER (Initial Stroke)
This tiny, faint stroke works its way toward earth in a series of short, zig-zag steps. Ionizing the air, it creates a faintly luminous path which succeeding strokes will follow.

2. FIRST FLASH
When the leader stroke nears the ground, an ionized streamer rises from the earth. When the two join, the ionized path from cloud to earth is completed, the leader reaches earth, and a brilliant main or return stroke occurs; the lightning flashes upward—while the charge moves downward.

3. SECOND FLASH
A second leader stroke appears after the first flash, followed by another return stroke, usually smaller than the first main flash.

4. TWENTY FLASHES
Up to twenty flashes composed of leaders and return strokes may follow the path ionized by the initial leader, but the average bolt flashes only twice. All this happens in less than half a second.

THUNDER
(Sound waves from expanding, exploding air)

RADIO AND LIGHT WAVES
(Lightning may be red, blue, white, green, yellow, black or orange.)

KING-SIZE BOLT
Diameter of this illustration (1¼ in.) is actual size of a large stroke. Average summer bolt is about ¾-in. in diameter.

FASTER THAN LIGHTNING?
...There isn't much that is. A lightning flash is usually 1,000 to 9,000 ft. long, but each stroke in a bolt lasts only from .00005 to .01 second. The stepped leader travels at an average 243 miles per second; the return stroke 61,400 miles per second. But for the mini-instant of its duration, a 30,000-ampere, 125-million volt bolt may peak at 3,750 million kilowatts—more than the combined peak capacity of every electrical power plant in the United States.

Figure L-1 Diagram of Lightning Bolt

LIGHTNING PROTECTION

L-1   HISTORY AT A GLANCE

Benjamin Franklin, in 1752, proved the identity of the electricity of lightning, *atmospheric electricity,* and ordinary electricity. He invented the lightning rod to be installed on buildings for lightning protection.

L-2   LIGHTNING

Lightning is an electrical discharge accompanied by thunder generally occurring during a thunderstorm (Fig. L-1).

Storm clouds, *nimbus clouds,* elevated approximately 3000 ft above the ground, containing protons with electric charges caused by violent air current, create thunder and lightning in the following manner:

1.   Masses of electrons with negative or positive electric charges created by violet air current gather on the upper part of the clouds.
2.   The opposite charges gather on the lower part of the clouds.
3.   The earth's mass of electrons, electrically charged positive and/or negative, are ready to rush up and contact their opposite charges in the clouds.
4.   The nonconducting air gap between the clouds and the earth prevents those electrons of opposite charges from colliding with each other if they are not powerful enough.

L-3   LIGHTNING BETWEEN CLOUDS

When a mass of electrons becomes powerful, with electric charges on one side of the cloud, it penetrates into the cloud and collides with opposite charges on the other side of the cloud, creating thunder and lightning within the cloud or between one cloud and another cloud.

L-4   LIGHTNING BETWEEN CLOUDS AND THE EARTH

When the mass of electrons in the clouds with positive or negative electric charges becomes powerful enough to penetrate downward through nonconducting air gaps, it collides with a mass of earth's electrons of opposite charges, creating spectacular lightning (Fig. F-2).

Figure L-2 Forked Lightning

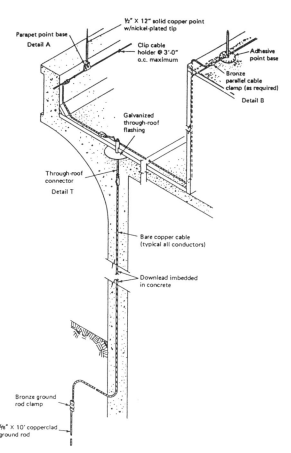

½" X 12" solid copper point
w/nickel-plated tip

Parapet point base
Detail A

Clip cable
holder @ 3'-0"
o.c. maximum

Adhesive
point base

Bronze
parallel cable
clamp (as required)

Detail B

Galvanized
through-roof
flashing

Through-roof
connector
Detail T

Bare copper cable
(typical all conductors)

Downlead imbedded
in concrete

Bronze ground
rod clamp

⅝" X 10' copperclad
ground rod

Figure L-3 Concealed System

L-5 TYPES OF LIGHTNING

In general, there are four types of lightning:

1. **Forked lightning.** Appears as a jagged streak (Fig. L-2).
2. **Sheet lightning.** Appears as a vast flash in the sky (Fig. L-2).
3. **Ball lightning.** Illuminates as a brilliant ball.
4. **Heat lightning.** Illumination from lightning flashes occurring near the horizon, often with clear sky overhead, and with the accompanying thunder too distant to be audible.

L-6 POWER OF LIGHTNING

A striking bolt of lightning can produce over 200,000 amperes of current, enough to illuminate 240,000 light bulbs of 100 W each.

Nikola Tesla in the early 20th century invented the **"Tesla coil"** which is a device to transmit electric energy without wires through the air. He was successful in his first experiment in Colorado, transmitting 100 million volts through the nonconducting air for a few thousand feet.

Lightning voltage has to be around 100 million volts in order to penetrate through nonconducting air.

The core of the bolt of lightning is a pure flow of electric energy about ¾ in. in diameter, and is surrounded by ionized air (Fig. F-1).

A strong lightning bolt can produce a temperature of about 27,000°F.

L-7 EFFECT OF LIGHTNING ON THE EARTH

A bolt of lightning hits any object on the earth that has the capacity to conduct electricity, such as trees, humans, animals, and metallic objects projecting above the ground, in order to penetrate to the crust of the earth.

L-8 EFFECT OF LIGHTNING ON STRUCTURES

Lightning bolts can hit a structure in four different ways:

1. Direct strike to the building.
2. Hit a tree near the structure and leap to the structure for better grounding.

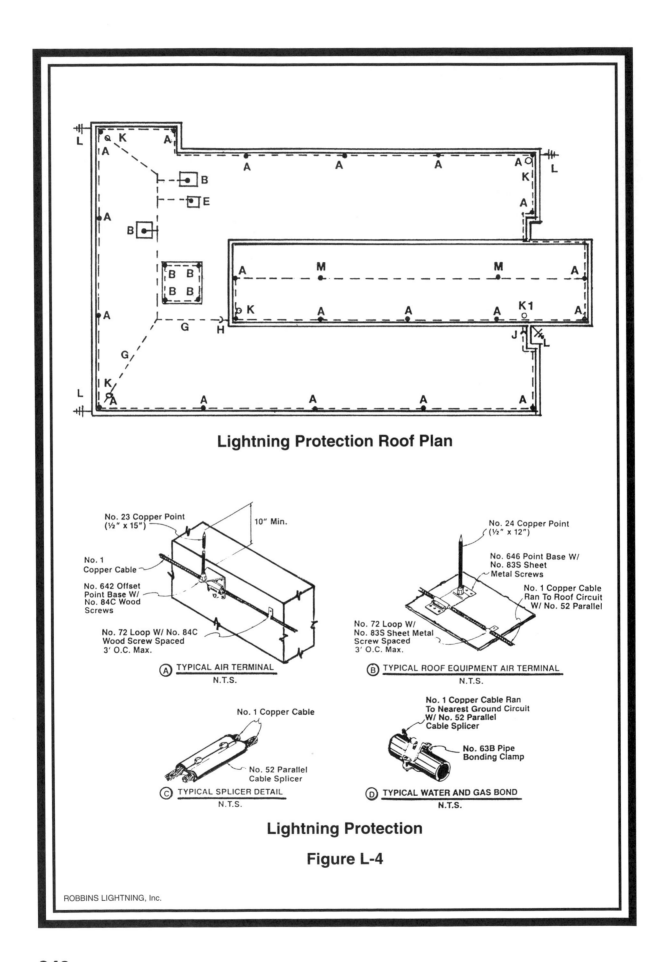

Lightning Protection Roof Plan

No. 23 Copper Point
(½" x 15")

10" Min.

No. 1
Copper Cable

No. 642 Offset
Point Base W/
No. 84C Wood
Screws

No. 72 Loop W/ No. 84C
Wood Screw Spaced
3' O.C. Max.

Ⓐ TYPICAL AIR TERMINAL
N.T.S.

No. 24 Copper Point
(½" x 12")

No. 646 Point Base W/
No. 83S Sheet
Metal Screws

No. 1 Copper Cable
Ran To Roof Circuit
W/ No. 52 Parallel

No. 72 Loop W/
No. 83S Sheet Metal
Screw Spaced
3' O.C. Max.

Ⓑ TYPICAL ROOF EQUIPMENT AIR TERMINAL
N.T.S.

No. 1 Copper Cable

No. 52 Parallel
Cable Splicer

Ⓒ TYPICAL SPLICER DETAIL
N.T.S.

No. 1 Copper Cable Ran
To Nearest Ground Circuit
W/ No. 52 Parallel
Cable Splicer

No. 63B Pipe
Bonding Clamp

Ⓓ TYPICAL WATER AND GAS BOND
N.T.S.

Lightning Protection

Figure L-4

246

3.   Hit a power line which is connected to the building.

4.   Strike metallic objects projecting above the roof of the building.

L-9   LIGHTNING PROTECTION FOR BUILDINGS

There are two types of lightning protection systems:

1.   **Concealed system** *(Fig. L-3).*   Commonly installed during the construction of the structure. The conductors are placed inside of the structural members and are grounded directly into the ground.

2.   **Semiconcealed system.**   Installed on existing structures. The conductors are exposed on the facade of the structure and are grounded directly into the ground.

Both systems contain five parts for complete lightning protection (Fig. L-4):

1.   **Lightning rods (air terminals).**   These must be minimum 10 in. in height and placed 20 ft o.c. along the parapet walls, on roof ridge. They also should be placed over any projection of the roof, such as chimneys, dormers, etc. (Fig. L-4"A" and "B").

2.   **Lightning arresters.**   These are devices for grounding electric service wires, telephone, and TV cables (Fig. L-5).

3.   **Tin-ins.**   These connect the vent stacks, plumbing pipes, gutters, air-conditioning units, and antennas to the conductors (Fig. L-4"F").

4.   **Lightning conductors.**   These are copper or aluminium cables interconnecting all rods, arresters, and tin-ins to the ground rods (Fig. L-4"K").

5.   **Ground rods.**   Minimum of two ground rods should be placed at opposite corners of the buildings (Fig. L-4"L"). They must be sunk a minimum of 10 ft into the moist soil. If the ground contains sand or gravel, a special grounding device should be used (Fig. L-6).

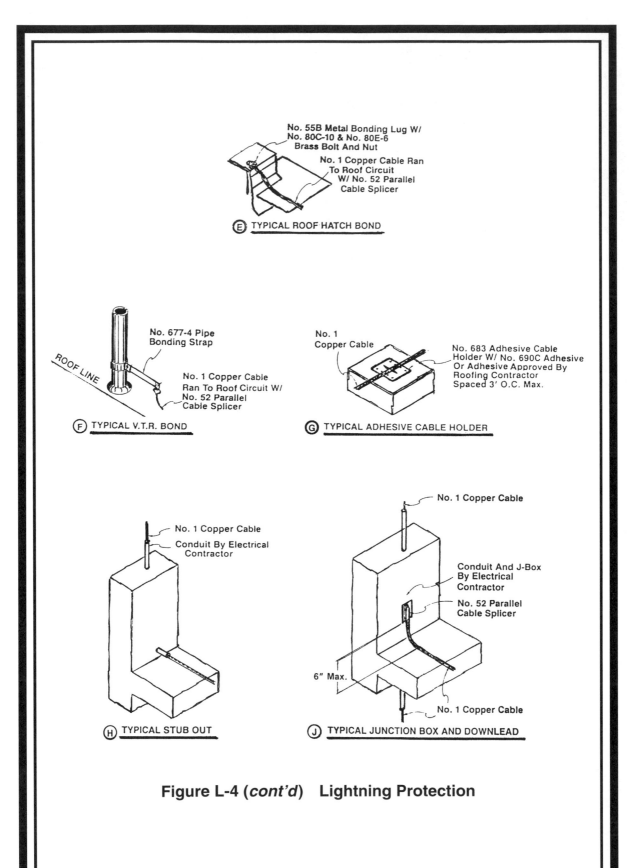

No. 55B Metal Bonding Lug W/
No. 80C-10 & No. 80E-6
Brass Bolt And Nut

No. 1 Copper Cable Ran
To Roof Circuit
W/ No. 52 Parallel
Cable Splicer

(E) TYPICAL ROOF HATCH BOND

No. 677-4 Pipe
Bonding Strap

ROOF LINE

No. 1 Copper Cable
Ran To Roof Circuit W/
No. 52 Parallel
Cable Splicer

(F) TYPICAL V.T.R. BOND

No. 1
Copper Cable

No. 683 Adhesive Cable
Holder W/ No. 690C Adhesive
Or Adhesive Approved By
Roofing Contractor
Spaced 3' O.C. Max.

(G) TYPICAL ADHESIVE CABLE HOLDER

No. 1 Copper Cable

Conduit By Electrical
Contractor

(H) TYPICAL STUB OUT

No. 1 Copper Cable

Conduit And J-Box
By Electrical
Contractor

No. 52 Parallel
Cable Splicer

6" Max.

No. 1 Copper Cable

(J) TYPICAL JUNCTION BOX AND DOWNLEAD

Figure L-4 (*cont'd*)   Lightning Protection

ROBBINS LIGHTNING, Inc.

L-10 INSTALLATION

All lightning protection systems, materials, and installations must comply with local codes. The work should be spot-checked by inspection services available from Underwriters Laboratories (UL).

The Lightning Protection Institute (LPI) has developed a program of instruction and certification for installers and designers.

L-11 SPECIFICATIONS

The outline of long- and short-form specifications for lightning protection is given in Fig. L-7. Make sure the following specifications and standards form a part of the specifications for the lightning protection of your building(s).

1. **Specifications and standards** by Underwriters Laboratories, Inc. Subject 96A (1983).

2. **Specifications and standards** by National Fire Protection Association NFPA No. 78 (1983).

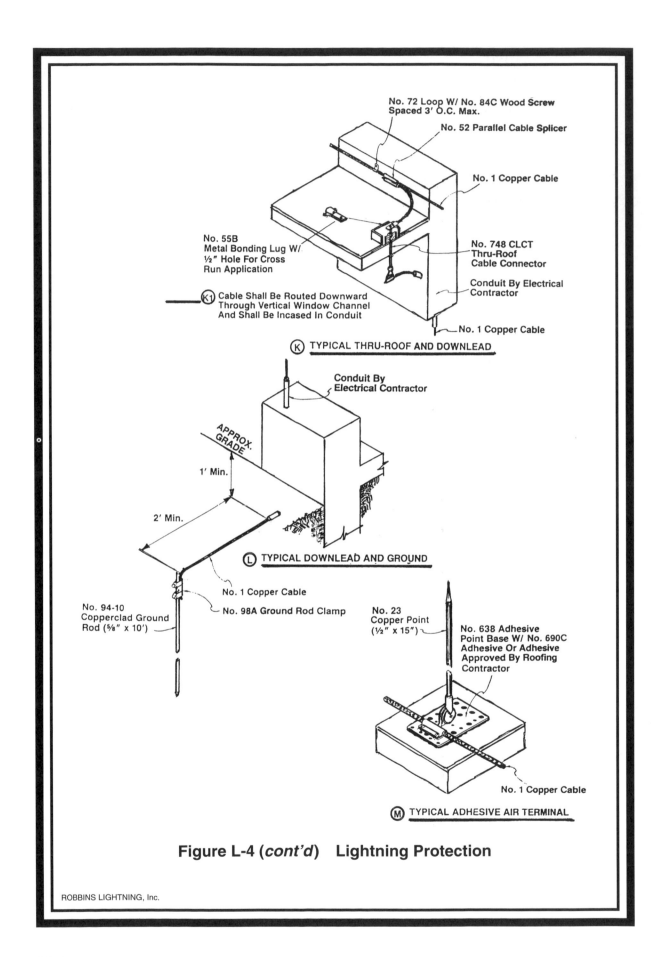

No. 72 Loop W/ No. 84C Wood Screw
Spaced 3' O.C. Max.

No. 52 Parallel Cable Splicer

No. 1 Copper Cable

No. 55B
Metal Bonding Lug W/
½" Hole For Cross
Run Application

No. 748 CLCT
Thru-Roof
Cable Connector

Conduit By Electrical
Contractor

K1 Cable Shall Be Routed Downward
Through Vertical Window Channel
And Shall Be Incased In Conduit

No. 1 Copper Cable

Ⓚ TYPICAL THRU-ROOF AND DOWNLEAD

Conduit By
Electrical Contractor

APPROX.
GRADE.

1' Min.

2' Min.

No. 1 Copper Cable

Ⓛ TYPICAL DOWNLEAD AND GROUND

No. 94-10
Copperclad Ground
Rod (⅝" x 10')

No. 98A Ground Rod Clamp

No. 23
Copper Point
(½" x 15")

No. 638 Adhesive
Point Base W/ No. 690C
Adhesive Or Adhesive
Approved By Roofing
Contractor

No. 1 Copper Cable

Ⓜ TYPICAL ADHESIVE AIR TERMINAL

Figure L-4 (*cont'd*)   Lightning Protection

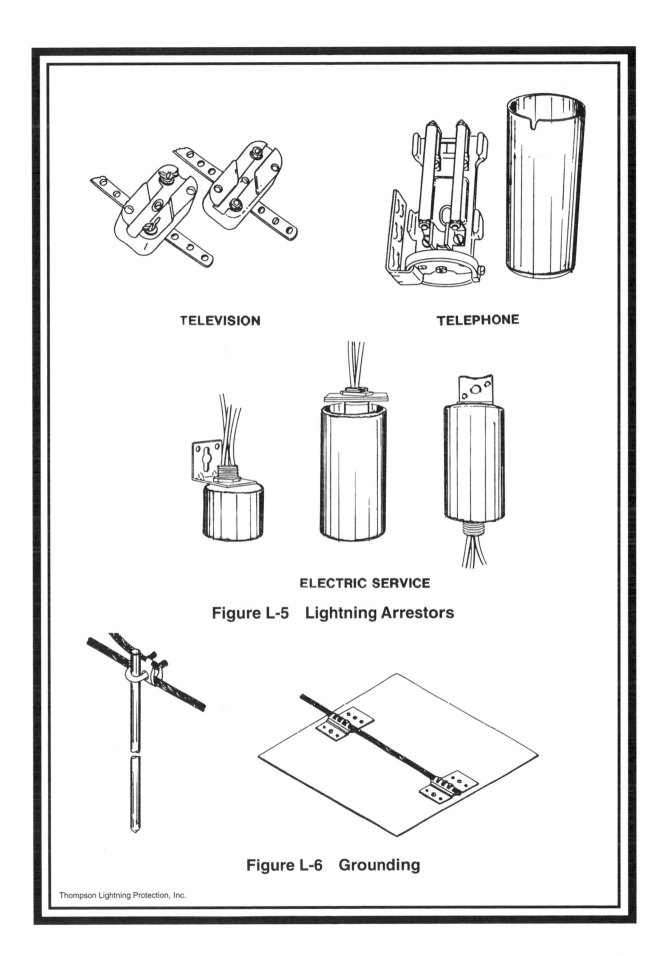

TELEVISION

TELEPHONE

ELECTRIC SERVICE

Figure L-5   Lightning Arrestors

Figure L-6   Grounding

SPECIFICATIONS:

LONG FORM—Scope: Furnish and install a complete Lightning Protection System in strict accordance with this section of specifications and the applicable codes specified herein.

Applicable Specifications: The following specifications and standards form a part of this specification:

    Underwriter's Laboratories, Inc. Subject 96A
       (1983)

    National Fire Protection Association NFPA No. 78
       (1983)

Standard Products: The System furnished under this specification shall be the product of a manufacturer regularly engaged in the production of Lightning Protection Systems and shall be the manufacturer's latest designs. Listing of the manufacturer in the Lightning Protection Section of the current edition of the Underwriters' Laboratories, Inc. "Electrical Equipment List" will be accepted as compliance with this requirement.

Materials and Equipment Schedule: Materials used in the installation of the Lightning Protection System shall be approved and labeled for Lightning Protection Systems by Underwriters' Laboratories, Inc. Prior to making the installation, a complete list of materials, catalog data and shop drawings shall be submitted to the architect or owner for approval. In the event any items of material or equipment contained in the schedule fail to comply with the specification requirements such items shall be rejected.

System Design: The System shall consist of air terminals, conductors, groundings and bonding of metal so designed to blend in with the appearance of the building that it appears as part of the building. The System shall be maximum concealed, semi-concealed or totally exposed as required to meet the approval of the architect and specifications for the individual type of building.

Conductors: Conductors shall consist of copper or aluminum of a grade ordinarily used for commercial electric work and shall be of a weight required by the specifications for the height of the building to be protected.

Air Terminals: Air terminals shall consist of solid copper or aluminum rod with a tapered point, not less than 10" in height. Rods shall be attached to the building with the proper base to adapt to the building design.

Groundings: Each downlead cable shall terminate in a grounding consisting of a rod, plate or cable to meet the requirements of the local soil condition and those of the applicable codes.

Bonding of Metal: All metal bodies such as ventilators stacks, pipes, gutters, downspouts, ducts, tracks, antennas, water pipes, ladders and other similar metal shall be interconnected to the main conductor System. Incoming electric and telephone service shall have a common ground with the Lightning Protection System.

Inspection and Acceptance: The Lightning Protection System shall be inspected by the architect or owner to determine conformance with this specification. No part of the system shall be concealed until inspected by the architect or owner. In addition the Underwriters' Laboratories Master Label "C" shall be delivered to the architect or owner before the completed installation is cleared for final payment. Any items found not to comply with the specification requirements shall be immediately replaced at no additional cost to the owner.

SPECIFICATIONS:

SHORT FORM–Furnish and install a complete Lightning Protection System which shall comply with the specifications of the Underwriters' Laboratories (UL 96A) and the National Fire Protection Association (NFPA No. 78). The Underwriters' Laboratories Master Label "C" shall be delivered to the architect-engineer-owner upon completion of the installation. Complete shop drawings of the proposed System shall be submitted to the architect-engineer for approval before installation is started.

UNDERWRITERS LABORATORIES MASTER LABEL SERVICE

The Master Label is evidence that the Lightning Protection System is properly made and properly installed.

Materials used for a Master Labeled System require UL listing marks. These listing marks are applied at the factory on all conductors, air terminals, and fittings. Any representative using our products must assume the responsibility of making the installation to Underwriters Laboratories specifications. Our engineered drawings will show the installer the correct method of installation.

Figure L-7   Lightning Protection Specifications

CONTENTS

Part 7

FIRE PROTECTION

F

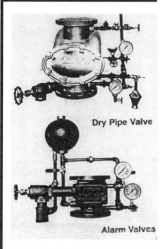

Dry Pipe Valve

Alarm Valves

Standard Spray

Bulb Sprinkler

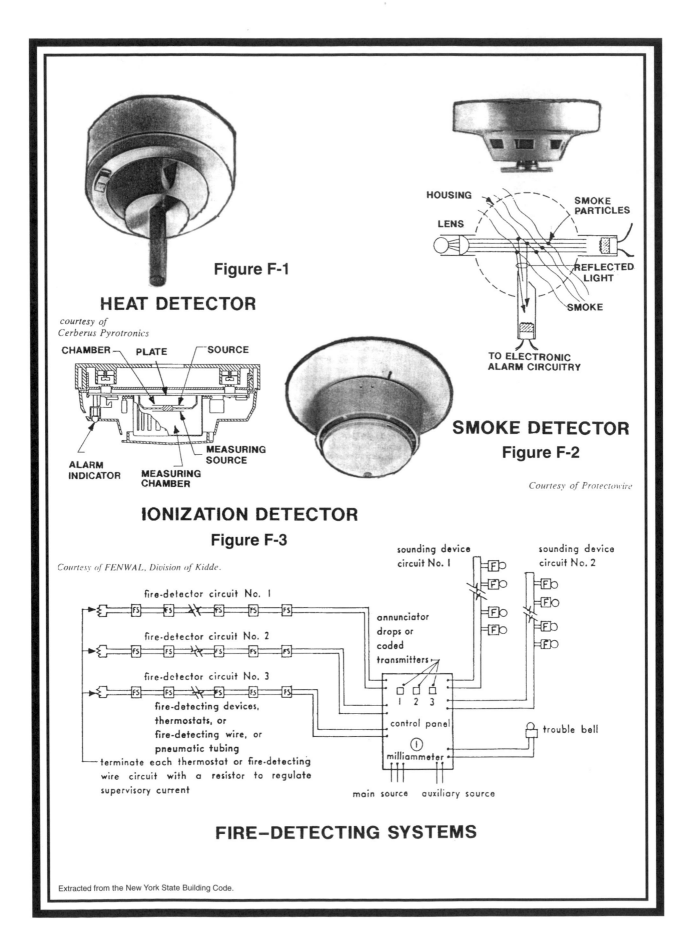

Figure F-1

HEAT DETECTOR

*courtesy of
Cerberus Pyrotronics*

HOUSING
LENS
SMOKE PARTICLES
REFLECTED LIGHT
SMOKE
TO ELECTRONIC ALARM CIRCUITRY

CHAMBER — PLATE — SOURCE
MEASURING SOURCE
ALARM INDICATOR
MEASURING CHAMBER

SMOKE DETECTOR
Figure F-2

Courtesy of Protectowire

IONIZATION DETECTOR
Figure F-3

Courtesy of FENWAL, Division of Kidde.

sounding device circuit No. 1
sounding device circuit No. 2

fire-detector circuit No. 1

fire-detector circuit No. 2

fire-detector circuit No. 3

annunciator drops or coded transmitters

fire-detecting devices, thermostats, or fire-detecting wire, or pneumatic tubing
terminate each thermostat or fire-detecting wire circuit with a resistor to regulate supervisory current

control panel

milliammeter

trouble bell

main source   auxiliary source

FIRE–DETECTING SYSTEMS

Extracted from the New York State Building Code.

FIRE PROTECTION

F-1 OBJECTIVES

The objectives of fire protection in any structure are to protect lives and property and to allow continuity of the operations in the building.

There is no such thing as a fireproof building. Any structure, regardless of materials used, can burn to ashes, depending on the amount and duration of the fire.

All codes require structures to be designed and constructed to resist the fire for 1, 2, or 4 hours, depending on the type of structure, height, and occupancy.

There are six essential elements for fire protection:

1. Early detection and alarm system
2. Means of egress
3. Compartmentation
4. Smoke control
5. Fire-suppression system
6. Emergency power

The building code specifies which one or combination of these elements should be used in a building. The requirements specified in the code are essential for the safety of the occupants and must be adhered to in the design phase, construction document phase, and construction phase.

F-2 FIRE AND SMOKE

When a fire starts in a structure, the first 5 minutes are more important than the duration of the fire for the following reasons:

1. Smoke can spread and overcome people in the first few minutes, long before the fire can reach them. Smoke moves more than 50 feet per minute and may kill people before they even notice the fire. When fire becomes visible, the speed of smoke may be over 100 feet per minute.
2. Fire spreads by radiation, known as **radiant plate,** across open and clear spaces in a second.
3. The speed of fire is approximately 15 ft/sec.

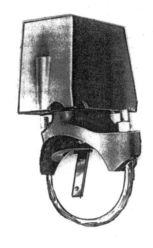

SPOT FIRE DETECTION UNIT
Figure F-4

Courtesy of Armtec/ Meggit Industries

WATERFLOW SWITCH
Figure F-5

Maximum ceiling temperature in degrees F.	Operating temperature in degrees F.	Rating
To 100.............	165	Ordinary
101 to 150..........	212	Intermediate
151 to 225..........	286	Hard
226 to 300..........	360	Extra hard

CLASSIFICATION OF FIRE–DETECTING DEVICES

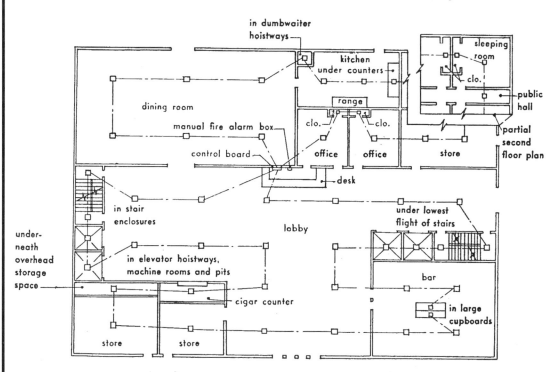

ARRANGEMENT OF FIRE–DETECTING DEVICES

Extracted from the New York State Building Code.

F-3 **FIRE STANDARDS**

The National Fire Protection Association (NFPA) generates standards covering all aspects of fire control. Their standards include over 260 documents.

The most widely used documents include:

1. **National Electric Code (NEC)**
2. **Life Safety Code (LSC)**

The local building department requires either all standards set forth by the NFPA to be followed or, in addition to their own standards, all or parts of standards of NFPA to be followed in the design, construction documents, and construction phases of the building.

F-4 **FIRE AND SMOKE DETECTION**

Immediate detection of fire and smoke in a building is essential. Early detection will prevent loss of life and property. Some of the commonly used fire-detection systems are as follows:

1. ***Automatic fire detection.*** This system is an audible and/or visible alarm: remote, local, or both. This system warns occupants to evacuate the building or to extinguish the fire.

2. ***Heat detector (thermal detector) (Fig. F-1).*** These are the simplest and most reliable fire-detection devices and are commonly used in buildings. They are also known as *temperature detectors.*

3. ***Smoke detector (Fig. F-2).*** When a fire starts before the flames actually surface, smoke is generated. These devices are best suited for areas within a building where an anticipated fire would produce a large column of smoke before the temperature of a fire is sufficient to operate heat detectors.

4. ***Ionization detector (Fig. F-3).*** Ionization detectors sense the products of combustion emitted during the incipient stage of the fire. They are more sensitive than heat and smoke detectors.

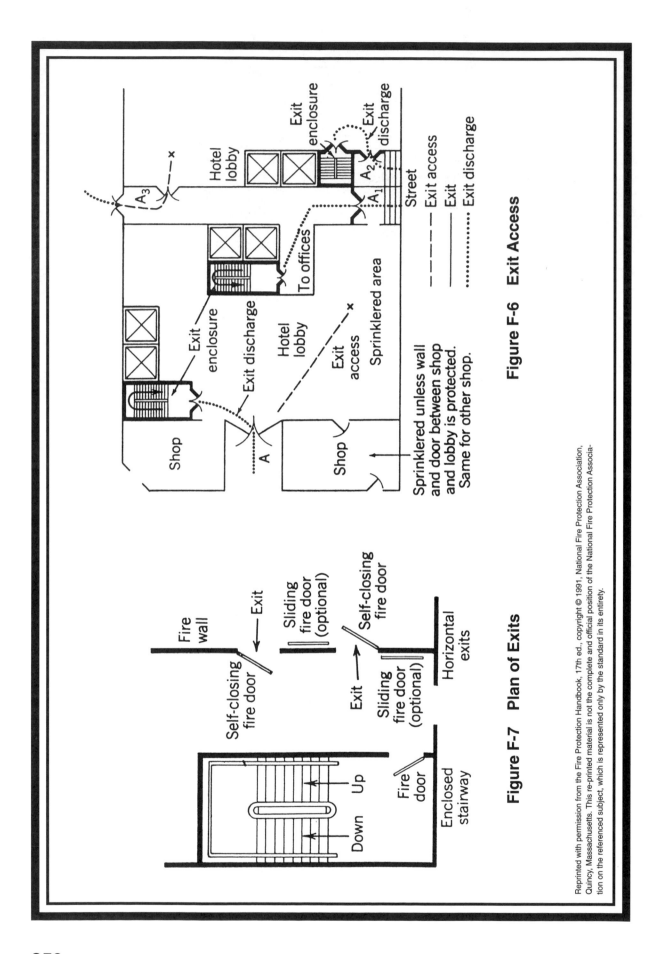

Figure F-6 Exit Access

Sprinklered unless wall and door between shop and lobby is protected. Same for other shop.

- - - - Exit access
——— Exit
· · · · Exit discharge

Figure F-7 Plan of Exits

5. ***Fire detector (flame detector) (Fig. F-4).*** These are the most rapid fire-detection devices available. They respond to the presence of either infrared or ultraviolet radiation, which are the characteristics of a fire.

6. ***Waterflow detectors (Fig. F-5).*** These are alarm-initiating devices used in structures which have complete or partial sprinkler systems.

F-5 FIRE SAFETY ELEMENTS

The main objective of fire safety elements is to prevent the fire from starting. These safety elements are:

1. Control heat-energy sources.

2. Control heat-energy transfer.

3. Control fuel response.

When fire starts in a structure, it must be suppressed and controlled as follows:

1. Detection of fire

2. Communication signals

3. Action to suppress fire

4. Response to site of fire

5. Initiation of suppressant

6. Control of fire from spreading

F-6 PROTECTION OF LIFE

In the case of fire in a building the most important and essential goal is to evacuate the occupants from the premises immediately. For designing a structure, the following guidelines are given for information only. The local code must be followed for the actual design.

1. Clear and define passageway to exit, **"exit access,"** which should be cleared of smoke as much as possible.

2. Exit access, exit enclosure, and exit discharge on the first floor of a multistory building is shown in Fig. F-6.

3. A clear view of exits and enclosed stairways allows occupants of the floors to escape the premises immediately (Fig. F-7).

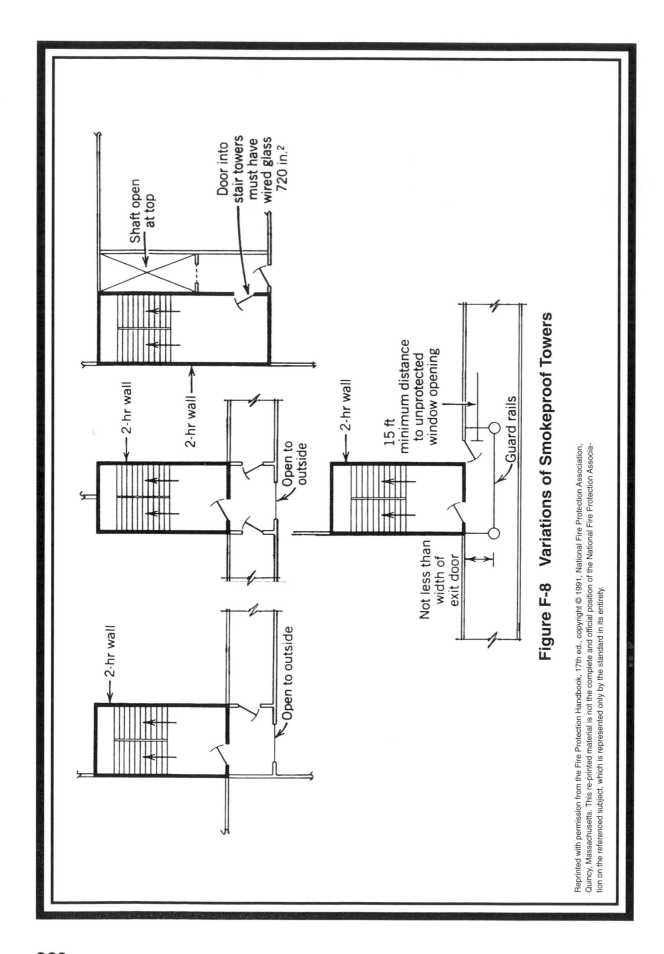

Figure F-8 Variations of Smokeproof Towers

Reprinted with permission from the Fire Protection Handbook, 17th ed., copyright © 1991, National Fire Protection Association, Quincy, Massachusetts. This re-printed material is not the complete and official position of the National Fire Protection Association on the referenced subject, which is represented only by the standard in its entirety.

4. A variation of smokeproof towers is shown in Fig. F-8.

5. The distances to the exits controlled by code are given in Fig. F-9.

6. Summary of "Life Safety Code" provision for occupants' load and capacity of exits is given in Fig. F-10.

7. Requirements for exit stairs are given in Fig. F-11.

8. Fire-rated doors are given in Fig. F-12*a* and rating-glazing requirements are given in Fig. F-12*b.*

Note: Check your local code before using the above figures.

F-7 EXTINGUISHING PROCESS

The most common means of fire suppression is the use of water supplied by

1. **Standpipe systems**

2. **Sprinkler systems**

Water removes the heat from fire and cuts off the oxygen supply from the source of combustion. It absorbs heat energy of the fire as it converts into steam and reduces the temperature of burning materials.

F-8 STANDPIPE SYSTEM

In multistory structures the hose from fire-fighting equipment cannot reach the upper floors; therefore, a standpipe system must be designed for such a structure. A schematic design of a standpipe system is shown in Fig. F-13, and the components for a standpipe system are given in Fig. F-14.

The local code and/or fire marshal specify the required gallons of water reserved in a reservoir for fire fighting and the pressure of water on the lower floors, which are maximum 80 psi.

F-9 SPRINKLER SYSTEM

Automatic sprinkler systems are commonly arranged in a grid pattern close to the ceiling in such a manner that the area which they are serving is fully covered (Fig. F-15).

There are four types of sprinkler systems which are commonly used:

1. ***Wet-pipe.*** The pipes used in areas which are heated in the winter are filled with water.

| Occupancy | Dead-End[a] Limit, Ft | Travel Limit to an Exit, ft | |
		Unsprinklered	Sprinklered
Places of Assembly	20[b]	150	200
Educational	20	150	200
Open plan	N.R.[c]	150	200
Flexible plan	N.R.	150	200
Health Care			
New	30	100	150
Existing	N.R.	100	150
Residential			
Hotels	35	100	150
Apartments	35	100	150
Dormitories	0	100	150
Lodging or rooming houses, 1- and 2-family dwellings	N.R.	N.R.	N.R.
Mercantile			
Class A, B, and C	50	100	150
Open Air	0	N.R.	N.R.
Covered Mall	50	200	300
Business	50	200	300
Industrial			
General, and special purpose	50	100	150[d]
High hazard	0	75	75
Open structures	N.R.	N.R.	N.R.
Storage			
Low	N.R.	N.R.	N.R.
Ordinary hazard	N.R.	200	400
High hazard	0	75	100
Open parking garages	50	200	300
Enclosed parking garages	50	150	200
Aircraft hangars, ground floor	20	Varies[e]	Varies[e]
Aircraft hangars, mezzanine floor	N.R.	75	75
Grain elevators	N.R.	N.R.	N.R.
Miscellaneous occupancies	N.R.	100	150

[a]Dead-end is an extension of a corridor or aisle beyond an exit (or exit access) that forms a pocket in which occupants may be trapped.

[b]In aisles.

[c]No requirement or not applicable.

[d]A special exception is made for one-story, sprinklered, industrial occupancies.

[e]See Paragraph 15–4.2 of Life Safety Code for special requirements.

Figure F-9   Life Safety Code Provisions for Travel Distances to Exits

2. **Dry-pipe.** Used in unheated buildings. The pipes are filled with compressed air or nitrogen. When a sprinkler head opens the water from the heated housing adjacent to the unheated area, it will rush to the open sprinkler head.

3. **Preaction.** Similar to a dry-pipe system except water is admitted to the pipe before any sprinkler head has opened.

5. **Deluge.** In this system, all sprinkler heads go on at the same time.

F-10 SPRINKLER HEADS

Sprinkler heads (Fig. F-16) operate with a heat-sensitive control, as follows:

1. **Metal alloys.** The low-melting metal will open the sprinkler head(s) at a temperature for which they are designed.

2. **Organic liquid contained in a glass.** When heated to certain designed temperatures, the liquid will expand and rupture the glass container and open the sprinkler head(s).

3. **Flow-control sprinkler.** The flow-control will shut off the water in the system when temperature at the ceiling is reduced.

The temperature setting of sprinkler heads should be a minimum of 25°F above the normal temperature of the ceiling.

The temperature setting of ordinary sprinkler heads is between 135 and 170°F, and for areas with high temperatures, between 155 and 355°F. All sprinkler heads should be replaced after they have been opened.

The water pressure in the pipes of a sprinkler system is 175 psi.

F-11 REQUIRED INSTALLATION FOR SPRINKLER SYSTEM

Required installation for sprinkler systems is as follows:

1. Fire department connection on each frontage of the building.

2. All water supplies should have a master alarm valve control.

3. Special firewall dividing protected area as required by the local code.

4. Floor drain as required.

When gravity tanks are used, the amount of water for operating the sprinkler system should be enough to operate 25 percent of the total sprinkler heads for 20 minutes.

Occupancy	Occupant[a] Load — Ft² per Person	Capacity of Exits — Number of Persons per Units of Exit Width[b] — Doors[c] Outside	Horizontal Exit	Ramp Class A	Ramp Class B	Escalator	Stairs
Places of Assembly							
Areas of concentrated use	15 Net	100	100	100	75	75	75
without fixed seating	7 Net						
Standing space	3 Net						
Educational		100	100	100	60		60
Classroom area	20 Net						
Shops and vocational	50 Net						
Day Nurseries with sleeping facilities	35 Net						
Health Care		30	30	30	30		22
Sleeping departments	120 Gross						
Inpatient departments	240 Gross						
Residential		100	100	100	75	75	75
Mercantile	200 Gross	100	100		60	60	60
Street floor and sales							
basement	30 Gross						
Other floors	60 Gross						
Storage-shipping	300 Gross						
Office areas	100 Gross						
Business	100 Gross	100	100	100	60	60	60
Industrial	100 Gross	100	100	100	60	60	60
Detention and Correctional occupancies	120 Gross	100	100	100	100[d] 60[e]		

[a] When actual maximum population count can be determined from plans, it can be substituted for these figures.
[b] An exit width is defined as 22 in.
[c] Not more than three risers or 21 in. above or below grade.
[d] 100 (down).
[e] 60 (up).

Figure F-10 Life Safety Code Provisions for Occupant Load and Capacity of Exits

F-12 OCCUPANCY HAZARD CLASSIFICATION

The purpose of a sprinkler system is the automatic discharge of water in amounts adequate to control the fire.

The areas controlled by sprinkler systems are divided into three categories according to the hazards involved (Fig. F-17):

1. **Light hazards.** Protection area per sprinkler is maximum 200 ft^2 and the distance between supply main and sprinkler and between sprinkler on each line is 15 ft.

2. **Ordinary hazards.** Protection area per sprinkler is maximum 130 ft^2 for noncombustible ceiling and 120 ft^2 for combustible ceiling, and the distance between sprinkler line and between sprinklers on a line is 15 ft.

3. **Extra hazards.** Protection area per sprinkler is maximum 90 ft^2 for noncombustible ceilings and 80 ft^2 for combustible ceilings, and the distance between lines and between sprinklers on a line is 12 ft.

Note: Check your local code before using Fig. F-17.

	New Stairs	Existing Stairs[a]	
		Class A	Class B
Minimum width clear of all obstructions except projections not exceeding 3½ in. at and below handrail height on each side	44 in. 36 in. where total occupant load of all floors served by stairways is less than 50	44 in. 36 in. where total occupant load of all floors served by stairways is less than 50	44 in.
Maximum height of risers	7 in.	10 in.	9 in.
Minimum height of risers	4 in.	7½ in.	8 in.
Minimum tread depth	11 in.		
Winders	See 5-2.2.5.	See 5-2.2.5.	See 5-2.2.5.
Minimum headroom	6 ft 8 in.	6 ft 8 in.	6 ft 8 in.
Maximum height between landings	12 ft	12 ft	12 ft
Minimum dimension of landings in direction of travel	Stairways and intermediate landings shall continue with no decrease in width along the direction of exit travel. In new buildings every landing shall have a dimension, measured in direction of travel, equal to the width of the stair. Such dimension need not exceed 4 ft when the stair has a straight run.		
Doors opening immediately on stairs, without landing at least width of door	No	No	No

[a]Classes A and B are defined as stairs having these dimensional characteristics in *existing* buildings.

Figure F-11   Requirements for Exit Stairs

Class	Rating	Location
A	3 h	Between buildings, or between separate fire areas in a single building
B	1 to 1½ h	Around vertical openings within buildings, such as stairs, elevator shafts, or mechanical chases
C	¾ h	In partitions between corridors and rooms
D	1½ h	Exterior walls with severe fire exposure from outside the building
E	¾ h	Exterior walls with light or moderate fire exposure from outside the building

ªTight-fitting doors will help stop the spread of smoke.

Figure F-12a   Fire-Rated Doors

Excerpted from *Fire Protection Handbook*, NFPA (1976).

A* 3 hr. rating; no glazing permitted.
B* 1 1/2 hr. rating; 100 sq. in. of glazing per door leaf.
C 3/4 hr. rating; max. 1296 sq. in. of glazing per light. Max. dim. per light — 54″.
   Min. dim. per light — 3″.
D 1 1/2 hr. rating; no glazing permitted.

E 3/4 hr. rating; Max. 720 sq. in. of glazing per light. Max. dim. per light — 54″.

*A, B & D doors are available with Heat Transmission Ratings of: 250°F
   650°F
   NOT RATED
*Available on Composite Doors only.

Figure F-12b   Rating-Glazing Requirements

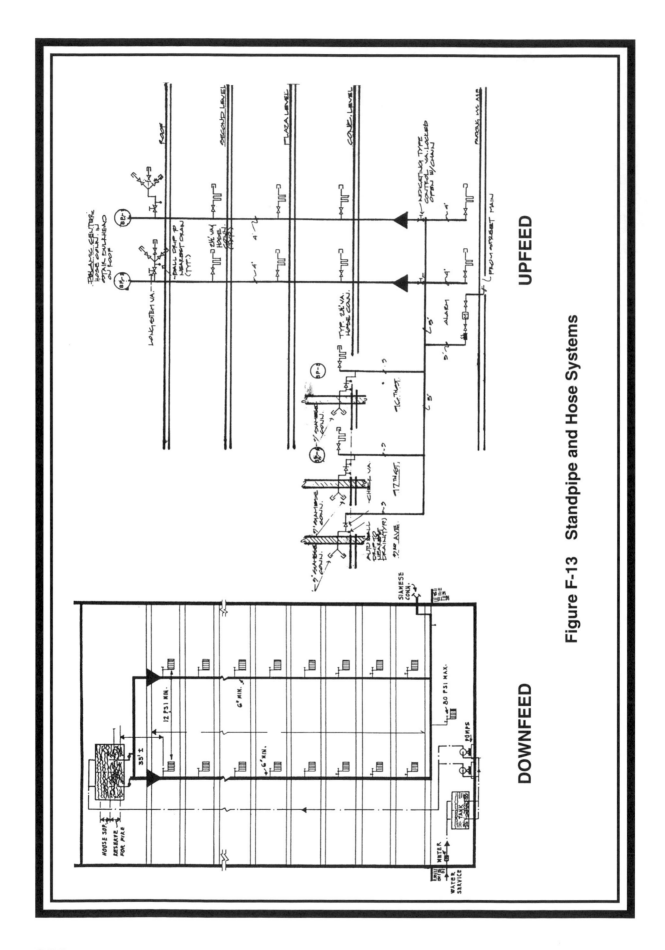

UPFEED

DOWNFEED

Figure F-13   Standpipe and Hose Systems

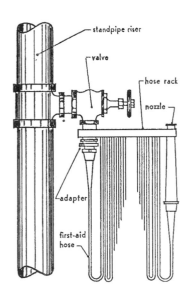

Typical hose 2½" diameter,
nozzle 1⅛", length 50–100 ft.,
200 gpm flow under pressure
by fire engines.

Hose Racks

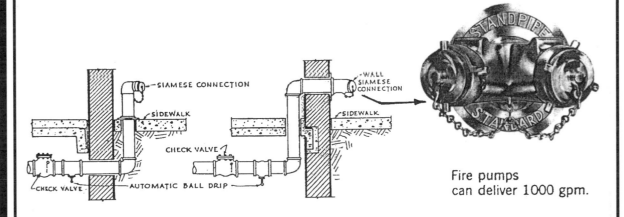

Fire pumps
can deliver 1000 gpm.

Fire Dept. Connection

Components for a Standpipe System

Figure F-14

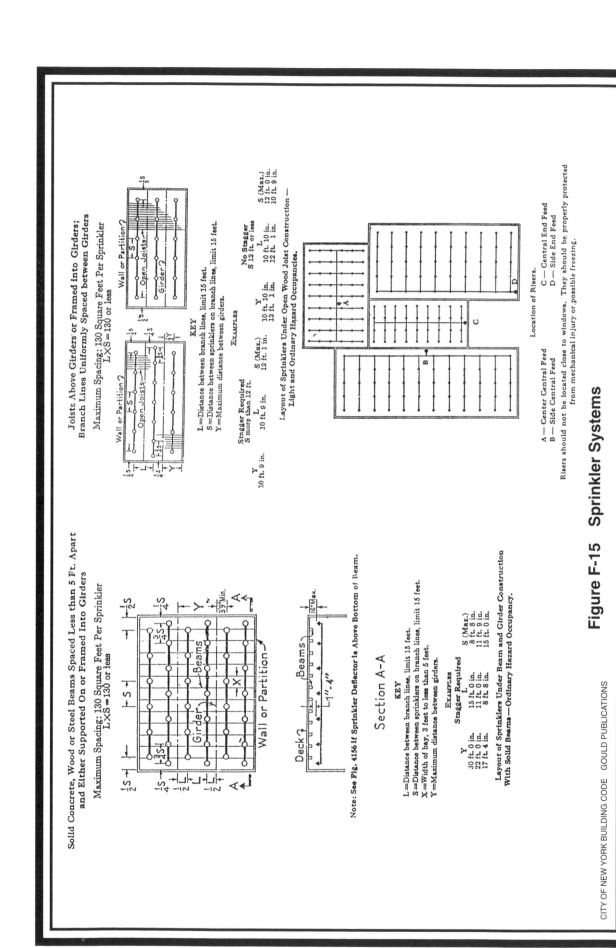

Figure F-15   Sprinkler Systems

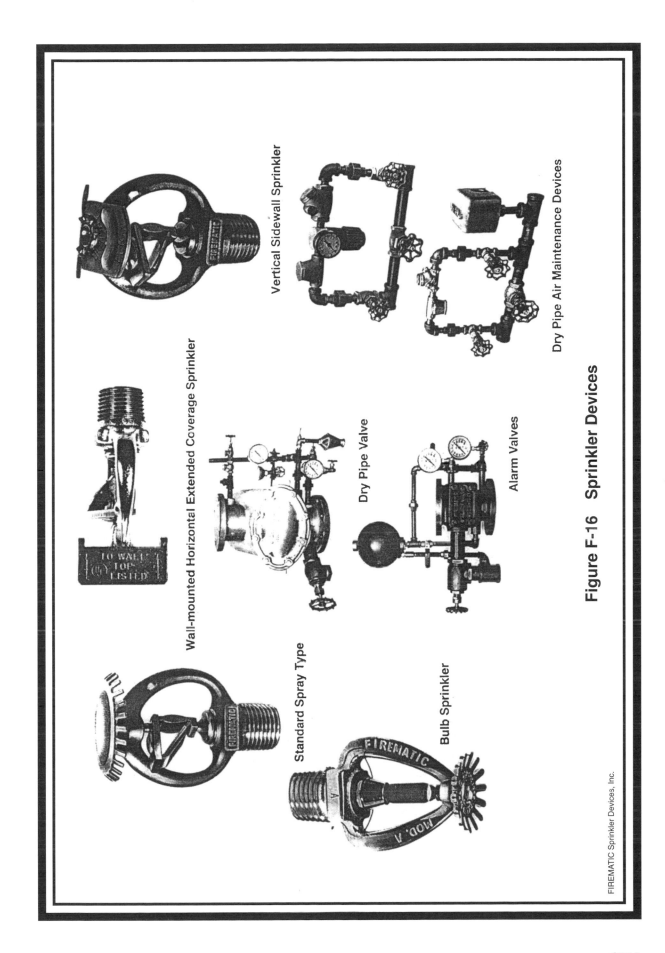

Vertical Sidewall Sprinkler

Dry Pipe Air Maintenance Devices

Wall-mounted Horizontal Extended Coverage Sprinkler

Dry Pipe Valve

Alarm Valves

Standard Spray Type

Bulb Sprinkler

Figure F-16   Sprinkler Devices

FIREMATIC Sprinkler Devices, Inc.

271

Classification of Occupancies

Occupancy classifications for this standard relate to sprinkler installations and their water supplies only. They are not intended to be a general classification of occupancy hazards. Examples listed below represent the norm for those occupancy types; unusual or abnormal fuel loadings or combustible characteristics may affect classification.

Light-Hazard Occupancies

Occupancies or portions of other occupancies where the quantity and/or combustibility of contents is low, and fires with relatively low rates of heat release are expected.

Light hazard occupancies include those having conditions similar to

Churches	Museums
Clubs	Nursing or convalescent homes
Eaves and overhangs (if combustible construction with no combustibles beneath)	
Educational	Office, including data processing
Hospitals	Residential
Institutional	Restaurant seating areas
Libraries, except large stack rooms	Theaters and auditoriums excluding stages and prosceniums
	Unused attics

Ordinary-Hazard Occupancies

Group 1—occupancies or portions of other occupancies where combustibility is low, quantity of combustibles is moderate, stock piles of combustibles do not exceed 8 ft (2.4 m), and fires with moderate rates of heat release are expected.

Group 1 ordinary-hazard occupancies include those having conditions similar to

Automobile parking garages	Electronic plants
Bakeries	Glass and glass products manufacturing
Beverage manufacturing	
Canneries	Laundries
Dairy products manufacturing and processing	Restaurant service areas

Group 2—occupancies or portions of other occupancies where quantity and combustibility of contents is moderate, stock piles do not exceed 12 ft (3.7 m), and fires with moderate rate of heat release are expected.

Group 2 ordinary hazard occupancies include those having conditions similar to

Cereal mills	Machine shops
Chemical plants—ordinary	Metal working
Cold storage warehouses	Mercantiles
Confectionery products	Printing and publishing
Distilleries	Textile manufacturing
Horse stables	Tobacco products manufacturing
Leather goods manufacturing	Wood product assembly
Libraries—large stack room areas	

Figure F-17   Relative Fire Hazard for Various Occupancies, as Related to Sprinkler Installations

Group 3—occupancies or portions of other occupancies where quantity and/or combustibility of contents is high and fires of high rate of heat release are expected.

Group 3 ordinary hazard occupancies include those having conditions similar to

Feed mills
Paper and pulp mills
Paper process plants
Piers and wharves
Repair garages
Tire manufacturing
Warehouses (having moderate to higher combustibility of content, such as
    paper, household furniture, paint, general storage, whiskey, etc.)
Wood machining

Extra-Hazard Occupancies

Occupancies or portions of other occupancies where quantity and combustibility of contents is very high and flammable liquids, dust, lint, or other materials are present, introducing the probability of rapidly developing fires with high rates of heat release.

Group 1—occupancies with little or no flammable or combustible liquids, such as

Combustible hydraulic fluid use areas
Die casting
Metal extruding
Plywood and particle board manufacturing
Printing (using inks with below 100F [37.8°C] flash points)
Rubber reclaiming, compounding, drying, milling, vulcanizing
Saw mills
Textile picking, opening, blending, garnetting, carding, combining of cotton,
    synthetics, wool shoddy or burlap
Upholstering with plastic foams

Group 2—occupancies with moderate to substantial amounts of flammable or combustible liquids, or where shielding of combustibles is extensive, such as

Asphalt saturating
Flammable liquids spraying
Flow coating
Mobile home or modular building assemblies (where finished enclosure is
    present and has combustible interiors)
Open oil quenching
Solvent cleaning
Varnish and paint dipping

Figure F-17(*cont'd*)   Relative Fire Hazard for Various Occupancies, as Related to Sprinkler Installations

CONTENTS

Part 8

BUILDING SERVICES

B

Sanitation and Disease

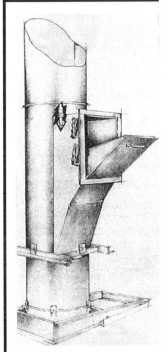

Odor Within the Building

Control and Removal of Waste

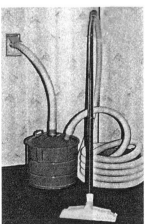

Central Vacuum Cleaning Systems

Snow-Melting Systems

BUILDING SERVICES

SANITATION AND DISEASE

B-1 DISEASE WITHIN THE BUILDINGS

There are many *microorganisms* in building(s) which are associated with infectious diseases.

In order for germs to survive and multiply, the body of a host such as people, animals, insects, and vermin is required.

The body of a host can be a disease carrier without becoming ill itself.

B-2 TRANSFER OF INFECTION IN A BUILDING

1. *Air-borne infection.* A droplet of *nuclei* formed during coughing will contaminate the air. A person inhaling the air can become infected when these nuclei enter his or her upper respiratory tract.

2. *From water and foods.* Infectious bacteria may exist in water and foods.

3. *From germ carriers.* Insects and vermin are germ carriers for diseases such as rabies and yellow fever.

Transfer of diseases may be related to the *character of buildings* we *inhabit*.

B-3 DISINFECTANTS WITHIN A BUILDING

Disinfection is the extermination of the causative microorganisms of disease. A substance which kills bacteria is called a *germicide.* An *antiseptic* is used to stop the growth and spread of germs.

Problem

The ultraviolet rays of the sun are disinfectant. However, some types of glass used in the windows of a building do not allow the sun's ultraviolet rays to penetrate into the structures.

Solution

Ultraviolet lamps have germicidal value and should be used in *air-handling equipment,* especially in *restaurants* and other buildings for disinfection.

Problem

Warmth and dampness contribute to bacteria growth.

Solution

1. Maintain dry surfaces in buildings in order to minimize the bacteria counts on room surfaces.

2. In bathrooms, kitchens, clinics, and hospitals, use smooth and impervious surfaces, as they do not absorb or hold water and are easy to clean.

3. Use light colors and proper and adequate illumination. It will help to observe soiled areas in order to clean them.

4. Proper ventilation in toilet areas not only ensures the dilution of offensive odors, but also helps to create dry conditions, which aids sanitation.

5. Scrubbing the surfaces with soap, etc., and hot water will help to remove bacteria and soiling.

B-4   MOSQUITOES, FLIES, INSECTS, RODENTS, AND VERMIN

Problem

1. Mosquitoes require a small body of water for breeding. A sag or any detail in the flat roof or gutter which can hold water is a good breeding area for mosquitoes.

2. Flies breed on any filth such as garbage or sewage.

3. Insects, rodents, and vermin are germ carriers for diseases such as rabies and yellow fever.

Solution

1. Design the flat roof and gutters, etc., to stay dry after rainfall.

2. Proper sewage and garbage disposal must be maintained inside and outside the building in order to prevent access to the refuse by flies.

3. Screen all openings of the building in order to stop air-borne insects from entering the premises. Use very small screen mesh such as wire cloth of 16-mesh (16 openings per inch).

B-5 COCKROACHES

Problem

Cockroaches or **crawling** insects require dark, damp spaces where food is available, such as cracks in kitchen floors, walls, and cabinets where moisture and food is readily available.

Solution

All spaces in kitchens and storage areas for food should be dry; all cabinetwork should have tight joints. Cold water pipes should be insulated against sweating. All holes in floor and walls of kitchen and food storage areas should be plugged.

B-6 RATS

Problem

Rats can enter into a frame building with ease because they like to gnaw on wood in order to keep their teeth short and sharp. Rats can climb up the rain leaders, pipes, etc., in order to gain entry to the building from high openings.

Solution

1. Foundations must extend a minimum of 2 feet below grade in order to prevent burrowing.
2. The bottom of a stud should be filled with concrete or sealed with metal flashing.
3. Stop rats from reaching food. If the source of food is reduced, the rat population will decrease.
4. Screen all openings with ½-inch hardware cloth in order to prevent rats from entering the building.
5. Use sheet-metal guards on rain leaders, pipes, etc., to stop rats from climbing to the roof.

B-7 TERMITES

Problem

Termites are small, soft-bodied, social insects of the order *Isoptera.* They have chewing mouth parts and undergo a gradual metamorphosis. Termites feed chiefly on the cellulose in wood, which the primitive species converts into sugar. They are either wood dwellers or soil dwellers; the wood dwellers cause approximately $43 million worth of damage annually in the United States. Termites attack only wood that is in contact with the ground or close enough to be reached by making enclosed runways from their underground galleries.

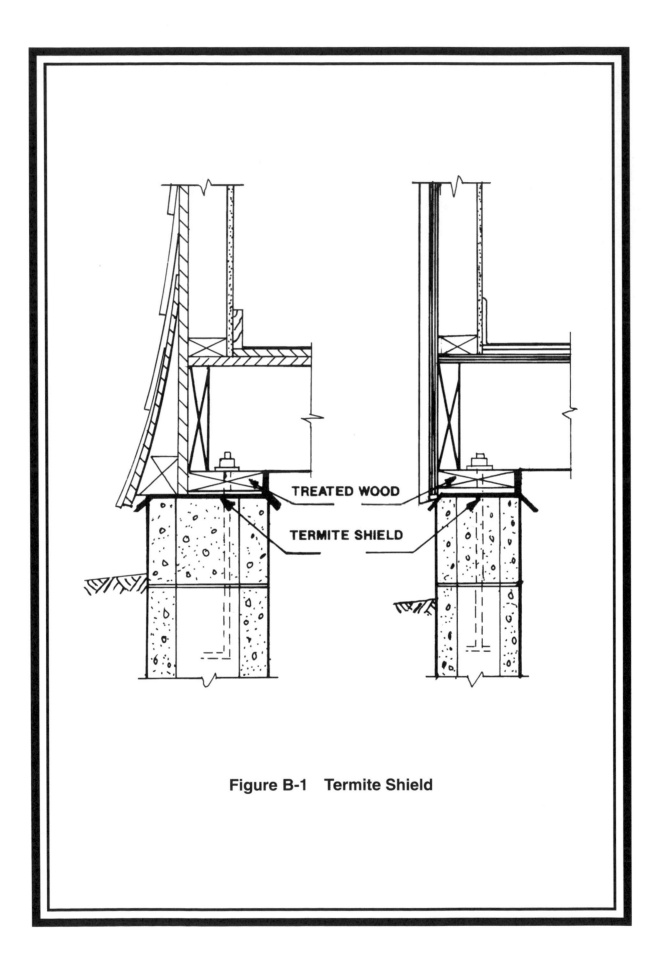

Figure B-1   Termite Shield

Solution

1. Use a concrete foundation.

2. No wood should be near the soil.

3. Use treated wood for that portion of the framing which is in contact with the foundation walls (Fig. B-1).

4. Use a **termite shield** between treated wood sill and foundation wall (Fig. B-1).

5. For more information on prevention and control of termites, see publications of the U.S. Department of Agriculture.

B-8   SANITATION WHERE FOOD IS PROCESSED FOR PUBLIC CONSUMPTION

All areas within a building where food is prepared or processed and served for public consumption must be designed and constructed in accordance with the rules and regulations set forth by public health authorities.

Some of the requirements which have architectural implications are given for information in the following (contact the Department of Health in your area for more up-to-date requirements):

1. Floor, walls, and ceiling must be easily cleaned.

2. They must not be able to absorb odors or dirt.

3. Flooring should be terrazzo, tile, or painted concrete.

4. Use glazed masonry for walls, or enamels and sheet plastic.

5. Use proper and adequate illumination.

6. Proper circulation of air is **required** in these areas; however, **recirculation** of air is **not permitted.**

7. Refrigeration storage is essential to alleviate food spoilage and retard the growth of disease germs.

8. All storage for food must be constructed in such a way as not to allow the entrance of the insects, pests, dust, and other air-borne contamination.

9. Water supply and sewage disposal must meet the requirements set forth by the Department of Health. Garbage must be kept in a separate room.

Note: Other buildings under public health control are (but are not limited to): hospitals, clinics, nursing homes, camps, swimming facilities, health clubs, etc.

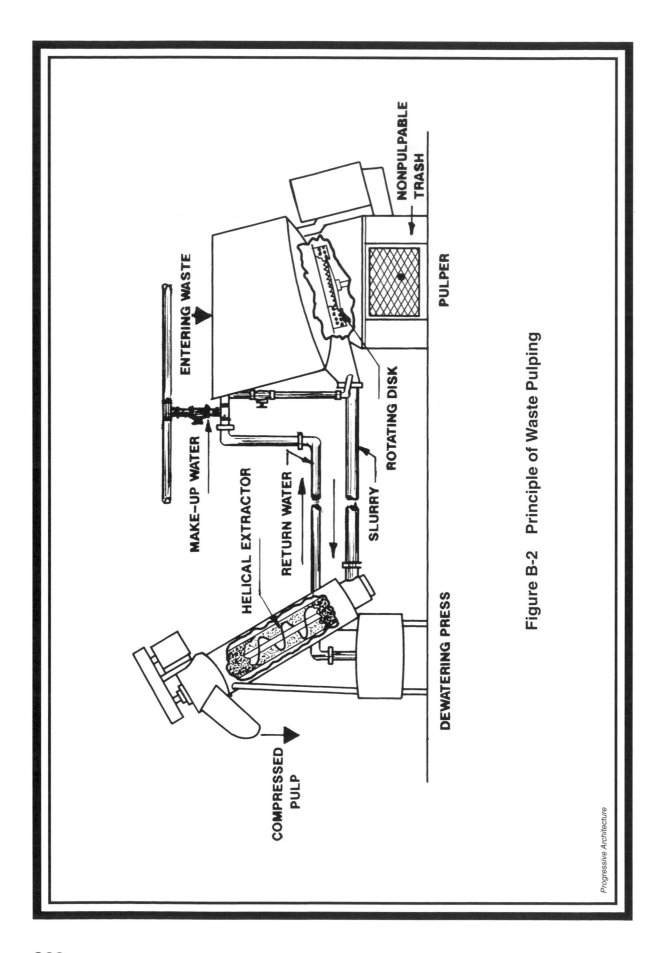

Figure B-2   Principle of Waste Pulping

ENTERING WASTE

NONPULPABLE TRASH

PULPER

MAKE-UP WATER

HELICAL EXTRACTOR

RETURN WATER

ROTATING DISK

SLURRY

DEWATERING PRESS

COMPRESSED PULP

ODOR WITHIN THE BUILDING

B-9   PROPERTY AND QUALITY OF ODOR

A substance must have adequate vapor pressure concentration in the air in order to produce odor.

Odors are usually the compound of sour, fruity, sweet, or rotten substances.

Odor is not visible, even with the strongest microscope, and its weight cannot be measured.

A small amount of odor will have a great environmental impact within a building.

The concentration of vapor pressure of some substances as low as one part in 100 billion will cause an odor.

B-10   CLASSIFICATION OF ODOR

Odors are classified according to the type of building and its characteristics:

1.   Typical inside air

2.   Typical outdoor air

3.   Perfume-type and other distinct pleasant odors

4.   Tobacco smoke and other smoke odor

5.   General industrial contamination

6.   Unburned and partially burned fuel

7.   Solvent vapors

8.   Sulfur dioxide, chlorine, and other acid gases

9.   Hydrogen sulfide, mercaptans, and other organic sulfides

10.   Ammonia, amine, and putrid odors

B-11   CONTAMINATION ODOR

Almost all irritants and toxic substances have odors. If these odors are eliminated, the undesirable vapor and harmful properties of the odor are also eliminated.

Smog, which is covering most of our cities and enters our buildings through ventilation systems or cracks and open windows, is the result of a photochemical reaction between (1) ozone and nitrogen dioxide and (2) hydrocarbons or organic substances.

B-12   MEASUREMENT OF ODOR LEVELS

There are five sensory scales for evaluating odor:

1.   *No odor*

2.   *Threshold level* (T.L.).   Sensation of odor is barely perceptible.

3.   *Definite level* (D.L.)

$$D.L. = T.L. \times 10$$

4.   *Strong level* (S.L.)

$$S.L. = T.L. \times 100$$

5.   *Overpowering level* (O.L.)

$$O.L. = T.L. \times 1000$$

The other scale used for evaluating odor is:

(+1) *Pleasant* to (0) *Not unpleasant* to (−1) *Objectionable*

The *scentometer* developed by the U.S. Public Health Service is used to measure the odor.

B-13   ODOR CONTROL IN BUILDINGS

Odors can be eliminated in a space within the building by the following methods:

1.   Removing the source of odor

2.   Dilution with outside air

3.   Using pleasant odors

4.   Using activated charcoal

Dilution with outside air is the most practical; however, it is expensive because the outside air must be heated in winter and cooled in the summer.

As is stated in G-11, the composition of air consists of 78.09 percent nitrogen, 20.95 percent oxygen, and 0.96 percent other gases.

Since we inhale oxygen and exhale carbon dioxide, we have to replace the stale air (air with little oxygen) created by the inhabitation of buildings with outside air constantly.

It is a good practice to exhaust 25 percent of the return air in an HVAC system and replace it with fresh air. This percentage is reduced in some buildings in order to save energy and, in some cases, oxygen is added to the return air; in this case, activated charcoal is used to eliminate odors.

In every building there are spaces which produce odors—such as kitchens, toilets, and laboratories. The portion of return air from HVAC system which is to be exhausted to outside air is first used to heat or cool these spaces.

Note: The return air from spaces which produce odor ***must*** be exhausted to outside air.

B-14 ODOR CONTROL METHOD

High odor-causing materials such as smoke and concentrations of odorants tend to accumulate on rugs, drapes, cloth, clothing, or surfaces of the room and can be removed only by volatilizing into the air.

The odor control system must continue to function after the odor has disappeared. Some odor control methods are as follows:

1. Scrubbing the areas containing odor with warm water and chemicals such as an alkali
2. Chemical oxidation using potassium permanganate, ozon, or chlorine
3. Absorption in activated charcoal
4. Absorption by an impregnated activated charcoal
5. Particulate filtration to remove odor-carrying particles

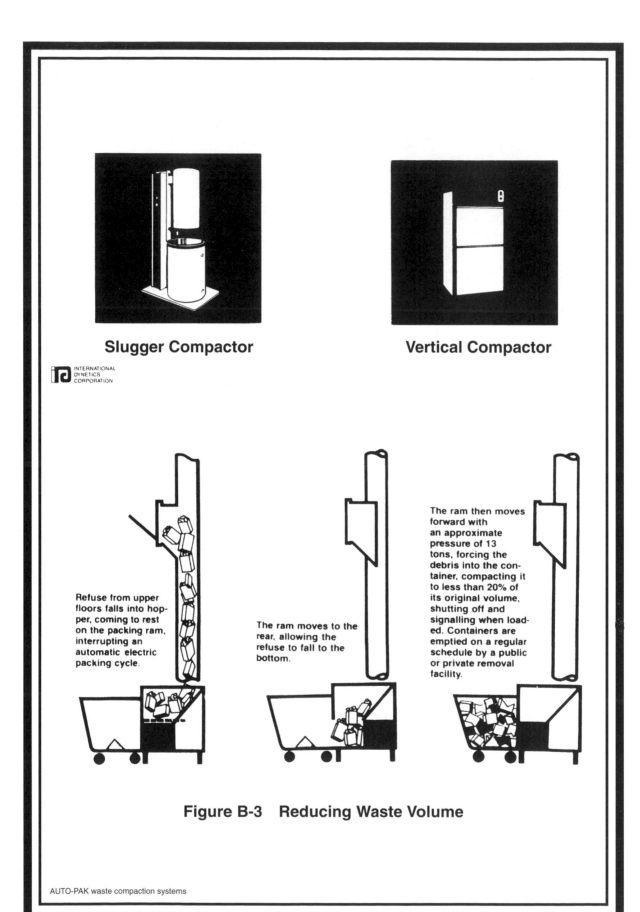

Slugger Compactor

Vertical Compactor

INTERNATIONAL
DYNETICS
CORPORATION

Refuse from upper floors falls into hopper, coming to rest on the packing ram, interrupting an automatic electric packing cycle.

The ram moves to the rear, allowing the refuse to fall to the bottom.

The ram then moves forward with an approximate pressure of 13 tons, forcing the debris into the container, compacting it to less than 20% of its original volume, shutting off and signalling when loaded. Containers are emptied on a regular schedule by a public or private removal facility.

Figure B-3   Reducing Waste Volume

AUTO-PAK waste compaction systems

CONTROL AND REMOVAL OF WASTE FROM BUILDINGS

WASTE WITHIN A BUILDING IS OF TWO TYPES:

1. **Water-borne waste (sewage)**

2. **Waste disposal from buildings (garbage)**

B-15   WATER-BORNE WASTE (SEWAGE)

Wastes include those from the human body, etc., which are disposed through the plumbing drainage system (discussed in Part 3, "Sewage Disposal Systems").

B-16   WASTE DISPOSAL FROM BUILDINGS

A remarkable increase has been taking place since early 1950 in producing packaging containing foods, drinks, household, and other needs. At homes or in buildings, such packaging will turn into waste and must be discharged through

1. **Municipal garbage collection system**

2. **Private garbage collection system**

The estimated refuse produced in different types of buildings is as follows:

1.	Apartments and hotels	2 lb/person/day
2.	Private homes	3 lb/person/day
3.	Restaurants	3 lb/person/day
4.	Hospitals	6½ lb/bed/day
5.	Schools	½ lb/student/day
6.	Office buildings	1 lb/100 sq. ft./day
7.	Cities and towns	3 lb/capita/day

B-17   PROBLEMS CREATED BY WASTE DISPOSAL

Case 1.   The population of New York City is approximately 8 million. The amount of garbage produced in New York City, using estimated refuse produced at 3 lb per capita per day:

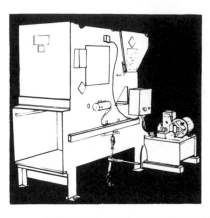

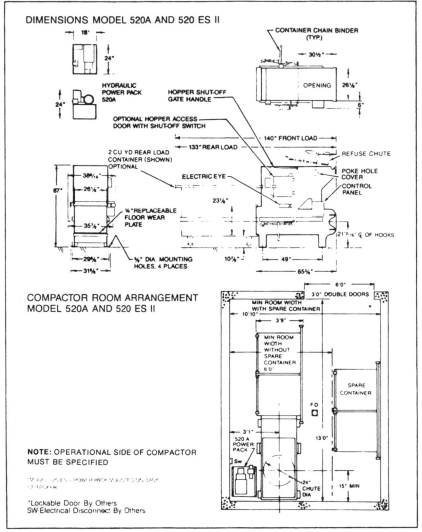

DIMENSIONS MODEL 520A AND 520 ES II

HYDRAULIC POWER PACK 520A

CONTAINER CHAIN BINDER (TYP.)

HOPPER SHUT-OFF GATE HANDLE

OPTIONAL HOPPER ACCESS DOOR WITH SHUT-OFF SWITCH

2 CU YD REAR LOAD CONTAINER (SHOWN) OPTIONAL

ELECTRIC EYE

¼ "REPLACEABLE FLOOR WEAR PLATE

⅝ " DIA. MOUNTING HOLES, 4 PLACES

OPENING

140" FRONT LOAD

133" REAR LOAD

REFUSE CHUTE

POKE HOLE COVER

CONTROL PANEL

C OF HOOKS

COMPACTOR ROOM ARRANGEMENT
MODEL 520A AND 520 ES II

MIN ROOM WIDTH WITH SPARE CONTAINER

MIN ROOM WIDTH WITHOUT SPARE CONTAINER

SPARE CONTAINER

3'0" DOUBLE DOORS

F D

520 A POWER PACK

SW

24" CHUTE DIA

15" MIN

NOTE: OPERATIONAL SIDE OF COMPACTOR
MUST BE SPECIFIED

*Lockable Door By Others
SW-Electrical Disconnect By Others

Figure B-4   Container Packer Compactor

INTERNATIONAL
DYNETICS
CORPORATION

$$8{,}000{,}000 \text{ c} \times 3 \text{ lb/c/d} = 24{,}000{,}000 \text{ lb/d}$$

$$24{,}000{,}000 \text{ lb/d} \div 2000 \text{ lb/t} = 12{,}000 \text{ t/d}$$

$$12{,}000 \text{ t/d} \times 365 \text{ d/y} = 438{,}000 \text{ tons of refuse per year}$$

lb = pound, c = capita, d = day, t = ton, y = year

Case 2. The total population of the United States is well over 250 million. Using this figure to calculate the amount of garbage and waste produced by all Americans:

$$250{,}000{,}000 \text{ c} \times 3 \text{ lb/c/d} = 750{,}000{,}000 \text{ lb/d}$$

$$750{,}000{,}000 \text{ lb/d} \div 2000 \text{ lb/t} = 375{,}000 \text{ t/d}$$

$$375{,}000 \text{ t/d} \times 365 \text{ d/y} = 136{,}875{,}000 \text{ tons of refuse per year}$$

The above two cases demonstrate that the accumulation of garbage and waste materials is capable of covering a good portion of our beautiful earth in less than 100 years if we continue to *abuse our* **environment.**

B-18   SOLUTION TO PROBLEMS OF WASTE DISPOSAL

The garbage and waste from buildings contain important resources, and we can help our environment and future generations by recovering those resources instead of burying them In landfills.

All garbage and waste contains:

1.   **Recyclable materials (B-19)**
2.   **Nonrecyclable materials (B-20)**

It is a **must** to separate **recyclable** from **nonrecyclable** waste in order to save energy and raw materials and, above all, to reduce the amount and volume of landfill.

B-19   RECYCLABLE MATERIALS

Recyclable materials include:

a.   ***Aluminum.***   Includes aluminum cans, foil, packaging, etc. The recovery of aluminum from waste saves over 90 percent of the energy needed to produce it in the first place. Production of aluminum is dependent upon electricity; recycling allows saving electrical energy and conservation of raw materials.

SERIES	INDUSTRIAL		HEAVY INDUSTRIAL		
PACKER MODEL	820	2144 HB	2560 HB	3885 H	5085 H
1. Standard Manufacturers' Rating	.75 cu. yds.	2.1 cu. yds.	2.5 cu. yds.	3.8 cu. yds.	5 cu. yds.
2. Rated Motor	5 hp 208V 3 ph 1725 rpm	10 hp 208V 3 ph 1725 rpm	10 hp 208V 3 ph 1725 rpm	20 hp 208V 3 ph 1725 rpm	30 hp 208V 3 ph 1725 rpm
3. Volumetric Compaction Rate	70 cu. yds./hr.	150 cu. yds./hr.	115 cu. yds./hr.	194 cu. yds./hr.	246 cu. yds./hr.
4. Cycle Time	19 seconds	31 seconds	51 seconds	39 seconds	39 seconds
5. Force Rating (ram face pressure) (Maximum)	35.4 lbs./sq. in.	26.2 lbs./sq. in.	40.9 lbs./sq. in.	47.1 lbs./sq. in.	47.1 lbs./sq. in.
6. Total packing Force (Maximum)	21,210 lbs.	37,700 lbs.	58,900 lbs.	84,700 lbs.	84,700 lbs.
7. Clear Top Opening	28.5" Wide × 25.938" Long	58" Wide × 39" Long	58" Wide × 39" Long	58.5" Wide × 48" Long	59" Wide × 60" Long
8. Chamber Length	26.312"	42"	42"	54.5"	68.5"
9. Ram Stroke (Maximum)	36"	51"	51"	74"	88"
10. Ram Penetration	9.687"	13"	13"	19.5"	19.5"
11. Discharge Opening	30¼" Wide × 27³⁄₁₆" High	62" Wide × 34" High	62" Wide × 34" High	60½" Wide × 40⁹⁄₁₆" High	60⅜" Wide × 40⁹⁄₁₆" High
12. Ground Height to Packer Floor	12³⁄₁₆"	16"	16"	15¹⁵⁄₁₆"	15¹⁵⁄₁₆"
13. Ram Face	30" Wide × 20" High	60" Wide × 24" High	60" Wide × 24" High	60" Wide × 30" High	60" Wide × 30" High

All Packer Installations Require Safety Disconnect per National Electrical & Local Codes (Supplied by Others).

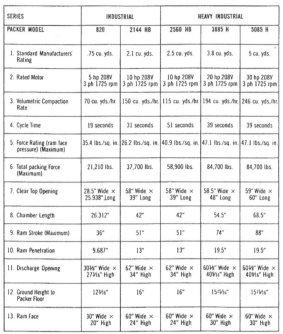

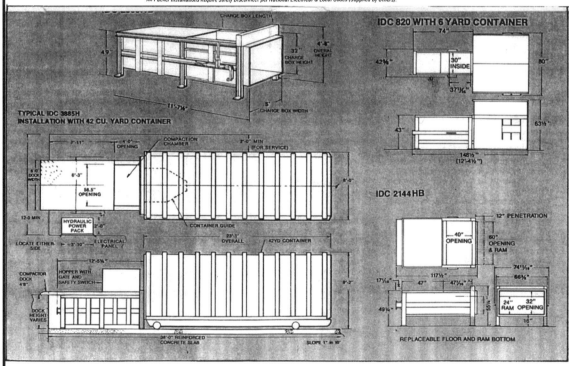

Figure B-5   Stationary Packers

b. **_Paper products._** Includes newspapers, magazines, paper bags, paperboards, etc. The recovery of paper products from waste saves over 50 percent of the energy required for pulp from virgin materials.

c. **_Steel._** Includes steel cans, packaging, etc. The recovery of steel from waste saves over 54 percent of energy in comparison to the use of raw materials.

d. **_Plastics._** Includes plastic bottles, cans, containers, etc. Recycled plastic cannot be used for food-related items according to USFDA regulations, but it can be used for building materials, sports, and toy products, etc.

B-20 NONRECYCLABLE MATERIALS

The nonrecyclable materials of garbage and waste can be used in the following ways:

1. **To produce heat energy (B-21)**
2. **For proper landfill (B-22)**

B-21 TO PRODUCE HEAT ENERGY

The recovery of heat energy from garbage and waste creates air pollution problems, but if it is done properly by use of required filters, It will save energy. For example:

Heating Value of Garbage and Waste

Mixture	Moisture contents	Btu/lb
Highly combustible	10%	8,500
Combustible	25%	6,500
Residential garbage	50%	4,300
Restaurants, hospitals, markets garbage	70%	2,500

B-22 FOR PROPER LANDFILL

To prepare the nonrecyclable portion of the garbage and waste, there are three systems which can be used:

1. **Incineration (B-23)**

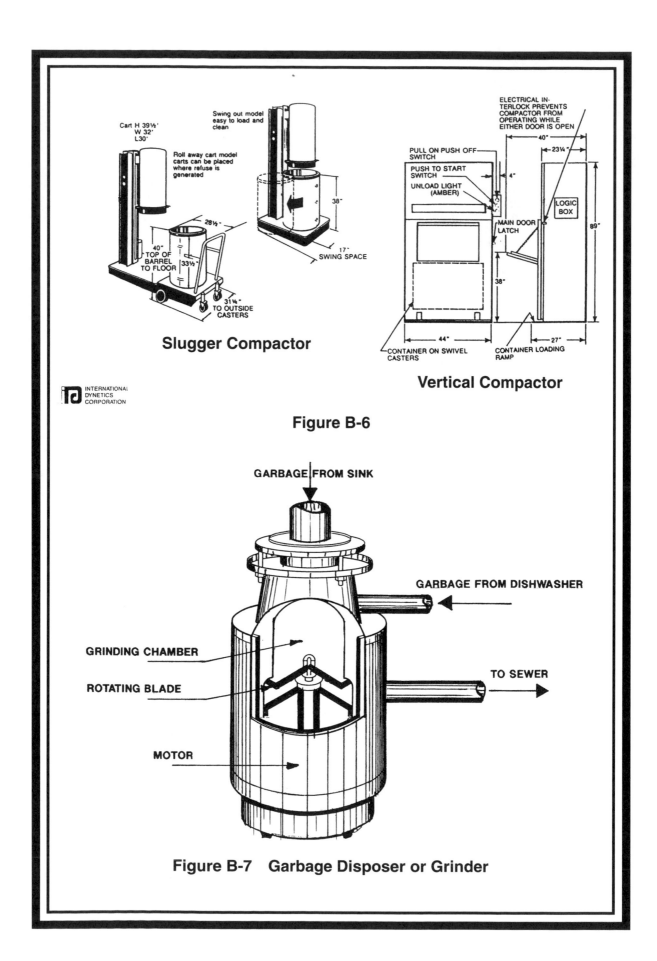

Slugger Compactor

Cart H 39½'
W 32'
L30'

Swing out model easy to load and clean

Roll away cart model carts can be placed where refuse is generated

38"

28½"

17"
SWING SPACE

40"
TOP OF BARREL TO FLOOR

33½"

31¼"
TO OUTSIDE CASTERS

INTERNATIONAL DYNETICS CORPORATION

Vertical Compactor

ELECTRICAL INTERLOCK PREVENTS COMPACTOR FROM OPERATING WHILE EITHER DOOR IS OPEN

40"

23¼"

PULL ON PUSH OFF SWITCH

PUSH TO START SWITCH

4"

UNLOAD LIGHT (AMBER)

LOGIC BOX

89"

MAIN DOOR LATCH

38"

44"

27"

CONTAINER ON SWIVEL CASTERS

CONTAINER LOADING RAMP

Figure B-6

GARBAGE FROM SINK

GARBAGE FROM DISHWASHER

GRINDING CHAMBER

TO SEWER

ROTATING BLADE

MOTOR

Figure B-7   Garbage Disposer or Grinder

2.   **Pulping of soil waste (B-24)**

   3.   **Compacting the waste (B-25)**

B-23   INCINERATION

Incineration is used to burn garbage and waste within the building in order to reduce its volume to ashes. This process causes additional problems of *air pollution.*

The ordinances in many cities, towns and villages throughout the country *do not allow* the use of incinerators, or their use is strongly restricted.

B-24   PULPING OF SOIL WASTE

Waste pulping is a relatively new system used to reduce the volume of nonrecyclable garbage and waste in buildings.

Pulping systems are designed in a variety of forms, shapes, and capacities; however, they operate on the same principal, as follows (Fig. B-2):

   1.   A rotating disk tears up the garbage in a bath of recirculated water.

   2.   The result is moved to the dewatering press where the rotating extractor squeezes the wet mass upward to eliminate 90 percent of its water.

   3.   The squeezed-out water is returned to a rotating disk and makeup water is added from the domestic water system.

   4.   A dewatering press squeezes waste which is almost dry, with only 20 percent of its original volume ready for landfill.

B-25   COMPACTING THE WASTE

The manufacturing of automatic waste compactors started in mid-1950. Today they are available through a nationwide organization of sales and installation specialists.

They are available in small sizes (1½ cu. ft.) to be used in the kitchen of a house, and on up to large, heavy industrial sizes (5 cu. yd.) (Figs. B-3 and B-4).

They are able to reduce the volume of nonrecyclable garbage and waste to 10 percent of its original volume. For multistory buildings, a *chute* is used for either automatic or manual operations (Fig. B-5).

293

Compactors are noisy, and they should be equipped with built-in sprays for both disinfecting and fire control.

A floor drain should be provided next to a compactor with a water hose for washing and cleaning the compactor.

B-26   GARBAGE AND WASTE IN SMALL BUILDINGS

In a residential or small building, recycling waste materials *must* be separated from the garbage and waste, ready for pickup separately.

Nonrecyclable garbage can be handled in three different ways:

1.   *Garbage cans* are the most commonly used method to move the garbage to the area where it is to be picked up by a municipal or private garbage collection system.

2.   *Garbage compactor.*   Placed under the counter or in a convenient place in or next to the kitchen, the compactor reduces the volume of garbage to approximately 10 to 20 percent of its original volume (Fig. B-6). The compactor must be equipped with a disinfecting spray control.

3.   *Garbage disposer.*   Also called a *garbage grinder,* a garbage disposer can be located under the sink and requires water and electricity. The water must be kept running during the grinding process. Approximately 4 gallons of water are required per minute of operation. This discharge of grounded waste is connected to the sewer system of the building (Fig. B-7).

Note: Many municipalities do not allow the discharge from garbage disposers to sewer mains.

If the house has a septic system, the Department of Health requires a larger septic tank. In this case, it really does not make sense to grind the garbage and send it to the septic tank and to create additional expenses to truck it out.

CENTRAL VACUUM CLEANING SYSTEMS

B-27   VACUUM CLEANING SYSTEM

This is the most effective system for cleaning many types of buildings, such as hotels, motels, institutional, and residential. It is more practical and safer than the portable type of vacuum cleaners and has a longer service life.

The system consists of:

1.   **Centrally located power vacuum unit (B-28)**
2.   **Distribution piping (B-29)**
3.   **Electrical requirements (B-30)**
4.   **Hose (B-31)**

B-28   CENTRALLY LOCATED POWER VACUUM UNIT

The power vacuum unit should be located at the center of the operation in the basement or utility space in an area which allows the exhaust air from the unit to be delivered to the outside air.

These units are available in many sizes with capacities for use in different applications. The smallest ones have a dirt capacity of 5 quarts at 95 CFM with 2-in. piping and the largest ones have a dirt capacity of 170 quarts at 350 CFM with 3-in. piping (Fig. B-8). CFM = cubic feet per minute.

B-29   DISTRIBUTION PIPING

Polyvinyl chloride (PVC) plastic piping and fittings are used to avoid corrosion. The plastic pipe size used is 2 inches for a dirt capacity of up to 27 quarts at 190 CFM, and 3 inches for a larger capacity (Fig. B-9).

B-30   ELECTRICAL REQUIREMENTS

The power vacuum unit has its own thermal overload fuse and switch.

The input power requirement is from 1 to 3 H.P. A separate circuit of 10 to 15 amp should be provided for small units, and 20 to 30 amp for the larger units.

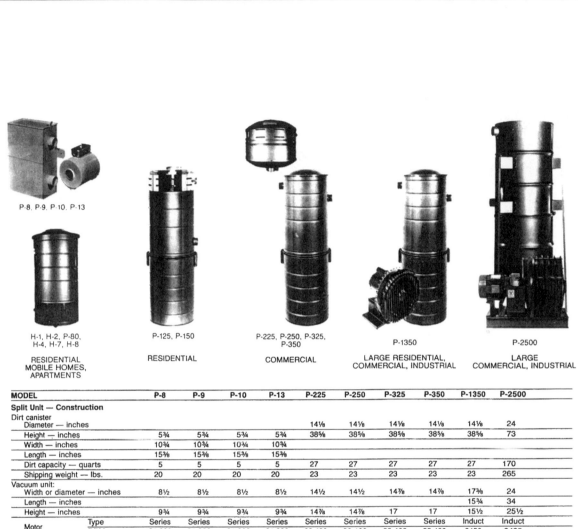

P-8, P-9, P-10, P-13

H-1, H-2, P-80,
H-4, H-7, H-8

RESIDENTIAL
MOBILE HOMES,
APARTMENTS

P-125, P-150

RESIDENTIAL

P-225, P-250, P-325,
P-350

COMMERCIAL

P-1350

LARGE RESIDENTIAL,
COMMERCIAL, INDUSTRIAL

P-2500

LARGE
COMMERCIAL, INDUSTRIAL

MODEL		P-8	P-9	P-10	P-13	P-225	P-250	P-325	P-350	P-1350	P-2500
Split Unit — Construction											
Dirt canister											
Diameter — inches						14⅛	14⅛	14⅛	14⅛	14⅛	24
Height — inches		5¾	5¾	5¾	5¾	38⅝	38⅝	38⅝	38⅝	38⅝	73
Width — inches		10¾	10¾	10¾	10¾						
Length — inches		15⅜	15⅜	15⅜	15⅜						
Dirt capacity — quarts		5	5	5	5	27	27	27	27	27	170
Shipping weight — lbs.		20	20	20	20	23	23	23	23	23	265
Vacuum unit:											
Width or diameter — inches		8½	8½	8½	8½	14½	14½	14⅞	14⅞	17⅜	24
Length — inches										15¾	34
Height — inches		9¾	9¾	9¾	9¾	14⅞	14⅞	17	17	15½	25½
Motor	Type	Series	Series	Series	Series	Series	Series	Series	Series	Induct	Induct
	RPM	21,000	21,000	21,000	21,000	22,400	22,400	22,400	22,400	3450	3495
Single	Voltage	250	250	120	120	120	250	120	250	230	
Phase	Amperage	3.1	3.1	6.3	6.3	11.5	6	21*	11*	16.6	
3-Phase	208V									10.6	24.8
Amperage	230V									9.6	21.6
at	460V									4.8	10.8
Sealed vacuum inches H₂O		90	90	90	90	110	110	110	110	110	100
CFM @ 2″ opening		95	95	95	95	110	110	200	175	190	350**
Type of filtration		Paper Bag	Paper Bag	Paper Bag	Paper Bag	Cyclone Sep.	Cyclone Sep.	Cyclone Sep.	Cyclone Sep.	Cyclone Sep.	Cyclone Sep.
Shipping weight — lbs.		12	14	12	14	27	27	40	40	109	360
Remote control circuit 24 volt		No	Yes	No	Yes	Yes	Yes	Yes	Yes	Yes	Yes

*Double Motor
**3″ Opening

Figure B-8   Vacuum Systems Selections

Vacu-Maid, Inc.

A system of low-voltage (24 V) wiring is used to provide open terminals at each hose station (Fig. B-9). When a metal cylinder at the end of the hose is inserted into the hole, it activates the switch and the vacuum unit starts to operate. HP = horsepower (746 watt), amp = ampere, V = volt.

B-31   THE HOSE

The hose used for a vacuum cleaner is a durable, lightweight plastic type, 25 to 30 ft in length and weighing approximately 5½ lb. (Fig. B-10).

B-32   SYSTEM PLANNING

First, prepare a preliminary design by using the floor plan of the building.

1. Indicate the areas to be vacuumed.
2. Locate the power vacuum unit at the center of the plan in a utility room or, if a basement is available, place the unit in the basement.
3. The location of the vacuum unit **must** allow the exhaust air from the unit to be discharged to the outside air.
4. The vacuum unit can be wall-mounted or freestanding.
5. The dirt canister must be accessible for emptying; it may be separated from the power unit and placed at the same location.
6. Draw a radius of 30 feet around the plug-in station; this is the range of a 28-foot hose which can be extended to 30 feet (Fig. B-11).
7. Use 2-in. PVC plastic piping (tubing) and fitting, which can fit easily in a 3⅝-in. space in the stud walls.
8. Tubing runs and fittings may run under floors, in walls, attic, or poured concrete, or they may be placed in masonry walls.
9. Use a short-radius fitting behind each inlet to block accidental pickup of large objects. All other fittings should have a large radius to prevent clogging.

After the preliminary design is completed, prepare a working drawing for the construction phase.

Typical industrial vacuum system specifications are available through the manufacturers.

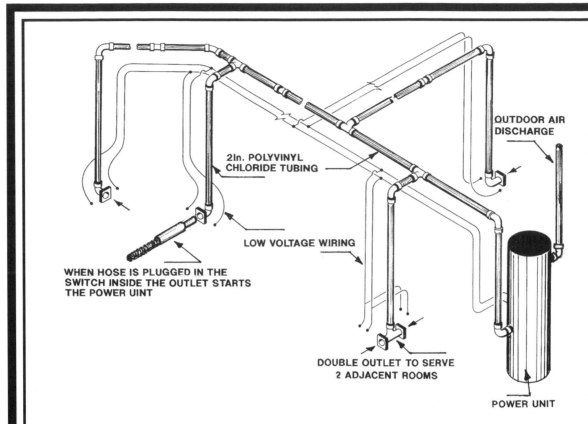

2In. POLYVINYL
CHLORIDE TUBING

OUTDOOR AIR
DISCHARGE

LOW VOLTAGE WIRING

WHEN HOSE IS PLUGGED IN THE
SWITCH INSIDE THE OUTLET STARTS
THE POWER UINT

DOUBLE OUTLET TO SERVE
2 ADJACENT ROOMS

POWER UNIT

Figure B-9   Principle of a Built-in Vacuum Cleaning System

Nautilus Industries, Inc.

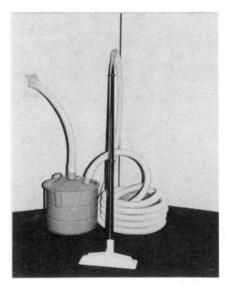

WET PICK-UP KIT

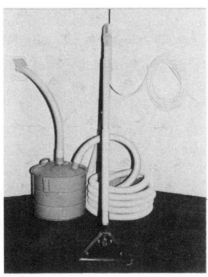

HOT WATER EXTRACTION CARPET
CLEANING KIT

Figure B-10

Vacu-Maid, Inc.

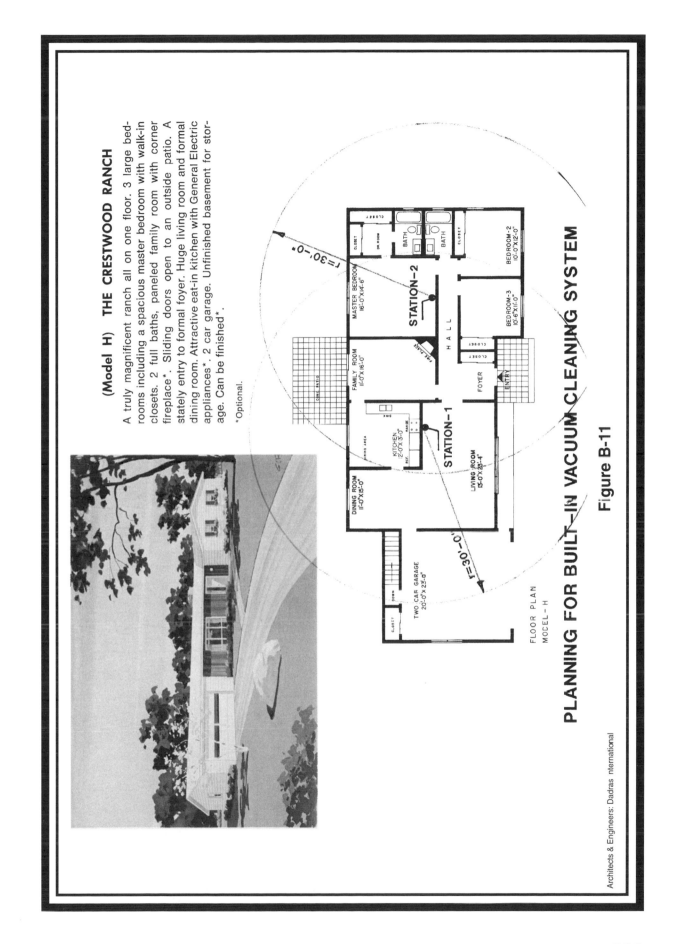

(Model H) THE CRESTWOOD RANCH

A truly magnificent ranch all on one floor. 3 large bedrooms including a spacious master bedroom with walk-in closets. 2 full baths, paneled family room with corner fireplace*. Sliding doors open to an outside patio. A stately entry to formal foyer. Huge living room and formal dining room. Attractive eat-in kitchen with General Electric appliances*. 2 car garage. Unfinished basement for storage. Can be finished*.

*Optional.

FLOOR PLAN
MODEL – H

PLANNING FOR BUILT-IN VACUUM CLEANING SYSTEM

Figure B-11

Architects & Engineers: Dadras International

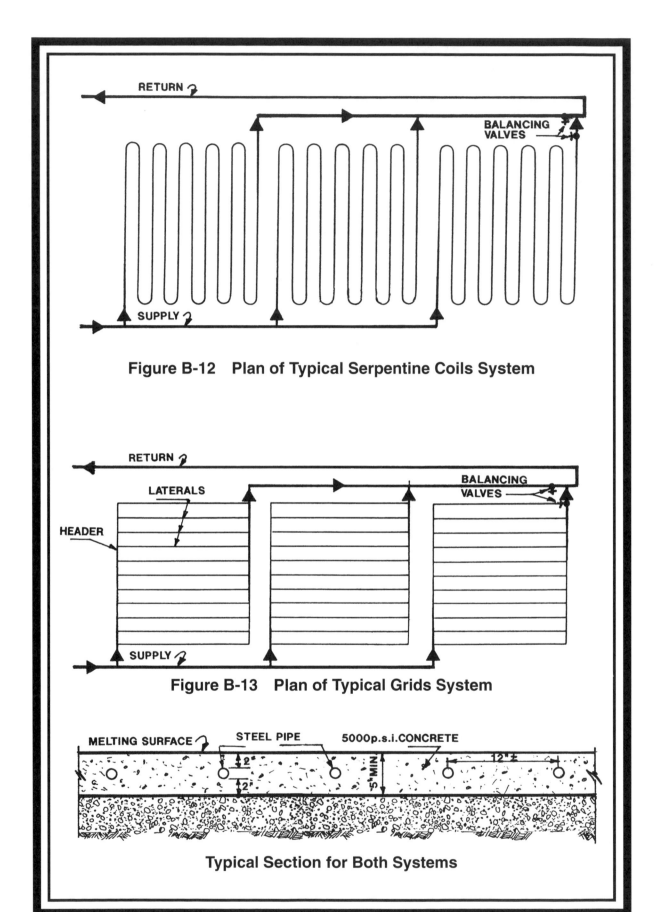

Figure B-12   Plan of Typical Serpentine Coils System

Figure B-13   Plan of Typical Grids System

Typical Section for Both Systems

SNOW-MELTING SYSTEMS

B-33   SNOW-MELTING SYSTEM APPLICATION

The snow can be cleared away (with difficulty) from walks and paved areas; however, the accumulation of snow next to a cleared area creates problems. In some cases, it has to be trucked away at a high cost.

A snow-melting system is used to warm the concrete slab in order to melt all the snow and ice on the sidewalks, paved areas around the buildings, balconies, etc.

The **thermal power** output for **snow melting** is 50 to 425 Btuh per sq. ft. of concrete paved area, depending on where the project is located. The factors governing the exact thermal power output are wind, temperature, humidity, the rate of snowfall, and heat-loss factors.

For example, 300 Btuh per sq. ft. is adequate heat to melt the snow in the New York City area.

There are two methods used for snow melting:

1.   **Snow-melting system by hot water panels (B-34)**

2.   **Snow-melting system by electric energy (B-35)**

In principle, a snow-melting system by electricity performs the same function as a snow-melting system by the hot water system. The cost factor, advantages and disadvantages of both systems must be evaluated before the choice is made.

B-34   SNOW-MELTING SYSTEM BY HOT WATER PANELS

The most effective design is not only to melt the snow, but also to keep the area *dry* in order to prevent the accumulation of ice.

Design Criteria

a.   Panels may be designed in two different ways:

    1. Serpentine coils design (Fig. B-12)

    2. Grids design (Fig. B13)

       Grids design is a better choice because of the many paths of flow in each grid. Also, it offers:

         1. Lower fluid friction in the pipe

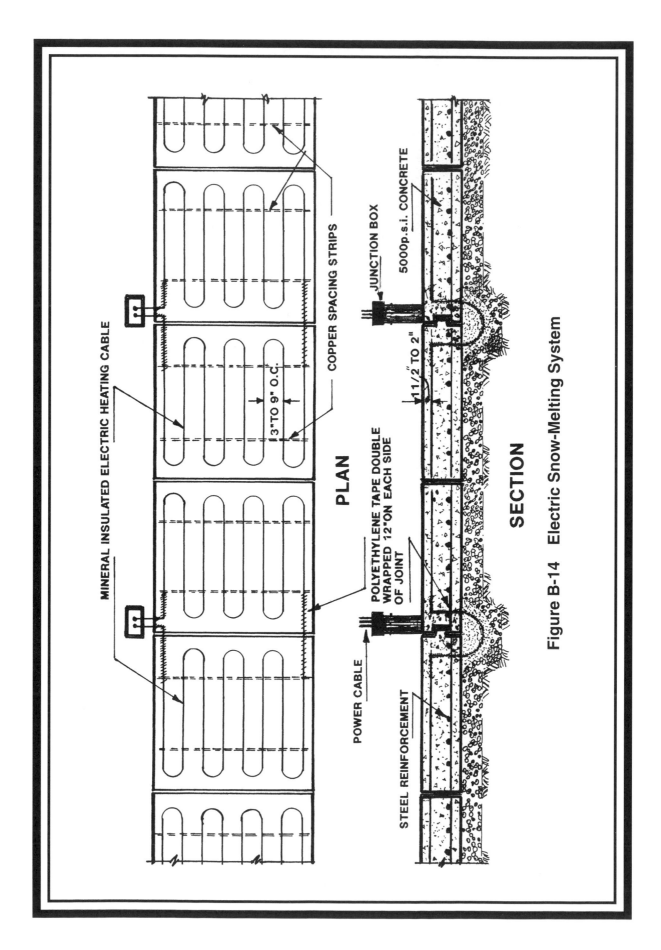

MINERAL INSULATED ELECTRIC HEATING CABLE

COPPER SPACING STRIPS

3" TO 9" O.C.

PLAN

JUNCTION BOX

5000 p.s.i. CONCRETE

1 1/2" TO 2"

POWER CABLE

POLYETHYLENE TAPE DOUBLE WRAPPED 12" ON EACH SIDE OF JOINT

STEEL REINFORCEMENT

SECTION

Figure B-14   Electric Snow-Melting System

2. Reduced circulating pump size

3. Lower energy used for pumping

b. There are three types of metals which can be considered for piping and fittings:

1. Steel is the best choice.

2. Wrought iron is good but it is more expensive.

3. Copper is not strong and rugged enough for this type of work.

c. Concrete slab used: Concrete slabs for the walks are 5 in. thick and should be dense concrete (5000 PSI).

d. Placing the panels (pipes) in the concrete: The pipes should be placed 2 in. below the surface and 12 in. center to center. They should be Schedule 80 steel pipe. The headers are 1½ in. in diameter and the lateral pipes ¾ in. (Fig. B-13). The pipes must be supported in place as the concrete is cast.

e. Testing the pipes and fitting: Testing of pipes and fitting must be done before casting concrete in place as follows:

1. Use nitrogen under 250 psi pressure over a period of 12 hours.

2. During the testing, a soap solution should be used to check for leaks.

3. Solution temperature should be 190°F.

4. All pipes should be kept under pressure during the concreting and continue for a least 36 hours after the concrete is poured.

f. Place valves at all low points for drainage, and use air vents at all high points to free the system from air.

g. A mixture of water and antifreeze, "**ethylene glycol,**" is used in the system to prevent freezing.

h. A separate hot water boiler is used for this type of operation.

B-35 SNOW-MELTING SYSTEM BY ELECTRICITY

Design Criteria

a. The concrete slab used for the walks should be a minimum of 5 inches thick and shall be dense reinforced concrete (5000 psi).

b. Resistance heating elements in concrete slab are of the mineral-insulated- (MI) type electric heating cable.

c. Heating cables are placed between 1½ to 2 in. below the surface of the pavement and 6 in. ± center to center.

d. When heating cables are to cross the expansion joint, they should be double-wrapped with polyethylene tape, 12 in. on each side of expansion joint, as is shown in Fig. B-14.

e. The junction box should be located in a dry location and a cable from the junction box to the heating cable must be double-wrapped with polyethylene tape.

f. Copper spacing strips should separate the resistance heating elements as shown in the plan (Fig. B-14).

The advantages of the electrical system are:

1. There is no need for the use of a boiler, pump, and other mechanical systems.
2. It is almost maintenance-free.
3. The initial cost is less than that of the hot water system.

The only disadvantage is the high cost of the electrical energy in many localities.

B-36 SNOW-MELTING SYSTEM BY HOT WATER OR ELECTRICITY

Before deciding which system should be designed for your project, a cost calculation must be made in order to determine which system is to be used (B-37 and B-38). After receiving the owner's approval, you may proceed with the design of the system.

The factors to be taken into consideration in order to determine the heating rate and the cost are wind factor, temperature, humidity, heat-loss factor, and the rate of a snowfall.

Based on current practices, the *thermal power output* for snow melting and also to keep the concrete pavement *dry* is 200 to 300 Btuh/sq. ft. around 40° north latitude.

B-37 COST CALCULATION FOR SNOW-MELTING SYSTEM BY HOT WATER PANELS

Example

A building in New York City has a paved area at its front entrance 30 feet long and 15 feet wide. The thermal power output required is 300 Btuh/sq. ft. What is the cost of operation per month if the system is to operate an average of 6 hours per day?

Oil No. 2 is $0.85 per gal.

Gas costs $0.86 per therm.

Solution

Step 1. Find the total thermal power output required per month.

$$30 \text{ ft} \times 20 \text{ ft} = 600 \text{ ft}^2$$

$$600 \text{ ft}^2 \times 300 \text{ Btuh/ft}^2 = 180,000 \text{ Btuh}$$

$$180,000 \text{ Btuh} \times 6 \text{ h/d} \times 31 \text{ d/m} = 33,480,000 \text{ Btu/m}$$

Btu = British thermal units, h = hour, d = day, m = month, g = gallons

Step 2. Using the formula given in W-51:

$$\text{Energy used} = \frac{\text{Btu required}}{\text{heating value} \times \text{efficiency}}$$

Using oil No. 2

From W-51, one gallon of oil No. 2 produces 141,000 Btu with 75 percent efficiency.

$$\text{Oil no. 2} = \frac{33,480,000 \text{ Btu/m}}{141,000 \text{ Btu/G} \times 0.75} = 317 \text{ G/m}$$

$$317 \text{ G/m} \times \$0.85/\text{G} = \$270 \text{ cost of oil No. 2 per month}$$

Using Gas

Step 3. From Fig. W-51, one therm of gas produces 100,000 Btu with 80 percent efficiency.

$$\text{Gas} = \frac{33{,}480{,}000 \text{ Btu/m}}{100{,}000 \text{ Btu/therm} \times 0.8} = 419 \text{ therms}$$

$$419 \text{ therms} \times \$0.86 = \$360 \text{ cost of gas per month}$$

B-38   COST CALCULATION FOR SNOW-MELTING SYSTEM BY ELECTRICITY

Example

Using the same problem given in B-37, electric cost is $0.12 per kW.

Solution

Step 1. Find thermal power output requirements per month.

Use the value found in Step 1 (B-37) 33,480,000 Btu/m

Step 2. From W-51, 1 kW of electricity produces 3,413 Btu with 100 percent efficiency.

$$\text{Electricity} = \frac{33{,}480{,}000 \text{ Btu/m}}{3413 \text{ Btu/KWh} \times 1} = 9{,}810 \text{ kWh/m}$$

$$9810 \text{ kWh/m} \times \$0.12/\text{kWh} = \$1178 \text{ cost of electricity per month}$$

Conclusion

Now that we know the advantages and disadvantages of both systems and the cost of operation, we can decide which system is the best for our project.

306

List of Tables

List of Charts

Index